RELIGION AND WORLDVIEWS

Religion and Worldviews: The Triumph of the Secular in Religious Education provides the first serious analysis and review of the Commission on Religious Education's proposed worldviews framework for the subject. It argues that religious education has an important contribution to make to the aims of liberal education and examines whether the shift to a worldview framework is capable of overcoming current weaknesses and initiating a new positive direction for the future. Chapters explore the role of worldviews in Religious Education, covering key debates including:

- Whether there is need for new legislation on RE
- The nature of professionalism and the role of 'experts'
- The extent to which there is educational value in study of the personal worldviews of students
- The role of the religious voice in RE
- The relation of religions to religious worldviews
- The aims of RE
- The relationship between the state and religion
- Consideration of the nature of a worldview
- The personal reflections of a member of the Commission on its proposals.

The chapters provide all that is necessary to understand and to evaluate the current debate on the appropriateness of a worldviews approach to RE.

Bringing together leading names in the field, this is essential reading for trainee and practising teachers of Religious Education, RE advisers and schools' leaders responsible for curriculum development.

L. Philip Barnes is Emeritus Reader in Religious and Theological Education, King's College London. He is the author of *Education, Religion and Diversity: Developing a New Model of Religious Education* (2014) and of *Crisis, Controversy and the Future of Religious Education* (2020), both published by Routledge.

RELIGION AND WORLDVIEWS

The Triumph of the Secular in Religious Education

Edited by L. Philip Barnes

LONDON AND NEW YORK

Cover image: © Getty Images

First published 2023
by Routledge
4 Park Square, Milton Park, Abingdon, Oxon OX14 4RN

and by Routledge
605 Third Avenue, New York, NY 10158

Routledge is an imprint of the Taylor & Francis Group, an informa business

© 2023 selection and editorial matter, L. Philip Barnes; individual chapters, the contributors

The right of L. Philip Barnes to be identified as the author of the editorial material, and of the authors for their individual chapters, has been asserted in accordance with sections 77 and 78 of the Copyright, Designs and Patents Act 1988.

All rights reserved. No part of this book may be reprinted or reproduced or utilised in any form or by any electronic, mechanical, or other means, now known or hereafter invented, including photocopying and recording, or in any information storage or retrieval system, without permission in writing from the publishers.

Trademark notice: Product or corporate names may be trademarks or registered trademarks, and are used only for identification and explanation without intent to infringe.

British Library Cataloguing-in-Publication Data
A catalogue record for this book is available from the British Library

Library of Congress Cataloging-in-Publication Data
A catalog record has been requested for this book

ISBN: 978-1-032-20618-9 (hbk)
ISBN: 978-1-032-20619-6 (pbk)
ISBN: 978-1-003-26443-9 (ebk)

DOI: 10.4324/9781003264439

Typeset in Bembo
by Apex CoVantage, LLC

CONTENTS

Preface   *vii*
Contributors   *ix*

    Introduction: From religions to worldviews   1
    L. Philip Barnes

1   The Religious Education Commission 2016–18:
    A view from the inside   18
    Anthony Towey

2   A new settlement? A defence of the 1944 Act   40
    Marius Felderhof

3   Who are the professionals in religious education?
    The Commission on Religious Education's side-lining
    of the religious voice   56
    Penny Thompson

4   Does the worldviews approach provide a new paradigm
    for religious education?   77
    L. Philip Barnes

5   The world is not enough: Religious education beyond
    worldview perspectivism   99
    Gert Biesta and Patricia Hannam

6　The philosophy of 'worldviews'　118
　　Roger Trigg

7　'Religion', 'worldviews' and the reappearing problems
　　of pedagogy　136
　　Daniel Moulin-Stożek

8　Worldviews – a threat to religious education but
　　ignored in science education?　152
　　Michael J. Reiss

9　Turning to worldviews education instead of religion –
　　helpful solution or even more problems? A perspective
　　from Germany　169
　　Friedrich Schweitzer

Index　*185*

PREFACE

As editor of *Religion and Worldviews: The triumph of the secular in religious education* I am delighted that so many prominent religious educators agreed to contribute essays: all invited were happy to contribute. This makes me think that there is a substantial body of opinion that does not agree with the current 'direction of travel' pursued by the Commission on Religious Education (CoRE) and the Religious Education Council of England and Wales. A well-funded 'charm offensive' by supporters of CoRE and the readiness of sympathetic grant-awarding charities, journal editors and official spokespersons for organisations concerned with religious education to commend (or possibly thwart criticism of) a worldviews approach to teachers is well under way and pressure to endorse the proposals of CoRE will no doubt grow. One can appreciate the readiness of some teachers to embrace CoRE, for how can so many 'experts' be wrong? Furthermore, repeating the rhetoric of CoRE that its proposals represent a new direction raises the possibility that the status of religious education among educators and the wider public will be raised and perhaps the perennial epithet of religious education as the 'Cinderella subject' of the curriculum will finally be overcome. But the 'crisis' in religious education and a longing for its resolution can precipitate lack of critical reflection and a rush to espouse ideas and solutions that will in time show themselves to further deepen the crisis rather than overcome it.

Ultimately, trust must be placed in Standing Advisory Councils on Religious Education and in classroom teachers to decide the direction religious education should take. There is much excellent teaching of religious education in schools; often by those who are prepared to develop their own ideas and implement their own strategies in contradiction of what is prescribed by 'experts'. Not infrequently those charged with the training of teachers inculcate ideas, pedagogies and even disciplinary frameworks (paradigms), ostensibly advanced in the cause of inclusion and of challenging bigotry, but which ultimately erase difference and misrepresent diversity; instead a secularist agenda is advanced where inclusion means 'all religions are equally true' or 'all are equally false' and where bigotry means the failure to accept the deliverances of the 'experts' and their ideological mentors. Opposing such powerful educational currents requires courage and determination, and an independent mind.

Finally, thanks again to my wife Sandra, who has supported me and (in her words) 'been my carer' for the last three years. It is thanks to her (and others) that I remain enthusiastic about life and work, and marital love.

St Andrew's Day, 2021

CONTRIBUTORS

L. Philip Barnes is Emeritus Reader in Religious and Theological Education, King's College London.

Gert Biesta is Professor of Educational Theory and Pedagogy in the Moray House School of Education and Sport, University of Edinburgh, UK; and Professor of Public Education in the Centre for Public Education and Pedagogy at the National University of Ireland at Maynooth, Ireland.

Marius Felderhof is Honorary Senior Research Fellow, Department of Theology and Religion, University of Birmingham.

Patricia Hannam is County Inspector/Adviser for Religious Education, History and Philosophy in Hampshire, UK.

Daniel Moulin-Stożek is University Assistant Professor in the Faculty of Education, University of Cambridge and Fellow and Director of Studies in Education, Jesus College, Cambridge.

Michael J. Reiss is Professor of Science Education at University College London, a priest in the Church of England, and President of the International Society for Science and Religion.

Friedrich Schweitzer is Professor of Religious Education, Protestant Faculty of Theology, University of Tübingen, Germany.

Penny Thompson is an independent researcher and writer on religious education and a former teacher of religious education in comprehensive schools.

Anthony Towey is Director of the Centre for Catholic Education, Research & Religious Literacy at St Mary's University, London.

Roger Trigg is Emeritus Professor of Philosophy, University of Warwick, and Senior Research Fellow, Ian Ramsey Centre, University of Oxford.

INTRODUCTION

From religions to worldviews

L. Philip Barnes

Early in 2012 the Religious Education Council of England and Wales announced that it intended to conduct a review of religious education to complement the government's review of the National Curriculum, which was initially planned in 2010. The government's rationale for not including religious education in its review is because there is local determination of its content, unlike other subjects whose content is nationally determined (as the name *National* Curriculum indicates). On this basis the distinction is often made between the 'basic' curriculum, which includes religious education, and the 'national' curriculum, which does not. In addition, although religious education is a statutory subject, parents enjoy a 'right' to withdraw their child from it, a right denied in the case of other subjects.[1] The government neither invited the RE Council, which is a charitable organisation representing groups concerned with religious education, to review the subject of religious education in school nor appointed official representatives to participate in or 'observe' the review process.

A review of religious education in England

The chief findings of the RE Council Review, which were published on 23 October 2013, were presented in two separate sections of the document: 'RE: A national curriculum framework' (11–28) and 'RE: The wider context' (29–46). The Review (2013: 8) acknowledged that there was a 'crisis' in the subject: 'The RE community has felt a sense of crisis despite government assurance' – which was only admitting what others had been saying, for example, Mark Chater, a year earlier.[2] The Review proposed (and set out the main features of) a new non-statutory national framework to replace the existing 2004 (non-statutory) framework, which has been widely used as a template by Standing Advisory Councils on Religious Education (SACREs) in their production of local agreed syllabuses. The Review also recommended that its proposed 'National Curriculum Framework for RE' should provide a new template for religious education in all schools, not just local authority schools, which are under a statutory obligation to follow an agreed syllabus (though legally they are not obliged to follow the recommendations of non-statutory documents), but also faith schools, academies and free schools. The fact that the proposed new framework intended to provide a curriculum model for all schools revealed the presumption of the RE Council to set the agenda for 'reform' and to control the subject in schools.

The findings of the Review proved controversial and were not well received. Prominent members of organisations and bodies that are affiliated to the RE Council claimed that their group did not have access to the document before publication and consequently could not endorse its recommendations and proposals; for example, this criticism was voiced by the then chair of the National Association of SACREs (see Barnes and Felderhof 2014). Criticism also focused on the new aims that were proposed. The Review abandoned the two attainment targets of 'learning about' and 'learning from', which are widely used in earlier documents and in curricular resources, in favour of three new aims (see below for discussion). The original distinction between 'learning about' and 'learning from' in attainment targets had been introduced to make it clear that religious education is not just a matter of transmitting information about the different religious traditions but also that pupils should be encouraged to engage with religious beliefs and values and to consider their personal relevance.

Three new aims were put forward: for pupils to (i) 'Know about and understand a range of religions and worldviews . . .'; for them to (ii) 'Express ideas and insights about the nature, significance and impact of religions and worldviews . . .'; and for them to (iii) 'Gain and deploy the skills needed to engage seriously with religions and worldviews . . .' (2013: 14–15). These new aims are puzzling. One might have thought that 'expressing ideas and insights' was an intellectual skill already covered by 'gaining knowledge and understanding of religions'. It is also difficult to know how to interpret the further demand that ideas and insights should be expressed 'reasonably' and with 'increasing discernment': how does one express how religious 'ideas . . . influence individuals and communities' reasonably? Is it that religious believers express some of their beliefs and ideas unreasonably and pupils should revise originally unreasonable beliefs and make them reasonable for educational purposes or is reasonableness a synonym for inoffensiveness?! The second aim, in turn, is not readily differentiated from the third, just as 'expressing ideas' cannot be easily separated from the supposed skill of 'articulating beliefs', a phrase that is used to expand the third aim. It is also difficult to grasp how 'knowing about and understanding' can be achieved or demonstrated separately from 'expressing ideas' or thoughts. A response may be that the three aims cannot in practice be separated from each other. The difficulty is that such abstract aims provide no clear direction for teaching and learning: they fail to make clear that pupil learning in religious education involves not just knowledge and understanding of religions but how religions relate to human experience, in particular to the 'lifeworld' (*Lebenswelt*) of pupils. Without this orientation, from the perspective of pupils, the subject is of limited relevance and value.

The failure to relate aims to educational outcomes is further illustrated by attending to some of the things that are said about the purpose of religious education (which in the Review is distinguished from aims). Religious education is said to contribute to education by 'provoking challenging questions about meaning and purpose in life, beliefs about God, ultimate reality, and these questions in turn 'develop in pupils an aptitude for dialogue' (2013: 14). But how does raising questions develop dialogue? Students might as easily develop an aptitude for nihilism, cynicism, and relativism unless one can be more positive about the value of studying religion. In 'enabling pupils to develop their ideas, values and identities', which is listed as a further purpose of religious education, can religious educators be indifferent as to which ideas, values and identities are formed by individual pupils? It appears that the perception of England as a plural and secular society has had the effect on those who drafted the Review document from being unable to identify how a student might develop or what personal qualities ultimately lead to an open, cohesive, tolerant and democratic society. If religious education is to contribute to the development of students and of society as the overarching aim of education demands, one must specify what bearing these religious matters should have for students' lives and their contribution to communities.

Finally, the Review was criticised for laying too much stress on students' developing and expressing their own views and not enough on acquainting them with the beliefs and practices of religion and with bringing pupils' views into dialogue with religion and allowing them to be challenged by the beliefs, values and commitments of religion. There was an all-pervasive individualism in the proposed new framework which meant that the focus of religious education was being shifted from religious content to that of the experiencing individual 'self' (see Taylor 1997). Simply put, religion was presented as extrinsic to the aim of pupils' self-development. Religious education is not chiefly about religion but about the autonomous, disengaged self that expands its horizons through being exposed to a range of viewpoints (in the hope that this, in itself, will challenge intolerance and prejudice). The word 'own' was used 72 times in the Review: 'own ideas', (2013:13); 'own feelings and experiences' (16), 'own narratives' (16), 'own . . . behaviour' (16), 'own needs' (16); 'own cultures' (16); 'own views' (18), etc. The intrusion of the word 'own' in contexts, where it would be more natural to state simply that pupils learn to express their views, their needs, and so on, suggests that everyone has his or her own view on things. What matters is that you have your own view and have the opportunity to express it. The implicit message is that religious truth is a subjective matter. The idea is not countenanced that there is objective truth in religion, things that are true for everyone, irresponsive of particular responses, and that viewpoints may be expanded, complemented or challenged by reflecting on religious beliefs, values and practices. These are some of the reasons why the Review was not well received by religious educators.

The Commission on Religious Education

Probably on account of criticism, within a few years of the publication of the original Review, the RE Council established a Commission on Religious Education (CoRE) and embarked on what was effectively a second 'review'; something not anticipated in the original Review. Why write a new National Framework and then immediately seek through a further review to 'overhaul religious education in schools' (quoting from CoRE's press release)?[3] The hope was presumably entertained that a revised panel of 'experts' (again solely appointed by the RE Council) would produce proposals that would attract more attention and have greater influence than the first set of proposals. We are told that the CoRE was 'established to review the legal, education, and policy frameworks for religious education (RE). . . . [The] review will be a wide-ranging, inclusive and evidence-based process designed to inform policy makers'.[4] (The reference to 'evidence-based process' is interesting because it is precisely the lack of engagement with research and the omission of reference to the research that influenced the decisions of the commissioners that have attracted criticism; see Schweitzer 2018.) An interim report, entitled *Religious Education for All*, was published in September 2017 and the final report, *Religion and Worldviews: The way forward*, was published in September 2018, with much 'pomp and ceremony', alongside the claim that it provided 'a new vision for the subject'.[5] Much remains of the original Review in the final Commission Report, for example, the expansion of religious education to include a study of secular worldviews at all key stages and the emphasis on the personal views and values of students, which is further expanded by CoRE into 'personal worldviews' and given even greater emphasis. Much, however, is also changed; for example, the Review presents itself as bringing forward proposals to enhance the work of SACREs in their production of local agreed syllabuses, whereas CoRE effectively 'disbands' SACREs, by relieving them of the production of agreed syllabuses; instead 'local advisory networks for religion and worldviews' are to be established with the purpose of 'providing information about sources of support' for religious education and with 'connect[ing] schools with local faith and belief communities and other groups that support the study of Religion and Worldviews in schools' (CoRE 2018: 16). It would be an illuminating exercise to trace the similarities and differences between the original Review, the interim report of CoRE and its final report, though this is not a matter that will be pursued here.

A number of organisations have thrown their weight behind the latest review and the RE Council has embarked on a well-funded (private) campaign to convince the 'religious education community', particularly religious education teachers, of the strength of CoRE's suggested 'reforms'. Gaining the support of teachers is crucially important, for although the central plank in the strategy of the RE Council was originally to convince the government that a new legal settlement is required to give statutory force to its proposed reforms (thus ensuring implementation in all maintained schools), the government has already indicated that new legislation on religious education is not on its parliamentary educational agenda. In an 'open' letter to The Very Reverend Dr John Hall, Chair of the Commission on Religious Education, the Secretary of State for Education, Damian Hinds MP, concluded that 'now is not the time to begin these reforms'.

> This would commit the government to radical changes which requires primary legislation; requires the development of new programmes of study for 'RE and Worldviews'; and leads to all schools having to implement a long-standing subject in our schools in a new way.[6]
>
> *(letter dated 6 December 2018)*

Two weeks later in the House of Lords, Lord Agnew, the Parliamentary Under Secretary of State for the School System, reaffirmed the government's position 'not to make further changes to the curriculum'. He added, 'we must decline to take forward the commission's vision for the future of RE in England' (Hansard, 17 December 2018).[7] At this stage it was clear that legislation along the lines CoRE proposed was not going to be introduced and that alternative strategies would have to be employed.

Interestingly, in his letter Damian Hinds MP referred to media coverage and correspondence that 'make it clear . . . that some stakeholders have concerns that making statutory the inclusion of "worldviews" risks diluting the teaching of RE. . .'.[8] There is no doubt that this statement reflected influential opinion, for example, that of the Board of [Jewish] Deputies and that of the Catholic Education Service. The Board of Deputies spoke of the Report as 'fundamentally flawed'; stating that it 'might be seen as an attempt by those hostile to faith to push their agenda of undermining rigour in religious education at a time when faith literacy could not be more important'.[9] The Catholic Education Service agrees and concludes that the quality of religious education is not improved by teaching less religion. It states that 'the scope of the subject' will become 'so wide and nondescript' that it will 'potentially lose all academic value and integrity'.[10] In quoting this extract from the Catholic Education Service, Lord Alton of Liverpool in the House of Lords debate on the Commission Report added that the proposed changes will also 'potentially depress religious literacy and understanding at a time when persecution of religious freedom has increased globally' (Hansard, 17 December 2018).[11] Few would deny this last point, for example, in all probability about 10,000 Christians worldwide are killed each year as a result of persecution and the number is increasing[12]; adherents of other religions and religious traditions are similarly persecuted, albeit not to the same extent.

The failure of CoRE to have its 'reforms' forced on schools through legislation is probably a good thing, both politically and educationally. If the reforms had been enacted, it would have been the first time in the history of education in England that one particular form of religious education would be given statutory force for all pupils, i.e. pupils in all types of schools. The law on religious education traditionally has allowed some degree of diversity of provision in religious education, for example, voluntary aided schools, which are mainly Catholic, and academies with a religious designation have at present the right to provide religious education in accordance with the provisions of the trust deed relating to the school or, where there is no provision in the trust deed, with the religion or denomination mentioned in the order designating the school as having a religious character. The concession is granted by CoRE (2018: 11) that alongside the proposed religion and worldviews curriculum schools can also satisfy the requirements of their trust deed, though given what CoRE requires to be covered, most commentators regard this as unrealistic, given the limited time usually allocated to religious education.

CoRE's proposals, if legally required, would also have had major implications for the role of representatives of local religious groups on Agreed Syllabuses Committees, which gives their members the opportunity to shape religious education according to local traditions and religious constituencies through the production processes. CoRE (2018: 11) called for Section 375 of the 1996 Education Act to be amended to remove the requirement for local authorities to follow their locally agreed syllabus and to remove the requirement for them to appoint Agreed Syllabus Conferences. Current syllabus conferences would then have been reconstituted as 'Local Advisory Networks for Religion and Worldviews', tasked with servicing the new centrally imposed curriculum ('National Entitlement'). The Networks will 'facilitate the implementation of the National Entitlement to the study of Religion and Worldviews in all schools within the local authority boundaries by providing information about sources of support available, and must connect schools with local faith and belief communities and other groups that support the study of Religion and Worldviews in schools' (2018: 55). The requirement that the Local Advisory Networks must limit their 'connection' to groups that support the new 'national entitlement' seems unnecessarily defensive and exclusionary. What does connection mean here and with which specific groups does CoRE believe Local Advisory Networks should not make connections? These collective measures would have undermined one element of local democracy, which is expressed through the formal challenge of bringing representatives of different religious groups and individuals together to negotiate and finally to produce an 'agreed' syllabus. There are political advantages in members of different religious and non-religious groups meeting together and then agreeing upon the form of religious education to be followed by schools in the local authority area. As was acknowledged in the original Review (2013: 35): 'There is a strongly held view [among 'contributors' to the Review] that local determination is good in principle. SACREs and agreed syllabus conferences (ASCs) continue to provide unique opportunities for local stakeholders, from many walks of life, to become actively involved in RE'. The occasion is potentially created for positive inter-religious encounters that may encourage wider encounters between 'ordinary' members of religious communities.

A serious educational disadvantage of removing the local production of syllabuses and appointing a small select body of national 'experts', proposed by CoRE (2018: 14), to determine the form and content of religious education would have been that the most important historical 'engine' of reform in the last 50 years would be lost. The transition from confessional to non-confessional, multifaith religious education was effected through the innovative work of Agreed Syllabus Conferences and teachers that took advantage of the freedom provided by legislation to introduce new ideas and innovative practices. Other examples could be cited – the City of Birmingham's innovative syllabuses of 2007 and 2021 that aligned religious education more closely with values and the moral development of pupils (see Barnes 2008). Imposed 'top-down' uniformity, however well-intentioned by its supporters, stifles innovation and ultimately compromises quality. The thrust of CoRE's proposed nationally mandated 'Entitlement', even if allowing for a degree of curriculum diversity, would still impose strict limits on innovation, as CoRE maintains that only what is consistent with its proposals and vision are appropriate for religious education in all schools. Syllabus diversity and diversity of provision have historically been shown to be the chief sources of positive reform and renewal in religious education.

The Worldviews Project

The only response available to CoRE, once it became clear that the government would not act to give statutory form to its proposals, is to convince 'the religious education community' that their adoption will improve the status and quality of religious education. Since its publication in 2018, CoRE, supported by the RE Council, has embarked on a well-funded campaign through meetings with interested bodies, training events, conferences, reporting survey results, commissioning research, and the production of classroom materials to win over the 'hearts and minds' of religious educators and those concerned with religious education. The RE Council (in part, in conjunction with TRS-UK, the 'professional association for Departments, Units and Subject Associations for the Study of Religion and Theology in the UK') has also initiated 'The Worldview Project', which is 'to support conversations in the RE community exploring the concepts of Worldviews in religious education'.[13] Phase one of the Worldview Project was to commission an independent academic literature review on the concept of 'worldview' in Religious Studies, Theology and cognate disciplines (Benoit et al. 2020). Phase two was a series of five online conversations in which religious education advisors, experts in religious education and academics from other relevant disciplines reflected on the academic international literature on worldviews. These conversations were written up by Amira Tharani as four short discussion papers (Tharani 2020). Phase three, which is now under way, will see the production of support materials for those responsible for writing religious education syllabuses. According to Professor Cooling '[t]hese materials will exemplify how different approaches to the worldview idea generate different types of syllabus appropriate for different contexts' (Cooling in Tharani 2020: 4).

This last comment by Cooling is noteworthy for it draws attention to what he regards as the 'open-ended' nature of CoRE's proposals for the curriculum. The root idea is that CoRE's vision can be instantiated in different ways – CoRE does not aim to establish a prescriptive curriculum (it even refuses to speak of its proposals as a 'framework'):[14] it may talk of a *National Entitlement*, but this entitlement is open to different interpretations. The comment by Cooling draws attention to the diversity of provision that is consistent, he believes, with the proposals of CoRE: *different* approaches (unspecified by Cooling), *different* interpretations of the meaning of worldview, generating *different* types of syllabuses, which are appropriate for *different* contexts. At this point he may claim support from CoRE's statement (2018: 32) that it provides 'a set of organising principles which form (*sic*) the basis for developing programmes of study'. CoRE also makes proposals about content. It provides a list of worldviews that are appropriate for study in schools though it excludes what some regard as worldviews that should be included on the list for possible study – global capitalism, communism and nationalism (2018: 75), for example. In other words, CoRE is not solely concerned with curriculum principles.

Leaving this aside, there are issues raised by the open-ended interpretation of what CoRE proposes for schools, and which Cooling expands upon. There is the matter of content and coherence. There isn't any specified common content or requirement for there to be common content: the programmes of study that make up a syllabus *can* differ (entirely) from other syllabuses; and according to Cooling the approaches to representing worldviews within programmes of study and syllabuses can also differ. But what then of coherence and progression? The first RE Council Review (2013: 37, 45) made much of 'securing coherence and progression': 'lack of coherence' is linked to 'confusion' and 'a lack of coherence' between agreed syllabuses is listed as one of the 'key issues that face[s] RE' (2013: 31 and 32). The Review praises the 2004 Non-statutory National Framework for its 'attempt to provide coherence for the subject at a national level' (2013: 49). Why has the principle of coherence been jettisoned and is this a positive educational development? By providing an extensive list of worldviews that may be studied (while acknowledged that the list is not exhaustive), CoRE has effectively evaded and neglected to answer one of the most difficult and controversial questions in religious education, that of the selection of content: do all worldviews have equal educational value and relevance? Of course CoRE's decision not to prescribe content beyond its support for a study of worldviews has apologetic appeal for its supporters: if it were to prescribe content or particular worldviews to be studied, contrary voices would be raised, better to abdicate responsibility for content selection to others (or as I anticipate, in the third phase of 'The Worldviews Project' to produce *illustrative* material only, again by-passing difficult questions about the relation of content to educational relevance).

Recently, Emma Salter (2021: 4) has attempted to defend CoRE from criticism, or more accurately, she believes criticism should be held in abeyance until we see the ways in which CoRE's 'National Entitlement influences curriculum design'. In her view to criticise at this point is to 'put the cart before the horse': the criticism is directed to Friedrich Schweitzer (2018) and myself (Barnes 2021). According to her, we do not yet know what a 'curriculum' (her term) faithful to CoRE's vision will look like; it is premature to criticise. Criticism at this juncture is inappropriate. This is because

> The National Entitlement as set out in the report is not a prescriptive curriculum framework or list of topics to be included, but rather 'a set of organising principles which form the basis for developing programmes of study'.
> *(Salter 2021; incorporating quotation from CoRE 2018: 32)*

But we do know a lot about the proposed content that the National Entitlement envisages. It is pedantic to say we do not know 'the topics', for we do know the religious and non-religious worldviews that are believed to be appropriate for study. CoRE lists 24 of them; and if we know the worldviews, we can with little imagination identify essential topics within particular worldviews, though no topic (or worldview) is prescribed. We do know that CoRE's 'set of organising principles', for example, justifies the study of paganism, existentialism and secularism (which is distinguished from agnosticism and atheism), alongside familiar and more numerically larger religions such as Christianity, Islam and Hinduism. We also know *how* these 'traditions' will be conceptualised and represented to pupils – they will be configured according to a worldview matrix, for this is what CoRE tells us is one of its central organising and innovative principles.

We also have a broad understanding of what a religion conceptualised as a worldview will look like, for the idea of a religion as a worldview has been around for a long time (see Naugle 2002) – it has particular appeal for philosophically inclined evangelicals (often following Bavinck 2019 [1904]), and it appeals to recent educators that want to include Humanism in the religious education curriculum.

> worldview refers to the cluster of beliefs a person holds about the most significant issues of life, such as God, the cosmos, knowledge, values, humanity, and history. . . . thinking of a worldview in terms of a basic conceptual system is critical.
>
> *(Samples 2017: 688)*

The literature on worldviews typically focuses on propositional beliefs 'about the nature of reality (metaphysics), the nature of knowledge and the method of attaining it (epistemology), and the nature of goodness and of a good life (ethics)' (Peterson et al. 2009: 64). The doxastic focus of worldviews is somewhat lost in CoRE's (2018: 4) definition.

> A worldview is a person's way of understanding, experiencing and responding to the world. It can be described as a philosophy of life or an approach to life. This includes how a person understands the nature of reality and their own place in the world.

It is further stated that institutional worldviews (in contrast to personal worldviews) are

> complex and dynamic. They may refer back to sacred texts or founding narratives and at the same time be fluid, adapting to new times and cultures. They *are made up* of practices, rituals, narratives, experiences, interactions, social norms, doctrines, artistic expressions and other forms of cultural expression, and should not be reduced simply to belief and practice but understood in all their complexity. Sometimes these may be expressed through complex institutional structures, while in other cases there may be much looser forms of identification.[15]
>
> *(CoRE 2018: 72, my emphasis)*

The description of what formal worldviews 'are made up of', while correct, does not fully capture what the study of worldview means and requires, which in educational terms is *study of the central beliefs and values* that give meaning to 'practices, rituals, narratives, experiences', and so on. Doctrines, as beliefs, are foundational to a worldview (or religion), unless CoRE has adopted an idiosyncratic interpretation of a worldview that excludes doctrines from being beliefs or that denies them the status of propositional attitudes. Consequently, it would be more accurate to say that the rituals, practices, narratives, and experiences of lived religions or of non-religious worldviews *express* their beliefs and doctrines. A worldviews approach to religious education, if it is to be faithful to its usual interpretation, should focus on the beliefs and the doctrines that give meaning and significance to the non-doctrinal aspects of a religion and consequently it is most naturally described as exemplifying an intellectual, philosophical approach (which is indicated by the title of some studies concerned with worldviews, for example, Hendrik M. Vroom's *A Spectrum of Worldviews: An introduction to philosophy of religion in a pluralistic world*, 2006).

CoRE and Cooling are acutely aware that a worldviews approach, with its inherent philosophical orientation, may not have wide educational appeal and it is not an approach well suited to religious education in primary schools (and probably beyond). Both therefore also urge giving attention to 'the lived experiences of adherents' (CoRE 2018: 76; Cooling 2020: 407), to 'the role of religious and non-religious ritual and practices, foundational texts, and of religious media, in both the formation and communication of experience, beliefs, values, identities and commitments. . . .' (CoRE 2018: 34). Such requirements, however, detract from (undermine even) CoRE's stated position that its proposals constitute a new worldviews approach to religious education. The study of worldviews, as currently practised, is not the study of 'everyday' lived religion or of religious texts, or of rituals and practices or of the influence of religions on the arts, and so on. CoRE could conceivably respond along with Lewis Carroll's Humpty Dumpty: 'When I use a word it means just what I choose it to mean – neither more nor less'. At the very least there is a tension between a worldviews approach and giving attention to 'lived religion' and the wider range of subjects that CoRE expects to be studied. Challenges emerge: too much focus on worldviews' beliefs and doctrines threaten to over-intellectualise religious education and make the subject uninteresting and inaccessible to the young; too little focus on worldviews compromises any suggestion of newness, which one of CoRe's central claims.

A further problem is that if emphasis is placed on 'non-doctrinal' aspects of worldviews, as is inappropriate to a worldviews approach, alongside the doctrinal, conceptual aspects, say the ritual, the experiential, or the social, this will effectively reinstate Ninian Smart's (1966 and 1968) seven-fold (originally six-fold) dimensional account of religion, which enjoyed significant influence in the 1970s and 1980s, to centre stage again in religious education (see Barnes 2000 and 2014: 65–78). Support for this interpretation is also found in CoRE's (2018: 37) claim that '[a]t school level, the study of worldviews is inherently multidisciplinary and should draw from as many of the . . . disciplines as possible'; in the same paragraph the disciplines relevant to religious education are identified as anthropology, area studies, hermeneutics, history, other human and social sciences, philosophy, religious studies and theology (it is doubtful whether all of these are strictly disciplines). Smart (1968) always insisted that the study of religion/religious studies was not a discipline, rather it was a 'field of study' that draws on different disciplines; he carried this conviction over into religious education. A good case can be made for the conclusion that CoRE is re-framing religious education according to the original vision of Ninian Smart. This prompts the question: how much is original in CoRE's proposals?

One final comment to add to these observations. We will have to wait to see the support materials produced for schools under Phase three of 'The Worldviews Project' before we can ascertain if it provides further evidence for interpreting CoRE's central commitments as representing a retrieval of the position of Ninian Smart. Nevertheless, in Mark Chater's edited collection, *Reforming RE: Power and knowledge in a worldviews curriculum* (2020), there is evidence to support this contention. Under Chater's direction some religious educators have anticipated the form of curriculum design and classroom material that they believe exemplifies what CoRE requires. Topics that are mentioned as appropriate for students to study include creation, reincarnation, sacred space (as reflected in sacred texts or teaching), prayer, fasting and Hajj in Islam (in the last case attention is to be given to the distinction between 'mythical and historical thinking', clearly echoing two of Smart's dimensions). There are some excellent suggestions for lessons and some insightful comments. It is almost impossible, however, to find any content or perspective that is novel and follows uniquely from a worldviews approach or any content that cannot be conceptualised using Ninian Smart's dimensional account of religion and its use to frame and plan lessons. Furthermore, there is a critical, philosophical element in many of the suggestions; again this reflects the position of Smart, at least in his early writings on religious education. In *Secular Education and the Logic of Religion* (1968), he argued that descriptive, historical studies of religion require to be supplemented by 'parahistorical' studies that focus upon the truth asserting nature of religion and provide students with opportunities to develop the necessary skills to evaluate religious beliefs and practices. It is acknowledged that the suggestions for classroom lessons in Chater's edited collection were not produced or endorsed by CoRE, though it does show what supporters of CoRE take to be required by materials to instantiate its proposals in the classroom, and again underlines the challenge CoRE faces in fulfilling its claims to newness.

The essays that follow consider different aspects of CoRE's proposed worldviews approach to religious education, offering analysis and criticism. Chapter 1 by Anthony Towey provides an 'insider's' account of the work of the Commission and why it 'may be that the subject [of religious education after CoRE] occupies a more contested space than ever'. Chapter 2 by Marius Felderhof challenges the idea that legislative change can 'fix' the problems of religious education. He argues that the existing 1944 Settlement is much more liberal and suitable for our secular, religiously plural society than the various proposals that have been forthcoming in recent reports, including that of the CoRE Report. Chapter 3, by Penny Thompson, considers how CoRE uses the word 'professional' and its proposal that nine professionals appointed by the Religious Education Council should oversee and determine the structure and content of the proposed new 'National Entitlement'. In Chapter 4 Philip Barnes challenges the apologetic refrain by supporters of CoRE (and Trevor Cooling) that it provides a new paradigm for religious education – a worldviews approach is neither new nor should be regarded as a paradigm, and as such offers limited prospects of overcoming the systemic weaknesses of English religious education. In Chapter 5 Gert Biesta and Patricia Hannam identify philosophical, theological and educational objections to a wordviews approach to religious education and develop an alternative proposal that seeks to take religion seriously in relation to itself and to the aims of education. Chapter 6, by Roger Trigg, traces the effect of prevailing philosophical assumptions on religious education since the 1950s, which has resulted in CoRE 'reducing' religion to a worldview that is indeterminate, fluid and highly personal. In Chapter 7 Daniel Moulin-Stożek considers the subject of pedagogy, setting his observations in the context of theoretical and empirical inquiries about religious education pedagogy stretching back to the 1960s. His critical analysis suggests that rather than solving pedagogical problems, CoRE's proposed new paradigm offers little in the way of new solutions to familiar challenges, while potentially putting the coherence and integrity of the subject at risk. Chapter 8, by Michael Reiss, reviews the role of worldviews in science education, and while not uncritical, takes a more sanguine view of the role of worldviews in religious education. The final essay, Chapter 9, brings a German perspective to bear on CoRE's proposals. Friedrich Schweitzer questions the shift in focus of religious education from religions to worldviews. Two main critical questions are raised, the first concerns the concept of worldviews, the second concerns the relationship between the state and religion.

Notes

1 A similar right of withdrawal applies to the Sex Education component within the broader subject of Relationship and Sex Education (DfE 2019: 11–12), though this is not taken as compromising the basic/national distinction which underlines the unique position of religious education in the school curriculum.
2 Originally available at www.reonline.org.uk/news/whats-worth-fighting-for-in-re.
3 www.commissiononre.org.uk/commission-on-re-press-release/ (accessed 2 December 2021).
4 www.commissiononre.org.uk/about-the-commission-on-religious-education/ (accessed 2 December 2021).
5 www.commissiononre.org.uk/commission-on-re-press-release/ (accessed 2 December 2021).
6 www.religiouseducationcouncil.org.uk/wp-content/uploads/2018/12/Letter-to-The-Very-Reverend-Doctor-John-Hall-from-Rt-Hon-Damian-Hinds-MP . . . -2.jpg (accessed 2 December 2021).
7 https://hansard.parliament.uk/lords/2018-12-17/debates/A497B8C8-9BE9-4975-95E3-91F4748A98AC/ReligiousEducation (accessed 2 December 2021).
8 www.religiouseducationcouncil.org.uk/wp-content/uploads/2018/12/Letter-to-The-Very-Reverend-Doctor-John-Hall-from-Rt-Hon-Damian-Hinds-MP...-1.jpg (accessed 2 December 2021).
9 www.bod.org.uk/bod-news/commission-on-re-report-is-fundamentally-flawed/ (accessed 2 December 2021).
10 www.catholiceducation.org.uk/component/k2/item/1003658-catholic-education-service-response-to-the-commission-on-religious-education-report (accessed 2 December 2021).
11 https://hansard.parliament.uk/lords/2018-12-17/debates/A497B8C8-9BE9-4975-95E3-91F4748A98AC/ReligiousEducation (accessed 2 December 2021).
12 Christian History Institute, 'Persecuted Christians today', christianhistoryinstitute.org/magazine/article/persecuted-christians-today; see also The APPG for International Freedom of Religion or Belief, 'How many Christians are killed each year because of their faith?', appgfreedomofreligionorbelief.org/how-many-christians-are-killed-each-year-because-of-their-faith/ (both accessed 2 December 2021).
13 www.religiouseducationcouncil.org.uk/projects/rec-discussion-papers-on-worldviews/ (accessed 2 December 2021).
14 The term 'framework' is used but only to refer to the principles governing religious education. CoRE (2018: 35) and Cooling confine the term curriculum to the collective subjects taught in schools; in their terminology the new subject of 'Religion and Worldview' is a core component of the broader curriculum. There are no compelling reasons for others to adopt this narrowing of usage: the term 'curriculum' can be properly used with different meanings

in different contexts; the context should make clear the range of its application. Other writers have happily used the term 'curriculum' in supporting the proposals of CoRE (see Chater 2020).
15 This account would serve better as a description of a religion rather than a worldview (see what follows below).

References

Barnes, L. P. (2000) 'Ninian Smart and the phenomenological approach to religious education', *Religion* 30(4): 315–332. Doi.org/10.1006/reli.2000.0291.

Barnes, L. P. (2008) 'The 2007 Birmingham Agreed Syllabus for religious education: A new direction for statutory religious education in England and Wales', *Journal of Beliefs & Values* 29(1): 73–81. Doi.org/10.1080/13617670801954601.

Barnes, L. P. (2014) *Education, Religion and Diversity: Developing a new model of religious education*. London: Routledge.

Barnes, L. P. (2021) 'The Commission on Religious Education, worldviews and the future of religious education', *British Journal of Educational Studies*. Doi.org/10.1080/00071005.2021.1871590.

Barnes, L. P. and Felderhof, M. (2014) 'Reviewing the Religious Education Review', *Journal of Beliefs & Values* 35(1): 108–117. Doi:10.1080/13617672.2014.884909.

Bavinck, H. (2019 [1904]) *Christian Worldview*. Wheaton, IL: Crossway Books.

Benoit, C., Hutchings, T. and Shillitoe, R. (2020) *Worldview: A multidisciplinary report*. London: RE Council. Available online: www.religiouseducationcouncil.org.uk/projects/rec-discussion-papers-on-worldviews/ (accessed 2 December 2021).

Chater, M. (ed.) (2020) *Reforming RE: Power and knowledge in a worldviews curriculum*. Woodbridge: John Catt.

Commission on Religious Education (2017) *Interim Report: Religious education for all*. London: RE Council. Available online: www.commissiononre.org.uk/wp-content/uploads/2017/09/Commission-on-Religious-Education-Interim-Report-2017.pdf (accessed 2 December 2020).

Commission on Religious Education (2018) *Final Report: Religions and Worldviews: The way forward*. London: RE Council. Available online: www.commissiononre.org.uk/wp-content/uploads/2018/09/Final-Report-of-the-Commission-on-RE.pdf (accessed 2 December 2020).

Cooling, T. (2020) 'Worldview in religious education: Autobiographical reflections on the Commission on Religious Education in England final report', *British Journal of Religious Education* 42(4): 403–414. Doi.org/10.1080/01416200.2020.1764497.

Department for Education (2019) 'Relationships education, relationships and sex education (RSE) and health education'. London: DfE. Available online: www.gov.uk/government/publications/relationships-education-relationships-and-sex-education-rse-and-health-education (accessed 2 December 2021).

Naugle, D. K. (2002) *Worldview: The history of a concept*. Grand Rapids, MI: Eerdmans.

Peterson, M., Hasker, W., Reichenbach, B., and Basinger, D. (2009) *Reason and Religious Belief*. 4th edn. New York: Oxford University Press.

Religious Education Council of England and Wales (2013) 'A review of religious education in England'. London: RE Council. Available online: www.religiouseducationcouncil.org.uk/resources/documents/a-review-of-religious-education-in-england/ (accessed 2 December 2021).

Salter, E. (2021) 'A critical reflection on the Commission on Religious Education's proposed National Entitlement to Religion and Worldviews in England and Wales', *Journal of Religious Education*, in press. https://Doi.org/10.1007/s40839-021-00150-w.

Samples, K. R. (2017) 'Worldview', in P. Copan, T. Longman III, C. L. Reese and M. G. Strauss (eds), *Dictionary of Christianity and Science*. Grand Rapids, MI: Zondervan.

Schweitzer, F. (2018) 'Sacrificing Cinderella: Will giving up religious education help to establish a more promising successor?' *Journal of Beliefs & Values* 39(4): 516–522. Doi:10.1080/13617672.2018.1542792.

Smart, N. (1966) *The Teacher and Christian Belief*. London: James Clarke.

Smart, N. (1968) *Secular Education and the Logic of Religion*. London: Faber.

Taylor, C. (1997) *The Ethics of Authenticity*. Cambridge, MA: Harvard University Press.

Tharani, A. (2020) 'The Worldview Project: Discussion papers'. London: RE Council. Available online: www.religiouseducationcouncil.org.uk/projects/rec-discussion-papers-on-worldviews/ (accessed 2 December 2021).

Vroom, H. M. (2006) *A Spectrum of Worldviews: An introduction to philosophy of religion in a pluralistic world*. Amsterdam: Rodopi.

1
THE RELIGIOUS EDUCATION COMMISSION 2016–18

A view from the inside

Anthony Towey

Introduction: owning an error

Although 'auto-ethnography' would not normally be my preferred methodology for academic discourse, it does seem the most obvious way for me to contribute to a volume dedicated to ongoing debates in religious education (Jackson 2016). As a member of the Commission on Religious Education convened by the RE Council 2016–2018, I participated fully in the discussions which led to the eventual report, *Religion and Worldviews: The way forward – A national plan for religious education*. And while I wouldn't go as far as to privilege auto-ethnography as an ontology of becoming, I think there is value in attempting an answer to the question 'what happened?' even if it entails 'writing dangerously' (Yoo 2019; cf. Gale and Wyatt 2019). My view on the Commission's work now is that it was more because of our ambitions rather than despite them that the Final Report had a mixed reception. Essentially, I think as Commissioners we gradually went beyond the evidence we gathered in an attempt to engineer a paradigm shift and present a 'game-changing' vision of the subject. In turn this undermined our ambition to build an 'irresistible coalition' of subject stakeholders without which it has proved difficult to present a coherent case for change to policy makers either at national or local level.

Although the religious education classroom has been famously described as 'a safe place to discuss difference', at the time of writing, entering the fourth year of post-Commission deliberation, it may be that the subject occupies a more contested space than ever. There is a sense of jeopardy as partisan positions are taken around the nature of the subject, pedagogy,

DOI: 10.4324/9781003264439-2

its predominant methodologies, its relation to faith sector stakeholders and its own designation. In what follows, I hope to explain why the Commission came to certain conclusions and, while 'owning' some of those consequences, make a number of irenic suggestions as to how the religious education community might find common cause once more.

Compromised consultation – in my end is my beginning

As the Commissioners gathered at High Leigh on 3rd November 2016 for the first of a scheduled six overnight plenary meetings, I was reminded of Eliot's famous phrase from *Four Quartets*, 'In my end is my beginning'. After the initial introductory session, we broke for coffee and in the fragmented way of such circumstances, I formed part of a random huddle where a delegate was already ascertaining from the Chair 'what they would say yes to'. Prescient readers may realise, 'they' referred not to fellow Commissioners but to Her Majesty's Government. In other words, already in the minds of more politically astute members of the group, a key consideration for the Commission was the extent to which the Department for Education (DfE) might be open to change. This was also, at least in part, in the minds of the secretariat who had already expressed a hope that the Commission would have the same effect as the Schools' Council Working Paper of 1971 which had given a new vigour and energy to both the profession and the subject at that time. The two audiences identified by the then Chair of the RE Council were to be:

> Teachers in need of a new, renewed and visionary sense of direction, and policymakers who understand the significance of the subject in British society and therefore can legislate and design policy on the basis of it.[1]

On reflection, I think this presented Commissioners with a problem, *ab initio*. On the one hand we were being tasked to consult widely and honestly with practitioners in the field and numerous stakeholders, but on the other hand we were being tasked to be visionary and offer a new direction for the subject. Essentially this risked a bias towards the novel and a bias against the current state of affairs, ultimately giving the Commission the disposition of a 'think tank' exploring ideas rather than a body driven either by research or by the schedule of consultation.[2]

For readers unfamiliar with the *modus operandi* of the Commission, 'consultation' took four main forms:

(a) Public Evidence Sessions held at various venues around the country. At these, practitioners, theorists and stakeholders usually made oral presentations to a selection of Commissioners. Sometimes including question and answer sessions and interaction between delegates, reports were compiled and circulated to all Commissioners. That said, it was never entirely clear what status such encounters enjoyed since they rarely seemed to set the tone or content of plenary Commission gatherings.

(b) Expert Invitees to Commission Gatherings by contrast did set particular agendas at particular points in the proceedings. Examples ranged from policy makers such as personnel from the Department for Education, researchers such as Adam Dinham and Martha Shaw from Goldsmiths (University of London) and stakeholders such as Nigel Genders and Derek Holloway from the Church of England education office. Presentations were normally followed by question and answer sessions with Commission delegates but often also fed forward into further discussions among the group itself.[3]

(c) The written call for evidence and the National Survey conducted in response to the Interim Report towards the end of 2017, together composed a third element in the Consultation (CoRE 2018: 81–97). There was vast interest from the religious education community with submissions to the survey alone numbering well in excess of 1,000 responses. Of these, over 600 replies were fully completed, collated and fed back to a plenary gathering of the Commission on 15th January 2018 by an independent researcher, Frances Lane, appointed for that purpose.[4]

(d) Visits to groups and organizations made by individual Commissioners to SACREs, schools and conferences offered a fourth somewhat eclectic element to the evidence which are listed on page 97 of the Final Report (2018).

If the methodology so described perhaps raises an initial question about how such a vast quantity of evidence range might be appropriately classified, calibrated and digested, a second arose from the make-up of the Commission itself. A nagging concern throughout our proceedings was that for all the theoretical and policy making expertise of the delegates, by the time the Commission completed its work there was only one member who was still actually teaching the subject to school age pupils. Moreover, given that the age-profile of the Commission was markedly older than the average age of religious education teachers, this risked both a professional and a generational bias in the reception of information by the Commission which was never entirely addressed.[5]

A possible way of rebalancing such asymmetry might have been to lay more emphasis on the evidence sessions and the questionnaire which attracted a healthy response among teachers across the country. Yet taking just three Commission conclusions (the National Entitlement, the role of stakeholders and the name of the subject), critics might conclude that the *modus operandi* of our Commission decision making ultimately served controversy rather than the cause of consensus building.

The national entitlement and 'the complex turn'

One of the clearest mandates supported by the survey evidence base and indeed all the forms of consultation was the widespread agreement that there should be a National Entitlement to a baseline curriculum in religious education for every pupil in every school between ages 5–16. At the public and expert consultations, this was either explicitly or implicitly affirmed, and in the survey there was strong affirmation that this should form a centrepiece of Commission recommendations. Some 72% of respondents supported the proposal outlined in the Interim Report (2017) and given that a further 13% thought it too detailed and 11% insufficiently so, it might be argued that this was something the Commission got just about right.

Underneath the surface, however, things are perhaps not so straightforward in terms neither of the provenance of the National Entitlement nor its reception. The idea of proposing a National Entitlement arose early in Commission discussions and had sufficiently taken shape to be 'trialled' by inclusion in the Interim Report released in Summer 2017. No other options were given – hence survey responders keen on a National Entitlement were somewhat bridled to that particular cart which itself had distinct corrective tendencies.

Perhaps best characterized as 'complexity over clarity', the new proposed patterning of religious education ran counter to pedagogical and policy shifts instigated by the Government in the 2016 Examination Reforms at Key Stage 4 and 5 (16+ and 18+ respectively) (see McGrail and Towey 2019). Based on theories of Powerful Knowledge associated with the work of Michael Young (2011), the DfE had argued that social mobility was best fostered in schools by information-heavy curricula as opposed to heuristic 'discover for yourself' approaches. In this way, pupils of whatever background could be enabled to go beyond the limitations of their own experience and lay hold of the great storehouse of human knowledge (Muller and Young 2019). Instead of trying 'to eat soup with a fork'[6] or in the case of religious education succumb to 'possibilitarianism' and risk merely 'having a chat' (Morgan 2015: 10), there would now be a chance for pupils to engage with great traditions while having the added bonus of custodians of those same traditions as their guide.

Although this latter aspect of the 2016 reform was an attempt to give credence to 'insider' views rather than privileging a theoretical 'outsider/phenomenological' view of religion associated with the work of Ninian Smart, for some Commissioners this was a misguided direction of travel. The 2016 reforms risked in this view not only the alienation of non-academically minded pupils but also the alienation of pupils not affiliated to the major faith traditions as well as 'nones' – those not linked to any faith position at all. Moreover, the 'insider methodology' was failing to acknowledge the complexity of the religious landscape and making an 'essentialist error' – reifying the doctrinal positions of religions while ignoring the infinitely complex ways in which religious identity and individuality were manifest 'in reality' (see Dinham and Shaw 2015; Smith et al. 2018).

By contrast, if the religious education classroom is primarily a place of self-discovery, a place where the formation of a personal *weltenschauung* ('worldview') in preparation for life should be the priority rather than preparation for any particular examination, then pedagogies serving that end should inevitably be profiled. At this point, in a somewhat *ex machina* move, three distinct patterns for the subject were set before the Commission. Of these, the first and third seemed obviously artificial confections but the middle did at least have the merit of an interior consistency and was readily identifiable with the Big Ideas project being developed by Barbara Wintersgill (2017) from the University of Exeter. Re-envisioning the entire subject, instead of a focus on 'the Big Six' religions, six 'Big Ideas' were to take centre stage, retaining its relevance to pupils precisely because its critical locus is the pupil.

> Schools should, through their RE programmes, aim systematically to prepare students for the spiritual and intellectual challenges of living in a world with diverse religions and beliefs as well as non-belief.
>
> *(Wintersgill 2017: 1)*

To underline the central importance this document had, Barbara Wintersgill was invited to present in person to the Commission in July 2017, but in terms of transparency and objectivity, circumstances were not ideal. The first two consultants acknowledged in the Wintersgill 'Big Ideas' project were in fact key protagonists of the Commission and were present throughout the discussion thereof. Moreover, it was impossible to drain the event of pedagogical polemic. We not only risked dissonance between heuristic curricula in KS1–3 and powerful knowledge curricula at KS4, we also risked policy ire on the part of the DfE, neither of which would prove entirely helpful in terms of consensus building.[7] Furthermore, as a

Commissioner not particularly wedded to the Big Ideas project, for me it did feel that we were needlessly limiting our understanding of the subject. Like a pre-prepared cricket pitch flown in and laid especially for a test match, this patterning of the subject was the wicket on which the Commission were being asked to play, with little proof outside a limited time-bound sample in the South West that it actually worked at all. The sub-structure of the National Entitlement was set in place and the 'game-changing' had begun with complexity rather than content as its refrain (see Cooling 2020: 411).

If one looks at the eventual proposed national entitlement it is hard not to notice the emphasis on difference, diversity and mutability which are mentioned explicitly in eight of the nine elements of the eventual national entitlement (my italics):

> (1) Matters of central importance are interpreted in *different times, cultures and places*. (2) That worldviews are *complex, diverse and plural*. (3) [beliefs] *may change* across and within worldviews (4) [and] *people may draw upon more than one tradition*. (6) Worldviews have *different roles* in making sense of lives and have (7) *different roles* influencing moral behaviour by appeal to (8) *various* sources of authority and must be analysed (9) in different ways through *a wide range of academic disciplines*.

Indeed, the only element of the national entitlement which doesn't explicitly advert to difference is (5) which nonetheless models complexity by clustering religious and non-religious ritual practices with texts and experience, beliefs, values, identities and commitments.

While at one level, the desire to emphasize complexity has its place in any subject discipline, that level tends to be at an advanced rather than at an introductory stage. Although Commission debates around positionality, how personal and group identity emerges in a societal/cultural milieu and the mutability of religious expression have perennial validity, a case could be made that they should be the omega point for the subject rather than its alpha. It left the Commission with four problems in terms of policy makers and practitioners.

(a) Whatever the merits of the National Entitlement idea, by deliberately adopting such an anti-essentialist stance, as Commissioners we were laying ourselves open to the charge that we were politically as well as pedagogically motivated, thus making it problematic for the legislature to accept, still less to impose on all schools.

(b) Moreover, such a move ran counter to 'cognitive load' theory which argues that when teaching new content and skills, explicit guidance, practice and feedback are more effective than requiring students to discover for themselves (Enser 2018).
(c) Since concerns about the subject expertise of teachers were a major talking point for the Commission, even making the subject appear more complex risked causing as many problems as it hoped to solve.
(d) In an anxiety to express complexity, the National Entitlement had managed to forget such notions as mystery, transcendence and paradox – all features that are part of the allure of religious traditions which even secular protagonists acknowledge.

Withal, the turn to complexity was not universally welcomed. It led one seasoned observer to remark that the step back from content in pursuit of objectivity risked 'losing sight of the subject altogether' and another describing the National Entitlement as an attractive proposition 'for Master's students'.[8]

Complexity and the othering of faith

As soon as the principle of a National Entitlement was agreed, the possibility of establishing an expert group funded by the DfE that would act as guardians of the subject was on the table. The argument was that religious education had academic credibility issues precisely because it was linked to confessional traditions rather than critical standpoints. Akin to bodies governing other National Curriculum subjects, the ambition was that this expert group would feed directly into Government via policy involvement in one direction while via curriculum design and resourcing facilitate practitioners in the other. Unfortunately, while such bodies are so constituted, say, in Sweden,[9] by opting to go down this route as Commissioners we risked alienating three constituencies naturally committed to the prosperity of religious education:

- First, national faith stakeholders such as the Board of Deputies, who, with the byline 'We are the Voice of the UK Jewish Community', had contributed resources for the 2016 GCSE Reform (Lawton 2016).
- Second, local faith bodies such as Statutory Advisory Councils for Religious Education (SACREs) whose unsung work supporting RE was a constant refrain during the evidence sessions.
- Third, believers themselves, who could be forgiven for thinking that faith itself was becoming a problem for the Commission.

Looking back, the day this latter question took centre stage at a Commission gathering proved particularly vivid.[10] It had just been announced that Damien Hinds, a practising Roman Catholic, had been appointed as Education Secretary. My recollection is that there was a perceptibly gloomy mood in the room, largely because it was presumed that the new Secretary of State would be a defender of the privileges of Faith Sector schools which applied not just to religious education curricula but also to vexed questions such as faith-based admissions criteria for new Free School foundations. Although I aired the possibility that it might be a case of 'Nixon goes to China' (whereby only someone with unimpeachable credentials in one camp can make concessions to the other side), discussions were somewhat stilted.[11]

In the afternoon, the refrain that faith schools were obsessed with indoctrination and produced narrow minded and intolerant pupils was voiced by two Commissioners. Mindful that nursery children at the local Catholic pre-school had recently enjoyed a series of lessons on Eid, Diwali, Hanukah, Christmas and Chinese New Year, I raised doubts that such claims were researched. I also remarked that references to 'the whiff of confessionalism' in religious education and aired the view that 'faith was the problem' on social media, was unhelpful. With mild astonishment I listened as evidence to the contrary was offered by one of my interlocutors who replied that they knew this to be true 'because I went to a Catholic school and I sent my children to one'. Moreover, the coffee break saw my other interlocutor circling all the way around the table to tell me to 'F★★k off' and threaten that if I didn't stop quoting him he 'would knock [my] block off.'

By way of reassurance, it needs to be said this exchange was the antithesis of the conviviality which typified the work of the Commission. However, it did cause me to absent myself from the rest of the day's proceedings and was in itself somewhat revealing of a latent hostility towards faith positions which does need some contextualization (see Gearon 2014: 111–131). Although it might seem far-fetched to outsiders that religious belief would somehow be perceived as the enemy of religious education, the argument was put forward that the very existence of the faith sector and its advantages in terms of resourcing and training was leading to an asymmetric provision which was rendering community school religious education a wasteland which only the direct intervention of the Commission could cure.

The problem with such a standpoint was that this view flew in the face of the evidence gathered by the Commission from around the country. For example, the Anglican programme 'Understanding Christianity' was repeatedly mentioned as a brilliant resource which could be successfully adapted at local level to help deliver religious education. Elsewhere, the fact that Catholic schools were allocating 10% of curriculum time to the subject meant that the Catholic Education Service were willing and confident they could deliver any eventual National Entitlement with the proviso that they weren't forced to!

Yet both deliberately and inadvertently, slowly, but inexorably, the Commission found itself extending the purview of its ambition. Hitherto the religious education in exempt faith schools would now come under the direction of the National Body of Religious Education Experts, accountable to Ofsted for the delivery of the Entitlement (CoRE 2018: 38–40). Likewise, the role of SACREs – Standing Advisory Councils for Religious Education made up of local faith groups – would be affected. They had been much discussed throughout the two years of Commission meetings and it was proving difficult to find consensus, one commissioner suggesting we should 'kill the dog' while others offered impassioned defence of their role. Ultimately, as deadlines for a Commission final draft hove into view, a somewhat immature proposal that they be reorganized and renamed Local Advisory Networks for Religion and Worldviews was sanctioned. Despite the quite remarkable work of SACREs in Birmingham and Leicester, they would no longer be required to convene Agreed Syllabus Conferences but the larger SACREs could offer resourcing aligned the National Entitlement (CoRE 2018: 52–57). As one delegate remarked, the journey from pupil National Entitlement to school national imposition was complete.

Ironically, this diminishing of stakeholder approved faith-based content had the effect of weakening one of the key attractions religious education had always enjoyed in the eyes of both parents and the DfE. Even if one doesn't subscribe to the view, that 'Modern Politics is a chapter in the History of Religions' (Gray 2008: 1), enhancing understanding of others through improving religious literacy has long been perceived as one of the most obvious beneficial side effects of the subject and had been given policy endorsement by the DfE reforms of 2016 which insisted that at least two religions be studied to examination standard.[12] Exemplifying its potential as a 'safe place to discuss difference', the Commission heard moving evidence from a pupil in Manchester that the subject had helped him be a better friend to a classmate during repercussions following the bombing at the Ariana Grande concert there.[13]

Linked to this helpful 'side-effect' of classroom religious education, it was not entirely clear that draining the subject of its religious content would increase its relevance to 'nones'. Relevance is surely in the eye of the beholder and even if there were no religious people in the UK, it might still be important to study faith as a global phenomenon – even more so in the 20 years since 9/11. War in the Middle East and Afghanistan, conflict in Africa and Myanmar need some knowledge of religion to foster understanding. Likewise, socio-sexual controversies in the West whereby faith has somewhat lazily been conflated with intolerance might demand some specific schooling in religious anthropology. Yet instead of engaging seriously with insider discourse, our *de facto* response as a Commission risked a marginalization of faith standpoints and an unwarranted diminution of the role of theology.

Mentioned last in the list of approaches applicable to the subject (CoRE 2018: 37), a number of Commissioners were uneasy about the criticality of theology despite the fact that the scholarly rigour of the subject has been the womb which birthed the Western University system itself. There was mild consternation when a representative of Ofsted giving evidence to the Commission opined that just as Geography should produce geographers, so Religious Education might be expected to produce theologians,[14] since for some delegates, such a thought was antithetical to the provision of a 'neutral religious education'. Although this *de facto* privileging of the agnostic position is philosophically untenable since everyone has a standpoint, a side-effect of such discussions was to return the nomenclature of the subject to centre stage and lead ultimately to a third radical suggestion by the Commission.

Complexity and the name change

Changing the name of the subject was a matter which accompanied the deliberations of the Commission throughout the two years of our meeting. When first discussed 'in house' the most popular option was 'Religion and Ethics' since not only does the acronym remain the same . . .

- it stakes a claim (which no other subject has formally done) for ethics.
- it is already a substantial and stimulating part of the current delivery via 'Big Questions'
- it is an aspect of RE that is always in the news
- it has traction with extra-mural agendas
- it is of interest to pupils of 'all faiths and none'
- it is a natural 'halakah'/'noble path' corrective to any (Western?) emphasis of doctrine over praxis
- it reflects the fact that ethical customs were connected to religion long before they are identifiable as a sub-set of Philosophy – a development Cicero accredits to Socrates in moving Greek thinking beyond epistemology.

So went the argument voiced by protagonists such as myself! However, far from being included in the next phase of discussions, a move towards 'Religion and Belief' appeared somewhat out of the ether and dominated Commissioner emails for a period of time across the autumn of 2017. At this stage 'worldviews' was not particularly on the horizon (*sic*) though a fellow Commissioner did acknowledge that 'this was what he was working towards'.

While intriguing suggestions such as 'Sophology' continued to be aired,[15] the most comprehensive sounding undertaken on nomenclature was the survey conducted the autumn of 2017. Here, for the record, is the breakdown:

Religious Education	30.39%	193
Religion and Ethics	2.05%	13
Religions and Ethics	1.89%	12
Religions and Worldviews	12.60%	80
Religion, Philosophy and Ethics	17.48%	111
Philosophy, Religion and Ethics	13.54%	86
Other	22.05%	140

It can be seen from the above that whatever our original affinity for it, 'Religion and Ethics' was not popular at all. 'Religious Education' arguably had the most support (30.39%) but not if one were to combine the suggestions of 'Religion, Philosophy and Ethics' with 'Philosophy, Religion and Ethics' (31.02%) edging towards a third of respondents. By contrast 'Religion and Worldviews' found favour with just one in eight.

So how did 'Religion and Worldviews' come to be anointed by we Commissioners as the chosen name for a revived subject? In my view it came about because of both pragmatism and an alignment of Humanist and Evangelical argumentation. In terms of practicalities, the secretariat rather than the delegates were bearing the pressure of expectation from the six-figure funding granted by bodies such as Culham St. Gabriel and the Hockerill Trust. Significant outcomes were expected and a name change could symbolize that. In terms of argumentation, while Humanists could align with 'worldviews' as a way of de-throning religion, for evangelical thinkers the idea that everyone has a worldview might de-throne the idea that agnosticism was an unbiased viewpoint. For both sides it cured the problem of relevance since life-choice was at the heart of the subject drama for everyone with the bonus that it would attract attention to the Final Report, 'be a game-changer' in the sector and help to justify the effort and expense of the Commission.

Hence even though it wasn't mentioned in the minutes of the Commission Meeting in late April 2018 and didn't appear in the draft of the Final Document circulated on 15th June, by the time the group met on 25th and 26th of that month, Commissioners were being asked to vote on a name change with 'Religion and Worldviews' one of two options on the table, the other being 'Religion and Belief'. Keeping the same name – despite that being the preference of a third of practitioners – did not appear to be an option. 'Religion and Worldviews' won the day – by two votes. The only serving teacher on the Commission was absent.

It was immediately predictable that this would garner headlines, which for some was seen as an advantage and for others a potential distraction. I think as a Commission we have to own the fact that we had struggled throughout for clarity on a definition for worldviews. It is not ideal when you need to explain what you mean with a special box, but that was where we found ourselves. Part of the problem for the Commissioners was that as the timeline demonstrates, 'worldviews' were inadequately discussed and submitted to insufficient scrutiny in terms of possible problems that might arise around pedagogy or assessment. Even such a basic distinction between personal and institutional worldviews invited complexity. While at one level it might help to classify their relative significance, it was an unstable distinction both for those whose institutional and personal self-understanding were closely identified and for those inclined to bound their personal autonomy contra any perceived institutional system. Time was running out; was there one last chance to change the game?

Eleventh hour plea – Cassandra speaks?

I was becoming increasingly concerned. By now on holiday in France, as a final appeal to colleagues on the Commission meeting for the last time on 7 July 2018, I penned the following. Better than any Bowdlerized summary, it captures my thinking in real time:

Dear Colleagues,

> Aim and Purpose (Othering)
> My first concern is best illustrated by a remark made towards the end of the last meeting. It went unchallenged when a senior Commissioner commented that our task was 'to wrest control' of the subject away from religious groups. While I am not particularly against a body of folk mapping how an NE might be taught, the idea that faith sector stakeholders should be excluded from how their tradition be taught is akin

to a body promoting foreign languages while banning native speakers. To me the most serious intellectual error implied by the Commission is that we believe (*sic*) in a mythical 'neutral position' which 'RE professionals' somehow occupy whereas avowedly religious people do not. Worse still, in this view, confessional stakeholders are suspected of working against the laudable aims of religious tolerance/community cohesion. The problem with this view is it ignores the fact that SACREs, faith schools and national stakeholder bodies demonstrate profound mutual commitment to differing religious traditions on a daily basis. This should be no surprise. People who love languages are likely to appreciate the subtleties, colour and expressions of other tongues.

Practicality (National Entitlement)
How has this affected our report? I think the upshot is that what we have gestated is a prolix/at times repetitive NE not primarily shaped by what should be our key area of concern (Community Multi-Academy Trusts), but which seems to have the long term aim of 'correcting' what some fear is happening in faith schools. From an 'end user' point of view, therefore, it worries me that our endeavour has quickly become impractical. A busy secondary Academy Head is being asked to allocate more time and find expert teachers to deliver a subject which is so variegated only faith schools would have time to master it. To boot, by deliberately not aligning the NE with the linear 'powerful knowledge' agenda behind the reform of public examinations at KS4 & 5, the Head teacher has to make a choice whether to shape KS3 to enable pupils' exam success or to serve a Commission ideal.

It is fanciful to think that the situation in Primary will be any better. We did not assay the situation at KS1 & 2 as we intended. Instead, as Commissioners who have spent a lifetime in the field, our one non-negotiable has been to emphasise the complexity of the subject from Day 1 in KS1. This confuses our arrival point with their start point and flies in the face of what we know to be widespread practitioner knowledge deficit.

Moreover, we have to embrace the fact that for many schools it might only be possible to deliver through the agency of peripatetic teams timetabled in drop down days etc. Hence whatever our aspirations for a National plan and reshaped SACREs, it might be advisable to include the funding of such teams as part of it.

Worldviews
Now at one level all the above already presents an issue before our attempt to rename the subject. Pace Trevor Cooling – a name change

is not a game change unless it has credibility – and I fear 'worldview' is not going to do what we want it to. Like 'meta-narratives' it might work among specialists as a theoretical term but if my unscientific canvas of national RE figures at the Clarke-Woodhead launch (2018) is anything to go by, it is going to fall flat.

I accept that the plural of anecdote is not data, but what makes us even more vulnerable in this regard is our repeated ill-considered binary of 'religious/non-religious' which bizarrely implies the decision for faith or otherwise is the central distinguishing feature of the subject. While this has a certain appeal to my inner Luther, I think it is astonishing in a document which purports to foster inclusivity.

In this regard I am genuinely baffled as to why some are reluctant to advert to extremely influential 'approaches to life' such as Marxism, Existentialism and Utilitarianism on the grounds that they may be unfashionable or have valency with religious positions. Almost anything would soften the binary which despite its good intent, Religion and Worldviews as a title doesn't quite manage.

Furthermore, as I have been at pains to point out, our almost unique non-religious exemplar, Humanism, means something very different on the continent of Europe and I'm not sure any of us would want to be party to an unqualified 'Brexit' definition.

The Danger of the Change
I am sympathetic that the move towards Worldviews is partly driven by the (unproven) idea it would be more attractive to "nones" but surely any perceived de-emphasis of the importance of religions will invite the question – why teach them at all? To be honest, this is my major concern, that the use of Worldviews will lead to either the DfE or busy Heads bundling this subject in with Citizenship or Relationships and Sex Education to be delivered through non-examined curricula during form sessions. The subject as we currently understand it would disappear.

Hence I'm not sure what colleagues think of the Clarke Woodhead suggestion, but if two reports opted for Religion, Beliefs and Values, that might have traction and preserve the best characteristics of the subject as it is currently understood. Our suggestion is fraught with far more risk.

Alas it was too late. The Commission met for the last time in the hallowed environs of the Jerusalem Chamber deep in the bowels of the Palace of Westminster. There was no intention to revise the key proposals of the draft. And in any case, there was no WiFi.

The report was launched on 12th September at Westminster. I remember being pleased to see colleagues and I was impressed, too, by the Dean's speech. John Hall had chaired all the proceedings with considerable élan and commendable patience. However, it may be of interest that in presenting the report, Dean Hall did not use the term 'irresistible coalition' even though I have reason to believe the phrase was in his script. In that moment, I concluded the Dean already knew, that despite the ambitions of the document, the eventual report would be incapable of constructing such or maintaining such an alliance, with all the risks that entailed.

Aftermath

'In the end is my beginning. . . .' After two months of false dawns, a letter was received from the DfE on 6th December 2018 and circulated to Commissioners a week later on the 15th. The ambition to influence the DfE had foundered on issues which mirrored salient concerns articulated above:

> First – in terms of the name change, while acknowledging that the Commission had worked hard, the first thing the Minister specifically pointed out was that he had essentially accepted that changing the name to 'worldviews' risked diluting the teaching of Religious Education.
>
> Second – in terms of othering the Minister deftly reaffirmed the statutory nature of the discipline but specifically argued that any diminution of the religious content of the subject would be undesirable since it 'fosters mutual respect and tolerance of those of different faiths and beliefs'.
>
> Third – in terms of National Entitlement. While addressing some of the recruitment and training needs through bursaries for training and specific funding of Subject Knowledge Enhancement, the Minister was not minded to revolutionize the subject along the lines of the National Entitlement at this time on the very practical grounds that teacher workloads were already under strain from the 2016 KS4 and KS5 reforms.[16]

As might be expected, the Commissioners were disappointed, as was the Secretariat anchored by Rudi Lockyer, to whom I wrote:

> This is very disappointing but was always a risk.
>
> As a Commissioner, my experience was that whereas back in January we were talking about an 'Irresistible Coalition', by Spring there was a perceptible change in direction that was looking for the report

first and foremost to 'be a game changer' and far less concerned about the potential reaction of NASACRE, CES, Board of Deputies. I still don't quite know why that happened. As I remarked on 20th July, thereafter I had a sense it was the correction of the perceived shortcomings of faith school approaches rather than the absence of RE in state schools that had become the salient concern.

I think your response is understandably robust, but it might be that we need to do more to plot a way forward. We don't have to regard the Report as the final word and it could be that with the right hermeneutic, it could still have immense traction.

Now certainly the question of hermeneutics has remained high on the agenda and as I write seems to be fulfilling a role in consensus building among the religious education community both at theoretical and practitioner levels. Trevor Cooling is a major protagonist in the debate using (what seems to me) Thiselton's re-presentation of Gadamer's original 'horizon' theory. Cooling sees hermeneutics as a way forward since it synthesizes both the knowledge and developmental aspirations of the subject (Cooling 2020: 411). Always thoughtful, I'm still inclined to think that the extent to which Trevor has continued to write about worldviews while claiming he had no influence on the deliberations of the Commission has the ring of the 'lady doth protest too much' (Cooling 2020: 409).

Meanwhile, the urge for implementation of the National Entitlement is being led by essentially the self-same Secretariat of the Commission[17] but by securing Templeton funding and engaging Stephen Pett as a resource writer, it has augmented its chances of success in two ways. First with regard to the National Entitlement, a new, less prolix version is in the pipeline and second, a subtle change in emphasis may prove salvific since it is likely to emphasize a 'worldviews approach' rather than be distracted by a renaming of the subject.[18]

This is to be welcomed since a focus on approaches resonates with the work of Gillian Georgiou and Kathryn Wright (2020) and Richard Kueh (2018). Ostensibly it solves the problem of managing an infinite range of content by marrying flexible methodology with powerful knowledge theory, so it could be said to have more political possibilities. It also reduces the risk of Cognitive Load which as noted above, is considered inimical to pupil learning. That said, in the simplified current tripartite lens form being proposed for schools, theology becomes understood as 'thinking through believing' while 'thinking through thinking' and 'thinking through living' are apportioned to philosophy and social science respectively.[19] This not only leads to specific problems with the notion of revelation and religious truth claims, it more generally opens up questions about curriculum identity and therefore the future prospects of the subject itself (Hannam and Biesta 2019).

In terms of othering, though the numbers attempting an examination award in the subject has continued to decline since the heights reached in 2010, it remains fashionable in some quarters to hold faith schools responsible.

> The faith sector influences R.E. in two ways: politically and economically. It has up until now had an effective veto over any attempts to reform R.E. nationally although this may be changing. And though far from monolithic, the faith sector is a solid market for the production and sale of resources, services training and qualifications. This power and influence has started to impact widely on the non-faith sector. Organisationally, R.E. is in the hands of producer communities, some of which are led and funded by faith-based organisations.
> *(Brine and Chater 2020)*

Cast as exemplars of economic and political control from which the subject needs to be liberated, faith groups constitute 'a mortal threat to religious education', a position which could also be both implicitly and explicitly deduced from reports published either side of the Commission's work (Clarke and Woodhead 2018; Clayton et al. 2018). In my view, such opinions are counter-factual and indeed are counter-productive. Energy should be expended instead on facilitating the delivery of religious education in places where it is currently not delivered rather than on unresearched assumptions that faith schools are fomenting rather than reducing prejudice and are harmful to community cohesion.

Meanwhile, despite the RE Council remaining four-square behind the name change, the inability of various reports and think tanks to find an agreed nomenclature has hampered its adoption. In this context, the relatively recent proposal by the Welsh Government to relaunch the subject as 'Religion Values and Ethics' risks upsetting everyone. Not only does it eschew the term Religion and Worldviews which the RE Council would prefer, it rejects the evidence of its own survey which suggested the subject should retain its name and removes the right of pupil withdrawal from parents – a rubicon which even the Commission did not dare to cross. All the while significant associations of religious education teachers in England (e.g. NATRE and ATCRE) have retained their pre-Commission designation[20] and my summary would be that despite its continuing prominence in the discussions of the RE Council, there is little evidence that schools see the incorporation of Worldviews into the subject name as a priority.

Concluding remarks

Rehearsing the journey made by the RE Commission, as delegates, it may be both salutary and timely to accept criticisms that we did not adequately:

Represent practitioners
Link our consultation with our conclusions
Incorporate positive aspects of Government policy
Make common cause with well-disposed protagonists
Represent the breadth of current educational theory

The upshot was that our Commission report failed to build the 'irresistible coalition' necessary to effect policy change. This is something of a shame, since the very first evidence session saw Anglicans, Catholics and Humanists agree on a fundamental point central to the concerns of schools and practitioners – viz. religious education must be properly academic and taught in every school.[21] I think this is a unifying principle which can help rebuild consensus. The subject itself is demanding and credible, and while every discipline has to confront the issue of classroom relevance, the religious wisdom of the world is at least as applicable to the everyday as the broad shores of science and the arts. In an epoch when it would appear that more young folk pray than their elders, we must be careful not to project our own diffidence onto others.[22]

Moving forward, to enable policy makers to take advantage of such basic principles of agreement, it would be wise to simplify the proposed National Entitlement, cease the 'othering of faith' and ease off lobbying for a name change. In terms of a benchmark Entitlement matrix, I think practitioners should be trusted to apply their knowledge attentive to

- Matters of central importance to a variety of religious and philosophical beliefs studied in their complexity, diversity and plurality. (Doctrines)
- Ways in which religious and secular rituals, festivals and artistic expression communicate identity, culture, mystery, transcendence and paradox. (Practices)
- How foundational texts and the ways in which they are interpreted can shape minds and lives. (Hermeneutics)
- The ways in which worldviews may inform moral behaviour and social norms. (Ethics)

Even if one can assume that there is rarely, if ever, only one expression of any given standpoint, far from marginalizing and even othering faith-based stakeholders, their role as 'native speakers' should be affirmed. I share some of the concerns about a content heavy curricula at KS4, but the 'insider turn' fostered by the 2016 reforms was a positive move which as Sushma Sahajpal remarked, has at last enabled her to speak about an elephant on its own terms rather than conceiving of it as a defective horse.[23] While the impact of SACREs is variegated and the importance of local ASCs differs from place to place, stakeholder groups are key to community cohesion and should be encouraged, not alienated. Better funding rather than their replacement would be a more collaborative path to pursue and foster the kind of outcomes which both policy makers and practitioners desire.

As regards 'Religion and Worldviews', at a time of acute vulnerability for the subject, it seems an unnecessary risk to impose a change in its name unless there is overwhelming support from schools and practitioners. 'Religious Education' is not perfect but may at least protect the subject from disappearing into a subset either of Well-being or of Critical Thinking.[24] Worldviews as an approach has merit but like current proposals around 'Lens Disciplinarity' and 'Big Ideas', any pedagogical methodologies should take root naturally rather than do violence to the mixed ecology of the subject by being made compulsory.

Last but not least, I would make a plea for Theology to be understood in its etymological sense, as thoughtful conversation about God, rather than a discipline that presupposes faith (Towey 2020).[25] I weary of pointing out that Richard Dawkins has made more money as a published theologian than as a published scientist:

> The word 'God' is a Theology in itself, indivisibly one, inexhaustibly various, from the vastness and the simplicity of its meaning . . . How can we investigate any part of any order of Knowledge, and stop short of that which enters into every order? All true principles run over with it, all phenomena converge to it; it is truly the First and the Last.
> *(Newman 1927 [1865]: 43)*

Far from bracketing out religious belief, the question of God is inclusive. It merits centre stage in the intellectual adventure requiring *a fortiori* a place on our school curricula, whatever we call the subject.

Notes

1 Trevor Cooling at the first session of CoRE, 3 November 2016, as recorded by Amira Tharani (2020: 39–40). It brought to mind a protest I once made at a Higher Education Change Academy meeting where it was presumed that as managers, our first step was to identify colleagues open to change. My own view was that the first step for a manager should be to ascertain whether the change in view was a good idea!

2 For the record I only missed one of these (York) and managed to attend gatherings in Exeter, Manchester and Birmingham as well events in London which included a 'plenary' style consultation event on 06/12/17.
3 Other expert presentations included Barbara Wintersgill (see below), Ofsted, Charles Clarke and Linda Woodhead, a Plymouth Teacher Network and the Catholic Education Service. Commissioners also attended and fielded questions at gatherings of the REC (Religious Education Council) and NASACRE (National Association of Statutory Councils on Religious Education).
4 It might be noted in passing that although there was money set aside for the Commission for research, to my knowledge, the survey was the only significant expenditure in this regard.
5 In retrospect, for example, it might have been wise to draft in two more teachers to the group during Year 2.
6 Head of Ofsted, Professor Daniel Muijs, at ResearchEd Conference, Durrington High School, 28/04/2018.
7 When asked whether her work might be construed as pedagogically opposed to the 2016 KS4 and KS5 reforms, with refreshing if astringent honesty, Barbara responded: 'Hell yes!'
8 Professor John Sullivan and Rev. Dr Duncan MacPherson respectively, quoted by Towey 2020: 143.
9 For further international comparisons see 'Toledo Guiding Principles on Teaching about Religions and Beliefs in Public Schools'. Available online: www.osce.org/odihr/29154?download=true.
10 15 January 2018.
11 Hinds would confirm Government control of Free Faith Schools admissions criteria on 11 May, 2018.
12 www.gov.uk/government/speeches/qualifications-and-curriculum-reform (accessed 5 December 2021).
13 The Manchester evidence session took place on 14 July 2017 at Trinity School, Hulme.
14 Mark Evans, 2 September 2017.
15 Dave Francis, reonline.org.uk/2013/12/16/time-to-ditch-religious-education-and-religious-studies-dave-francis/ (accessed 5 December 2021).
16 The correspondence is accessible here: www.commissiononre.org.uk/commission-chair-responds-to-secretary-of-state/.
17 Trevor Cooling, Rudi Lockyer and Amira Chilvers-Tharani constituted the Secretariat to the Commission of which Denise Cush was a key protagonist.
18 This was confirmed most recently by evidence shared by Cooling and Pett at an RE Council meeting on 16 November 2021.
19 See www.schools.norfolk.gov.uk/-/media/schools/files/teaching-and-learning/religious-education-agreed-syllabus/norfolk-religious-education-agreed-syllabus-2019.pdf (accessed 5 December 2021).
20 National Association of Teachers of R.E. and Association of Teachers of Catholic R.E. respectively.
21 Derek Holloway, Philip Robinson and Andrew Copson on 23 February 2016 at Grey Coat Hospital School, Westminster. They likewise agreed that any formative dimensions of the subject were to be regarded as secondary.
22 See www.bbc.co.uk/news/uk-58681075.
23 Giving evidence to the All Party Parliamentary Group on Religious Education, April 2016.

24 I do have a fear that we will make it too dangerous to teach and end up with Theology in faith schools and a form of Mindfulness and Citizenship elsewhere.
25 In one sense it can be argued that faith rather than theology needs re-imagining. Newman long ago pointed out that 'faith' (or 'trust' if you prefer), is an epistemological fundament – e.g. 'I haven't been to Paris recently, but I know (trust) it is still there.' As contemporary theories of 'Fuzzy Epistemology' confirm, a form of faith grounds common discourse and is part of what Newman describes as a *Grammar of Assent*.

References

Brine, A. and Chater, M. (2020) 'How did we get here? The twin narratives', in M. Chater (ed.) *Reforming R.E.: Power and knowledge in a worldviews curriculum*. Melton: John Catt.

Clarke, C. and Woodhead, L. (2018) *A New Settlement Revised: Religion and belief in schools* (Westminster Faith Debates). Available online: http://faithdebates.org.uk/wp-content/uploads/2018/07/Clarke-Woodhead-A-New-Settlement-Revised.pdf (accessed 5 December 2019).

Clayton, M., Mason, A., Swift, A. and Wareham, R. (2018) 'How to regulate faith schools'. Impact Pamphlet 25. Philosophical perspective on education policy. Retrieved from Wiley Online library: Doi/pdf/10.1111/2048-416X.2018.12005.x (accessed 5 December 2021).

Commission on Religious Education (2017) *Interim Report: Religious education for all*. London: RE Council. Available online: https://www.commissiononre.org.uk/wp-content/uploads/2017/09/Commission-on-Religious-Education-Interim-Report-2017.pdf (accessed 2 December 2020).

Commission on Religious Education (CoRE). 2018. *Final Report: Religions and worldviews: The way forward*. Available online: www.commissiononre.org.uk/wp-content/uploads/2018/09/Final-Report-of-the-Commission-on-RE.pdf (accessed 2 December 2021).

Cooling, T. (2020) 'Worldview in religious education: Autobiographical reflections on *The Commission on Religious Education in England: Final report*', *British Journal of Religious Education* 42(4): 403–414. Doi:10.1080/01416200.2020.1764497.

Dinham, A. and Shaw, M. (2015) *RE for Real: The future of teaching and learning about religion and belief*. London: Goldsmiths.

Enser, M. (2018) *Teach like Nobody's Watching: The essential guide to effective and efficient teaching*. Carmarthen: Crown House.

Gale, K. and Wyatt, J. (2019) 'Autoethnography and activism: Movement intensity and potential', *Qualitative Inquiry* 25(6): 566–568. Doi.org/10.1177%2F1077800418800754.

Gearon, L. (2014) *On Holy Ground: The theory and practice of religious education*. London: Routledge.

Georgiou, G. and Wright, K. (2020) 'Disciplinarity, religion and worldviews: Making the case for theology, philosophy and human/social sciences', in M. Chater (ed.) *Reforming RE: Power and knowledge in a worldviews curriculum*. Melton: John Catt.

Gray, J. (2008) *Black Mass. Apocalyptic religion and the death of Utopia*. London: Penguin.

Hannam, P. and Biesta, G. (2019) 'Religious education, a matter of understanding? Reflections on the final report of the Commission on Religious Education', *Journal of Beliefs & Values* 40(1): 55–63. Doi:10.1080/13617672.2018.155433.

Jackson, R. (2016) 'A retrospective introduction to religious education: An interpretive approach', *Discourse and Communication for Sustainable Education* 7(1): 149–160. Doi.org/10.1515/dcse-2016-0011.

Kueh, R. (2018) 'Religious education and the "knowledge problem"', in M. Chater and M. Castelli (eds) *We Need to Talk About Religious Education: Manifestos for the future of RE*. London: Jessica Kingsley.

Lawton, C. (2016) *GCSE Judaism*. London: Board of Deputies of British Jews. Available online: www.bod.org.uk/resources/resources-publications/ (accessed 5 December 2021).

McGrail, P. and Towey, A. (2019) 'Partners in progress? An impact study of the 2016 religious education reforms in England', *International Studies in Christianity and Education* (special issue: 'Critical Christian intersections between higher education and schools') 23(3): 278–298. Doi.org/10.1177/2056997119865569.

Morgan, J. (2015) 'Michael Young and the politics of the school curriculum', *British Journal of Educational Studies* 63(1): 5–22. Doi.org/10.1080/00071005.2014.983044.

Muller, J. and Young, M. (2019) 'Knowledge, power and powerful knowledge re-visited', *The Curriculum Journal* 30(2): 196–214. Doi.org/10.1080/09585176.2019.1570292.

Newman, J. H. (1927 [1865]) *The Idea of a University*. Chicago: Loyola University Press.

Smith, D. R., Nixon, G., Pearce, J. (2018) 'Bad religion as false religion: An empirical study of UK religious education teachers: Essentialist religious discourse', *Religions* 9, 361(11): 1–19. Doi:10.3390/rel9110361.

Tharani, A. (2020) 'The Commission and its recommendations', in M. Chater (ed.) *Reforming RE: Power and knowledge in a worldviews curriculum*. Melton: John Catt.

Towey, A (2020) 'Grammar of dissent? Theology and the language of religious education', *New Blackfriars* 101(1092): 135–152. Doi.org/10.1111/nbfr.12542.

Wintersgill, B. (2017) *Big Ideas for Religious Education*. Exeter: University of Exeter.

Yoo, J. (2019) 'A year of writing dangerously: A narrative of hope', *The International Journal for the Practice & Theory of Creative Writing* 16(3): 353–362. Doi.org/10.1080/14790726.2018.1520893.

Young, M. (2011) 'The return to subjects: A sociological perspective on the UK coalition government's approach to the 14–19 curriculum', *The Curriculum Journal* 22(2): 265–278. Doi.org/10.1080/09585176.2011.574994.

2
A NEW SETTLEMENT?

A defence of the 1944 Act

Marius Felderhof

Of late, talk of a 'new legal settlement' for religious education has been raised in various circles, virtually exclusively, it must be said, amongst members of the education profession and academics. For example, the 'Westminster Faith Debates' included a pamphlet entitled, 'A New Settlement: Religion and Belief in Schools' (2015), now more recently reissued as 'A New Settlement Revised: Religion and Belief in Schools' (Clarke and Woodhead 2018). Other studies have come up with remarkably similar suggestions (Dinham and Shaw 2015: 1; Butler-Sloss 2015: 37). A few years earlier the second recommendation of the Religious Education Council's Review of Religious Education in England (2013: 32) was to 'pursue with policy makers the challenges around the existing "settlement" for RE'. Not surprisingly the Commission on Religious Education (CoRE), one of two successor reports of the original Review, duly recommended changes to the legislation on religious education (2018, Recommendations 2, 4 and 8). The outstanding question is whether a 'new legal settlement' would address the weaknesses of religious education or do these weaknesses stem from elsewhere that have little to do with the original settlement? Indeed, closer attention to the original settlement would show it to be best fitted for our secular and religiously plural society. This is the position defended here.

To those who are less familiar with current educational rumblings, the 'settlement' refers to an agreement in 1944 between the government and some of the historic providers of schooling, namely, the Church of England and other (mainly, but not exclusively, religious) bodies, about the funding, provision and character of schooling. The agreement was expressed in the 1944 Education Act, sometimes known as the Butler Act. It is this Act

DOI: 10.4324/9781003264439-3

which is now seen, by some, to be an obstacle to a deeper change in the character of religious education and, importantly, to an alternative philosophical basis for schooling[1] as a whole in England.

It is interesting to note that neither of the original parties to the settlement (whether it is the government or the main historic providers of schools),[2] appear to have called for the revision of legislation, or for revisiting the original settlement. The discontent with the original settlement does not issue from them. This lack of interest can be attributed to the fact that the main elements of the original settlement have suited them all. The key provisions have therefore remained in place despite the many vicissitudes in education. For example, the governments of both persuasions have accepted rather than challenged a continuing role for the historic providers, even within the creation of whole new categories of schools; academies, free schools, and studio schools. They have also retained the important features of requiring a provision for religious education and collective worship in schools. Admittedly the precise funding arrangements, curricular prescriptions and freedoms with respect to admissions, together with the role played by local authorities, have changed over time. These changes, however, did not affect the more foundational provision for faith schools (properly speaking 'schools with a religious character') nor the overall legal requirement for religious education and collective worship[3] in schools.

Admittedly, there have been practical influences on the provision of religious education and collective worship in schools, (especially on those without a religious foundation), since educational changes in 1944. There has certainly been a significant impact on the *perception* of the place and role of religious education and collective worship with the introduction of a national curriculum, the EBacc and the provision of free schools and academies. The introduction of a national curriculum gave the impression that the religious education determined locally was less significant. The exclusion of religious education from the EBacc gave the impression that the subject did not really matter. Academies and free schools were offered greater freedom to devise their own school curriculum, including the curriculum for religious education and thus the opportunity to digress from the local agreed syllabus. The loss of local authority control over schools made the work of local Standing Advisory Councils on Religious Education (SACREs) and local Agreed Syllabus Conferences increasingly irrelevant. It is this changing situation in the provision of educational institutions, in the criteria for judging schools, in the curriculum, in the governance and control of schools and in admissions that has given wider credence to the appeal made to lawmakers to revisit 'the settlement'.

However, it is important to differentiate the minor adjustments (those that might usefully be made on the order of the Secretary of State for Education to render the original legal settlement more effective, e.g. the inclusion of religious education in the EBacc, additional support for the training of religious education teachers, etc., from those more radical, foundational changes that are sought by means of a change in education law. The envisaged more radical, foundational changes could in effect alter the place of religious life in the public square and the co-operation of religious institutions with government for the common good. It will be maintained here that with minor adjustments reforms could be addressed fairly easily without the upheaval of altering the foundational settlement and the need for a change in the law.

Those protagonists, who nevertheless persist in calling for the more foundational change requiring a change in the law, are driven not so much by institutional changes in education as the perception of changes in society (see Butler-Sloss 2015: 15ff) and, much more importantly, their perception of the ideal of what constitutes religious education in a secular context. The secularisation of society, it is suggested, requires religious education to change from its interest in developing the character of young people, drawing on and using the resources of religious faith (as in the 2007 Birmingham Agreed Syllabus), to one that focuses increasingly on secular ideologies under the supervision of a select, centralised professional body. In brief, the critics' goal is primarily to change religious education into the secular study of religions and additionally into the study of those ideologies that vaguely resemble religions. Secondarily, they wish to wrest the control of religious education away from local authorities and communities and to locate it in the religious education profession. In their eyes the legal nomenclature, 'religious instruction' in the 1944 Act and 'religious education' in the 1988 Education Reform Act, suggests an agenda unsuitable for a secular society. The obsession in various reports (Dinham and Shaw 2015: 1; Clarke and Woodhead 2018: 48; CoRE 2018: 11), with changing the name of the subject *in law* is at heart a desire to change the essence of the subject. Such change is impossible, so long as religious communities still exercise significant influence.

The determination to change the law may have a price. It runs the serious risk of initiating a change that cannot be controlled. Those seeking change are all too readily joined by the traditional antagonists to religious life who, overtly or covertly, resent any expression of religious faith in 'the public square', and hence in schools. These antagonists strive assiduously to limit, control and circumscribe religious faith and thus limit people's basic human right to express publicly their religious sensibilities and to transmit these sensibilities to their children. In effect, those calling for a change in the law may be opening the door to an intolerant secularism and a decisive shift away from the influence of religiously interested people and institutions.

The 1944 Act and its critics

There must be considerable caution when unpicking a settled state of affairs in society. This caution might be represented dismissively as conservatism and fear of change, but there are more positive reasons for preferring the existing settlement to what is being proposed as an alternative. The reasons may be stated simply. Where one may fairly describe the 'religious' provisions of the 1944 Act as: (i) responsive and religiously sensitive; (ii) permissive and plural; and (iii) consensual; its critics, on the other hand, are more often than not: (i) reactionary and secular; (ii) illiberal and narrow; and (iii) complacent and paternalistic. If offered a policy choice between these two sets of descriptions, one suspects that most British people would prefer the former, the existing settlement, over that demanded by the critics. The question is: 'Are these descriptions warranted?'

Responsive and religiously sensitive vs reactionary and secular

In what sense is the 1944 Act 'responsive and religiously sensitive' whereas the critics are 'reactionary and secular'? The 1944 Act was formed in a period of crisis. The horrors of the rise of Nazism (and communism) were perceived as challenging the very foundations of Western civilisation and its values. The legislators saw religious life as part of the solution, hence the early syllabi could speak of sharing the 'best values that Christianity has to offer'. The teaching is not so much *about* Christianity; it is much more concerned with what Christianity is about (an important shift in focus),[4] i.e. guiding and supporting pupils in living with integrity with the resources that Christian traditions have to hand. To come to understand what a religion might be about demands a profound religious sensitivity and criticism that takes religious understanding seriously. This does not mean that one must be religious to have such sensitivity or to engage in such religious (self)-criticism. One might follow the example of Ludwig Wittgenstein (1980; Malcolm 1983) who demonstrated a profound appreciation of religious ways of thinking and acting, whilst saying that he himself did not think or live like that.

It is clear that in the eyes of the critics of the 1944 Act, the challenge facing society and its educational institutions is a very different one. Religious life is seen to be not so much part of the solution as the source of the problem (see Butler-Sloss 2015: 33–35). Religions help to form and define the identities of individuals and the communities they serve. Given the different traditions, there are going to be different identities and recognisable social groups. The assumption is that the differences will inevitably lead to conflict. The fear of conflict demands a reaction. The envisaged solution to conflict is to teach *about* them in the hope that the more one knows *about* them the more tolerant and accepting one will be. The very different possibility that an increased knowledge *about* religions and beliefs may sharpen one's perceptions and one's objections to whoever happens to be 'other' or different is not considered to be a natural outcome (as recognised by Dinhan and Shaw 2015: 3).

The expectation of tolerance from the study of religions appears to be based on a two-fold mechanism. The first is to study religions using methodologies without religious presuppositions and to engage in such study 'neutrally' and 'objectively'. In adopting a methodology *outside* the religious frame of reference one is deliberately locating the pupil within a secular perspective and, perhaps inadvertently, fostering a non-religious identity. This secularity supposedly avoids the attributed latent antipathies and antagonisms within situations of religious pluralism. The second mechanism is to blur the boundaries of the identities. This is easily achieved by highlighting the pluralism within a specific religious tradition and by adopting secular concepts and frameworks that range across religious traditions[5] and, extending the frameworks even further to include so-called non-religious worldviews, such that the identity differences between them become less significant, inconsequential or even somewhat arbitrary. Any religious education that takes this form of the study of religions is rightly considered to be reactionary in adopting a position which sees religions as a problem to which a reaction is required and promotes the solution of a secular outlook that has been prevalent for the last 40 to 50 years.

If conflict between communities is the primary issue, the solution may not be to relativise or subvert religious identities through a secular form of religious studies. One might instead aim to focus on what religions are about, viz., to understand 'the good' and to live with integrity. Religions share this interest and will readily support each other to remove injustices and engage in peace building and to remind communities of their religious commitments that exhort them to selfless service, to voluntary suffering, to loving one's enemies and to do good to those who hate you. A vision of a deeper religious life might in fact inspire conflict resolution.

Permissive and plural vs illiberal and narrow

It is clear that those who devised the 1944 Education Act were acutely aware of the existence of religious pluralism and of the presence of many in society who did not identify with any religious tradition. Much of the religious pluralism at that time arose between Christian denominations and also between forms of Judaism. But the solutions created by the Act are equally applicable to the deeper pluralism and secularism of our current age. The on-going existence of independent schools, together with the possibility of voluntary aided and controlled schools alongside county schools in the maintained sector created a diversity of provision ideally suited to a plural democracy. It was grounded in a deep suspicion of fascist and communist nation states that had used their school systems to promote a supposedly unifying state ideology, not uncommonly against the wishes and interests of parents.

The existence of independent schools avoided a state monopoly in education. On the other hand, in the maintained sector voluntary aided schools (and to some extent controlled schools) enabled religious communities to devise their own ethos and curriculum in schools that could support and sustain their characteristic life at relatively modest additional costs[6] to these communities. There was to be a more general religious ethos in county (community) schools through the provision of collective (i.e. public) worship at the start or end of the day. The religious instruction was to be done according to an Agreed Syllabus, an agreement based on negotiations in a conference between the (i) local authority, (ii) teachers, (iii) the Church of England and (iv) other religious denominations. Those parents, or groups, who were still not satisfied with the Agreed Syllabus would be given access to school premises to provide their own religious instruction (at their own cost).

The freedom of religion, or from religion, was fully recognised by also granting parents the right to withdraw their children from religious instruction and from collective worship. The latter was facilitated by requiring collective worship to be held at the beginning or end of the day. Teachers were similarly granted the freedom to be excused from providing religious instruction or to participate in collective worship without any risk of a financial (or other) penalty. It is clear that in these provisions of the Act, the legislators were bending over backwards to accommodate all those of any religious persuasion and of none. The Act is positively permissive by facilitating religious communities in education and it is openly plural by avoiding any whiff of religious coercion. The only complaint that may be laid against the 1944 Act is that it is too permissive and opens the door to too many possibilities, ideologically and religiously, i.e. those positions that might harbour an extremism that denies others equal rights to their way of life.

The objection may be raised that the permissive pluralism of the 1944 Act was rooted in an apparently unwarranted assumption, namely, that any serious exploration of religious life, and that any pursuit of what it might mean to live a truly religious life, will comport generally with the insights and widely held values of the Christian tradition. The later accusation that the religious education following the 1944 Act was 'confessional' (a term used in a pejorative way) is grounded in this assumption. And it is accurate only insofar as the religious education of the post-1944 period sought to transmit those values to young people largely by means of the familiar scriptures and practices which supported them. A more practical pluralism would draw on a wider range of texts and practices to support the same values.

The critics of the existing settlement are not content to draw on the permissive pluralism of the Act, instead they have systematically sought to narrow it. Where the Act provides scope for dissent, the critics seek to limit it. This they do in four ways. First, they seek to limit or preferably eliminate the possibility of withdrawal from religious education (for criticism, see Barnes 2020: 139–163). They simply find it difficult to imagine that there might be a good reason[7] for withdrawing from their secular version of the ideal religious education. Second, they seek to nationalise or centralise religious education. Removing religious education from the orbit of local authorities is an effective way of limiting diversity and eliminating any dissenting views of what constitutes 'good' religious education. Third, they seek to 'professionalise' religious education. Where the Act envisages agreement between politicians, teachers and religious bodies at a local level, the critics seek to restrict the formation of a religious education syllabus to selected religious education teachers and academics in the appropriate fields. It is the job of politicians simply to guarantee the supply of money for the subject and to leave the key decisions to the 'experts'. On the other hand, it is apparently the duty of leaders and representatives of religious bodies to acknowledge that they are tainted by self-interest and limited in their understanding of what is 'educational'. Without diminishing the importance of experts, this planned 'professionalisation' (see Chapter 3 in this volume) is a profound narrowing of input and opinions. Fourth, the critics are so convinced that they are able to define the key features and 'entitlements' of what might pass for 'good' religious education that they are happy to impose these on *all* schools whether they be independent, 'faith' schools or academies and free schools, that is to say, any educational institution that might dare to differ in their understanding of education and its appropriate curriculum.

The critics might have taken advantage of the liberality of the 1944 Act to persuade others of their vision of the ideal religious education but they have failed lamentably to do so. Their demand for new legislation stems solely from their frustration and desire to impose it on all. Having chosen this route as the best way of realising their aim, they show themselves to be fundamentally illiberal and narrow in the sense of not admitting alternative or wider views.

It may be protested that the critics of the settlement in the 1944 Act are motivated by the goal of opening religious education to 'other religions', to 'belief' and to so-called 'non-religious worldviews' (Butler-Sloss, 2015: 34). Hence their desire for a re-designation and re-definition of the subject in law. In this respect, it might be claimed, the critics are much more open-minded than those who are content with the key features of the 1944 Act that have been continued in current legislation. Yet this claim is contested. The permissiveness of the Act leaves ample scope for the consideration of faiths other than the Christian faith, and much will depend on precisely what is meant by 'belief' and 'worldview'. Any close examination of religious life cannot avoid, *inter alia*, considering loss of meaning, doubt, temptation, scepticism, reasonableness, prejudice, critiques and antagonists, so that much is already admitted as permissible material. The question is what is excluded in the original settlement that a redefinition of religious education in law would permit?

Consensual vs complacent and paternalistic

As regards county (community) schools, it is clear that the 1944 Act expects a consensual approach by prescribing a process of establishing an Agreed Syllabus Conference to determine the precise syllabus to be used in any local authority community school. Such a conference might simply adopt the Agreed Syllabus of another authority or exploit the ideas of others where it suited. Given the diversity of parties from whom agreement must be sought, one can expect many different voices. In addition to the diversely committed religious voices, one can also expect those of atheists, agnostics and sceptics from within the committee of local authority representatives or from the committee of teachers, with their respective political and educational interests. The entire process is quite simply designed to be inclusive and moderating of the more radical and extremist voices.

Diverse local authorities have defined needs and resources in their area. This may ensure a degree of pedagogical rootedness without condemning them to being narrowly parochial. Furthermore, the process in the existing law is responsive by admitting requirements for revision and re-assessment. It is not surprising, therefore, that local authorities, which became increasingly religiously plural, would design an Agreed Syllabus fit for a religiously plural population, such as that of Birmingham in 1975. Subsequent revisions in the Syllabus in Birmingham in 1995 and 2007 sought to address other perceived deficiencies. The current legal arrangements have, therefore, proved their worth and adaptability to a changing world.

In contrast to this consensual process, critics of the settlement, who seek to prescribe a defined entitlement in law, will in doing so sacrifice the adaptability currently available. They will be imposing the rigidities of a definition of religious education that happens to be in fashion in the 'religious education community' at a specific point in time. Further, the process of local agreement is to be abolished in favour of the decisions of selected professionals. Any reference to the role of other interested parties is couched in such a way that they are essentially powerless to have any real influence on shaping the religious education curriculum. Hence the accusations of paternalism; it is a matter of the very few telling the many what is good for them.

It may be the case that many local authorities and volunteers across the country will be content to hand over the responsibilities laid upon them by the current law to the 'experts' nationally if the associated financial responsibilities are also shifted to central government. The truth is that the central government is unlikely to be any more generous than local authorities in the funding of religious education unless they are fully persuaded of the merit of what is proposed to be delivered in the curriculum. Excluding the politicians from the decision making process about the content of religious education is unlikely to be helpful.

However, the critics may believe they have just such a vision of religious education as to convince and inspire the government into believing that the selected professionals have just the recipe to abolish supposed religious ignorance and conflict, a recipe moreover that is essential to human flourishing, individually and communally. But this is where the complacency of the critics is so striking. The proposed recipe or ideal of religious education is not so very different from that commended by the RE Council's Review (2013) or from the Non-Statutory National Framework for religious education published in 2004, which was actually incorporated into most Agreed Syllabi. It has, in fact, failed to convince many schools and parents of the need for such religious education. The result is that many schools simply do not provide religious education and parents do not demand it.

The recipe for religious education commended by the 'religious education community' is in fact not so very different from the vast majority of Agreed Syllabi that had emerged since 1975. This self-acclaimed recipe has presided over a period of sustained secularisation in British society and may itself have been a major contributory factor. The subversive and secularising impact of this form of religious education is such that even the religious communities do not clamour for its provision in schools in places where it is not being delivered. Yet in letters to the Secretary of State for Education, the RE Council on behalf of the 'religious education community' was prepared to claim that the religious education in Britain is the envy of other countries. It may (arguably; though see Barnes 2014: 10–24) be envied in other countries but not in many of our English schools it seems.

There is an urgent need to explore what form of religious education will gain the support of parents, schools and religious bodies, for such support will not fail to catch the eye of politicians. As Birmingham has proved with its 2007 Religious Education Syllabus, the local authority *will* provide funding and its schools and academies *will* embrace it and deliver it. The faith leaders in the city are on record of having actively supported and defended the 2007 Agreed Syllabus. Teachers and schools can deliver religious education with confidence precisely because of the communal, political and religious support the Agreed Syllabus commands. To abandon the processes prescribed in the 1944 Act in favour of some form of professional paternalism is to abandon the strengths gained by a democratic discipline.[8] It is the teaching profession that gains when it engages seriously with grassroots at local level and with interested parties. Giving these parties a real say in the curriculum through the process of agreement is both more testing and more rewarding. To assign the 'non-professionals' a consultative role without decision-making powers is a sure way of turning them away and isolating teachers.

The incoherence of the critics

The concerted efforts on the part of the critics of the original settlement to define or re-define religious education raises many basic issues. The references to 'religion and belief' or to 'religion and non-religious worldviews' have many pitfalls. For the sake of brevity, only three will be touched on here. They are identified here as: (i) scope; (ii) judgement; (iii) self-knowledge.

Scope

Looking at the work of one of the early scholars in the field of comparative religion, J. G. Frazer's *The Golden Bough*, one notes that the 3rd edition (1906–1915) runs to 12 thick volumes. He does not claim to have covered the full range of human religiosity but his study is confined to select phenomena from the early history of humankind. Those 12 volumes are a reminder that there is virtually no limit to what there is to study and comprehend in the field. Without willing to deny the intrinsic worth to be found in all such study, the ordinary teacher and lecturer in the field are faced with a different problem. Given the nature of the community in which the school is located, the ages and aptitudes of the children in the class, and, most importantly, the time available for teaching, they raise the question what *must* be taught? Presented with a vast field that embraces not only many religions and many disciplines, teachers may feel inadequate to the task. Have they mastered the field sufficiently to evaluate what it is important and what is secondary? Enlarging the scope to include so-called 'non-religious worldviews' (and there are many) will not help without a clear rationale for including areas, such as environmentalism and dialectical materialism which are substantively different from religions or which have little to do with religious sensibilities.

Education is not just about gathering together and organising the relevant data in a field of knowledge, it must also be about developing children in a fashion that enables them to live with integrity. The children need information, certainly; they need to learn to make good judgements too; they need to able to feel appropriately and deeply; and they need to be able to act rightly. Education is not merely mastering fields of knowledge, but it is also about developing character and, besides this, education has many other goals and objectives. Some may dismiss these aims as instrumentalist, yet they are intrinsic to religious life itself, if not to the secular study of religion. Those, who are engaged in setting out 'entitlements', or in planning an examination course, or in writing a syllabus for teaching, are inevitably making value judgements. These value judgements should be openly set out, tested and accepted widely. Claims to be promoting tolerance by knowing *about* religion and belief, or merely commending a neutral and objective study of 'religion and belief', are simply self-deluding. They may be promoting an intolerance of religious life or a form of individualistic consumerism.

Judgement

One of the functions of a serious education is not only to increase one's knowledge and to appreciate complexity but it is also to exercise judgement. In the exercise of judgement of what is deep or shallow, true or false, awesome or pedestrian, reasoned or non-rational, and so forth, one may also create social disagreements since there is not always a clear, or agreed, view. Hence conflicting judgements may be perceived to be subversive of tolerance and indicative of a failure to accept the other. The rejection appears to be implicit in regarding the view and opinions that another may have as wrong, shallow, pedestrian, wicked or irrational.

A proffered but confusing solution may be to regard the religious education judgements solely as one's 'own' personal and private matter. And those who differ have their own opinions to which they are 'entitled'. But, of course, if these 'private' judgements do not arise through, or out of, public conversations, e.g. between teachers and pupils in the classroom, but occur solely through a private, subjective exercise that is 'wholly one's own', then they do indeed become personal and subjective, and perhaps as such do not need to be taken very seriously. Apart from the trivial sense of one's 'own' opinion being simply the opinion one happens to have, the word, 'own', can be understood in two very different ways. To 'own' an opinion is to become responsible for it and to answer for it in the public square, i.e. one does not hold the opinion at second hand or derivatively. Or one can use 'own' in the sense of being a purely private matter. In this case, it creates the space for extremism to flourish since private judgements are, in principle, unchallenged and away from public scrutiny. This, of course, also includes the extremism of those who would ban religious life from the public sphere.

Self-knowledge

In schoolgirl(boy) physics one may have studied the forces exercised in the use of a lever and have come across the thought experiment by Archimedes. He suggested that if only he had a standpoint far enough away from the world and a lever long enough, he could move the earth. This Archimedean standpoint has suggested an idealised model for certain forms of 'academic' study, namely, that of withdrawing one's self from the world to gain an objective view of the totality. It is a heuristic device for removing one's own interests and biases from the picture one attempts to make of the world, in effect, to gain a 'truer' picture or understanding. It is sometimes forgotten that this 'academic' approach is merely a device to ensure greater honesty and integrity in one's thinking. It is also forgotten that the Archimedean standpoint is an idealisation that does not exist in reality. There is no place in space to stand, or for using a very, very long lever to apply to the earth. Nor is there a way of removing the thinker from the world in which (s)he finds (her)himself. The eye may not be part of the field of vision but the eye is nevertheless an integral part of seeing and what is seen.

As living beings, humans are so to speak, thrown into the world; who they are and what they live for, shape what it is they think they understand. The goal of understanding, therefore, demands a process of self-reflection and self-knowledge in much the same way that the aspiring psychoanalyst must first submit him or herself to the process of psychoanalysis. This process of self-reflection and self-knowledge may be encountered in St Augustine's *Confessions* or in Leo Tolstoy's *A Confession* (original 1882). St Anselm referred to the same process when he conceived of theology as 'faith seeking understanding', establishing or showing what it means to live religiously. In effect, it is coming to grips with the matter of who you are and what you live for and live by, and the very context in which you exist. Without this self-knowledge, the intellectual case that is made may be presented under false colours, claiming an authority and impartiality that is undeserved. It is essential to recognise that one cannot step outside one's own 'worldview'; this is implicit in the very meaning of the concept of 'worldview' as it is all embracing.

A serious problem in the critics' case is the unexamined assumption that all the different religions are just so many species of the genus called 'Worldview'. It is further assumed that various ideologies, such as materialism, are yet further species of the same genus, 'Worldview', only they are to be considered a 'non-religious' species of the same genus. The assumption ignores significant differences. These supposed 'worldviews' are denominated, 'non-religious', one suspects, mainly, or only, because they do not draw on the concept of 'God'. However, this is a rather thin understanding of religion or even of significant differences between religious traditions, e.g. between 'semitic' and 'dharmic' faiths, as well as between these and their supposedly non-religious counterparts. There is no suspicion that religion might be *sui generis*. The assumption that they are all in the end nothing but so many different worldviews is little more than a sloppy generalisation.

Then there is the implicit suggestion that people somehow choose between them (Butler-Sloss, 2015: 13–14), but this is precisely what people do not and cannot do with any honest definition of 'worldview'.[9] At best, one can enlarge one's understanding, perhaps by purloining concepts and practices from others. One might try to resolve contradictions, search for greater coherence, look for relevance, universality and greater impressiveness (Brummer 1981: 139) in the account one is able to give of oneself in the world. One might even undergo a conversion in which one's 'worldview' undergoes a radical shift or re-organisation. What one does not do is step outside one's 'worldview'. In short, a 'worldview' is not one theory amongst others between which one might choose on the basis of independent evidence. If the concept of 'worldview' means anything, it is one's 'worldview' that determines what constitutes evidence, (just as much as it determines what constitutes 'education').

On the other hand, if one re-defines a 'worldview' as something chosen then one can be sure it has little in common with 'religion'. In a religion, it is the person who is called or 'chosen'. For example, a religious person may obey or rebel against the command of God, but he or she does not choose for it to be a 'command of God'.[10] Nor does the 'command of God' have the status of human legislation that one may alter at will. Those who conflate religion and 'non-religious worldviews' need to re-examine their terms and their preconceptions, i.e. embark on a difficult exercise in self-knowledge to appreciate where they stand. This exercise is what confession means in its proper sense.

Conclusion

The call for a change in the settlement is misguided. It fails to recognise the tolerant pluralism built into the 1944 Act. More often than not the call for a new settlement abandons the religiousness of religious education in favour of something much more ill-defined, demanding a range of skills that few, if any, possess. It puts in place an incoherent concept of 'worldview' that is grounded in a secular methodology, and in a secular agenda, which subverts religious understanding. The change in the conception of what religious education supposedly should be, fails to appreciate the political rationale for including religious education in the school's curriculum. Like many disciplines or fields of study, e.g. geology or anthropology, religious *studies* has intrinsic worth, but this is not yet an argument why all children should study religious education from the ages of 5 to 18. The real rationale for religious education relates to the essence of religious life, which is to deepen the values to be transmitted to the next generation, values which may save them from oppression, meaninglessness and isolation in some rampant anti-social individualism or unthinking collectivism.

Notes

1 The provision of collective worship in school reflects a possible conception of what education ultimately means and what it is for. It counters a conception that education is provided solely for utilitarian reasons, e.g. to prepare pupils for work or to help them earn a higher income in adulthood.
2 It is important to distinguish the religious leadership of the Church of England from its Board of Education.
3 It does not help the discussion if the requirements in law are misrepresented, e.g. para. 4.17 of Butler-Sloss (2015) where it speaks of compulsory collective worship, when in fact the compulsion is on head teachers to provide it. No-one is compelled to worship.
4 The shift in focus that frequently takes place in religious education should not be underestimated. It is one thing to learn that Sikhism demands *sewa* (selfless service), it is another thing to ask what such service might mean to a 10 year-old, 16 year-old or 74 year-old Sikh. Or to ask what selflessness might mean and how this might relate to 'losing one's self' or to the self love implicit in summary of the Torah provided by Christ, 'to Love God and to love one's neighbour as one's self'. In exploring what religions are about, religious education is directly about the spiritual, moral, social, and cultural development of pupils and of society and only indirectly about the study of religions.
5 Describing baptism as a rite of passage may be an example of a shift in meaning from the specifics of a religion to a secular generalisation. It should be noted that the description of Christian baptism as a rite of passage fails utterly to capture the meaning assigned to baptism within Christian liturgy.
6 A 'faith' school was never entirely free or wholly maintained at public expense. Contributions to the capital costs of schooling were expected, and many religious communities made considerable sacrifices to raise these costs.
7 It is notable that in the Act the parent does not have to provide a reason for withdrawing their child.
8 Note the comments of National Association of Standing Advisory Councils on Religious Education (2018: 2) on the CoRE Report: 'We feel that some of the evidence presented has been chosen to put one view forward, that of a centralising curriculum narrative, without local democratic checks and balances in place.'
9 In relating the concept, 'Worldview', to the German word *Weltanschauung* as CoRE does, they should also have considered related words, such as *Weltbild* or *Weltprojekt* to have discerned important elements of the definition. *Weltanschauung* is more a view of life or an attitude to life than a view of the world which could be taken to be a *Weltbild*, literally a world picture. CoRE has a curious understanding of a 'worldview'. It states (2018: 24) that 'a person's worldview is likely *to influence and be influenced* by their beliefs, values, behaviours, experiences, identities and commitments' as if it was a separate entity. It would have been better if they had said that a 'worldview' *is* one's 'beliefs, values, behaviours, experiences, identities and commitments'.
10 In the imagery of Moses at the burning bush, either the bush is not burning with the Divine or one takes off one's shoes in the presence of holiness, either the theophany is authoritative or there is no theophany.

References

Augustine, St (1994 [1886]) *The Confessions of St Augustine*, in P. Schaff (ed.) *A Select Library of the Nicene and Post-Nicene Fathers of the Christian Church*, Vol. 1. (27–207). Edinburgh: T & T Clark; Edinburgh/Grand Rapids, MI: Eerdmans.

Barnes, L. P. (2014) *Education, Religion and Diversity: Developing a new model of religious education.* London: Routledge.

Barnes, L. P. (2020) *Crisis, Controversy and the Future of Religious Education.* London: Routledge.

Brummer, V. (1981) *Theology and Philosophical Inquiry: An introduction.* London: Macmillan.

Butler-Sloss, E. (2015) *Living with Difference: Community, diversity and the common good.* Cambridge: Woolf Institute. Available online: corablivingwithdifference.files.wordpress.com/2015/12/living-with-difference-online.pdf (accessed 6 December 2021).

Clarke, C. and L. Woodhead (2015) *A New Settlement: Religion and belief in school.* London: Westminster Faith Debates.

Clarke, C. and L. Woodhead (2018) *A New Settlement Revised: Religion and belief in schools.* Westminster Faith Debates.

Commission on Religious Education (2018) *Final Report: Religions and worldviews: The way forward.* London: Religious Education Council of England and Wales. Available online: www.commissiononre.org.uk/wp-content/uploads/2018/09/Final-Report-of-the-Commission-on-RE.pdf (accessed 6 December 2021).

Dinham, A. and M. Shaw (2015) *RE for Real: The future of teaching and learning about religion and belief.* London: Goldsmiths College and Culham St Gabriel.

Frazer, J. G. (1906–15) *The Golden Bough*, 3rd edition. London: Macmillan.

Malcolm, N. (1993) *Wittgenstein: A religious point of view?* London: Routledge.

National Association of Standing Advisory Councils on Religious Education (2018) *Response to CoRE Final Report.* Available online: nasacre.org.uk/file/nasacre/1-533-response-to-core-final.pdf (accessed 6 December 2021).

Qualification and Curriculum Authority (2004) *Religious Education: The non-statutory national framework.* London: QCA.

Religious Education Council of England and Wales (2013) *Review of Religious Education in England.* London: REC.

Thompson, P. (2004) *Whatever Happened to Religious Education?* Cambridge: Lutterworth Press.

Tolstoy, L (1987 [1882]) *A Confession, and Other Religious Writings.* London: Penguin Classics.

Wittgenstein, L. (1979) *Remarks on Frazer's* Golden Bough, edited by Rush Rhees. Harleston: Brynmill Press.

Wittgenstein, L. (1980 [1977]) *Culture and Value*, edited by G. H. von Wright. Oxford: Blackwell.

3

WHO ARE THE PROFESSIONALS IN RELIGIOUS EDUCATION?

The Commission on Religious Education's side-lining of the religious voice

Penny Thompson

The meaning of the word 'professional'

It might be thought that the meaning of the word 'professional' is straightforward and certainly apart from one interesting paragraph in the Commission on Religious Education (CoRE) Report there is no discussion or explanation of the way in which the term is used. Educational researchers, however, have pointed to different nuances that the word may convey. An article about music education begins: 'The general concept of a "profession" or a "professional" is so loose and general that the idea can often be more confusing than helpful' (Regelski 2008: 2). Regelski illustrates three different ways in which the term may be used and demonstrates some ambiguities. First, a professional is paid for their expertise as opposed to an amateur who is not. I have a friend who is a trained musician and takes pupils to earn a living. She does not consider herself a professional musician because she is not paid to play the violin. She plays happily in an amateur orchestra. However, she considers herself a professional *teacher* as she is paid for giving private lessons. A problem with this is that her capabilities as a musician are downgraded (in her own eyes too) and undervalued yet she is a fine musician. Second, a professional may be someone who has a calling or is strongly attracted to a particular occupation. It may have a religious connotation: an individual is 'professed' after taking vows. Still today one hears people talking about teaching (and other careers) as a vocation. On this understanding anyone who feels called to engage in teaching (for example) is a professional. Historically a problem with this interpretation has been that it has justified low pay since a teacher is living out a vocation.

And to pay someone for what God (it may be) calls one to do seems to sully one's calling. Religious orders have often worked in poor areas without asking for payment. Third, the word professional may be used to indicate expertise, knowledge and skill in a particular area. My husband is very skilled at DIY. He can do practically every job that could be required around the house; I sometimes tease him and suggest that we should hire a professional to do some job or other. To which, if he falls into the trap, he replies 'but I am a professional'.

Regelski (2008) goes on to consider how social theorists have understood the term. Some theorists argue that the term professional should be restricted to occupations where there is a sense of calling followed by long and rigorous study, but not applied to manual jobs. Regelski refers to Weber who described the esoteric knowledge gained within the medical profession meant that communication between doctor and patient was not to be made available to lawyers or others. Here a professional is thought to belong to a group whose knowledge must be guarded for fear of misuse by the less qualified. In the 20th century functionalism became the leading theory:

> The function of a profession was to provide a unique and specialist competence of practical value. The profession becomes the authoritative source for judgements in its particular realm. Thus only professional peers or regulatory professional bodies that represent the profession can evaluate competence, not laypersons.
>
> (Regelski 2008: 5–6)

Here the word professional acts to mark out those who possess a certain status and competence not held by non-professionals. It is a claim to territory as well as a guarantor of standards.

Recent social theorists, according to Regelski, emphasise the way professions may act as a special interest group, exerting power over their members. This may lead to the subduing of conflicting perspectives within a profession or imposing a particular ideological stance that is advanced at the expense of others. Internal competition for resources and recognition amongst professionals in a field of study, Bourdieu (quoted in Regelski) argues, is natural but the danger is that professionals seek to create monopolies over rival paradigms or teaching methods.

The professional in the religious education literature

Before going on to consider how the word professional is used by CoRE, I briefly survey discussions in recent religious education literature. There is a considerable body of writing on the matter which may be summarised as covering (a) how an individual develops the qualities to become a professional religious education teacher, (b) how the collective body of teachers achieves and maintains the status of a profession, and (c) how teachers handle conflicts between their personal beliefs and professional commitments.[1] There is a prior question as to whether it is correct to use the word profession at all in relation to teachers. David Carr for example (quoted in Conroy 2016: 165–166) has argued that at best teaching is a 'para-profession' because there is no clear body of knowledge to be mastered as is the case of a lawyer or doctor; teachers do not have control over their domain but must bow to decisions that are made in the public sphere. On the basis of extensive discussion of professionalism in Germany, Klaus-Peter Horn (2016: 131) concluded that teaching is a semi-profession, for similar reasons as those given by Carr. Horn (cf. Regelski earlier in this paper) begins his article by raising the question as to whether terms to do with professionalism 'obfuscate more than they reveal' (Horn 2016: 130). James Conroy, after a section outlining cultural changes which have impacted the notion of teaching as a profession, points to the difficulty for religious education teachers in asserting a professional identity because of uncertainty about what constitutes professional knowledge. He writes of the 'disappearance of the epistemic ground for RE' and a 'reduction of RE to opinion' (Conroy 2016: 174). He identifies a turn to philosophy and ethics and away from religion. The turn to worldviews that CoRE proposes might be viewed as another example of a shift away from religion as a field of study in its own right.

A model for the study of the professionalisation of religious education

Important work on professionalism in religious education in the UK has been carried out by Rob Freathy and Stephen Parker. They have developed a comparative model for international research into the professionalisation of religious education (Freathy et al. 2014, 2016, and Parker et al. 2016). This work does not directly question the status of religious education as a profession but does see the need for clarification. In an article entitled 'Towards international comparative research on the professionalisation of Religious Education' (Freathy et al. 2014), the authors deplore the lack of conceptual clarity found in notions of the teacher as a professional and say that this is no less true with regard to religious education. The research model of Parker et al. has been applied to the history of religious education from the early 20th century to 1973. Their articles provide a detailed and fascinating account of the development of religious education over this period which might be equally well described as a history of religious education. The aim is to describe the 'professionalisation' of religious education over time. Professionalisation is defined as 'the historical and institutional processes by which teachers of RE, as a collective occupational body, assumed their specific professional shape and characteristics over time' (Parker et al. 2016: 201). The process of professionalisation can be viewed through three related concepts (Freathy et al. 2014: 228) which are:

(1) specialist knowledge relating to religious education;
(2) self-organisation and internal politics;
(3) initial and continuing development of teachers.

All three aspects are readily to be seen throughout the period under review. The Swanwick conference of 1934 was instrumental in setting up the Institute of Christian Education (ICE). '[The ICE] fulfilled a role in organising RE professionals, and in developing and promoting what we have called orientative knowledge, subject-specific content knowledge and knowledge of subject-specific pedagogical methods (Parker et al. 2016: 213). One of the key figures in the setting up of the ICE was Basil Yeaxlee, a Congregationalist minister who became editor of *Religion in Education*, the journal published by ICE from 1934. Parker writes that the early editorials of the journal 'demonstrate coverage, however unevenly, of all the constituent elements of professional knowledge (Parker et al. 2016: 215). The Swanwick conference on education was attended by around 179 university lecturers and college teacher trainers, head teachers, teachers, missionaries, clerical and lay representatives of the churches and at this period contributors to the journal represented a similarly broad constituency. All such parties contributed to the professionalisation of religious education in the first half of the 20th century.

The 1944 Education Act formalised the structure of the local authority Agreed Syllabus Conferences (ASCs) and Standing Advisory Councils for Religious Education (SACREs). Parker et al.'s comment on this is largely positive. These bodies

> contributed to the professionalisation of RE/RI teachers by providing 1) an organisational process by which teachers, along with others might determine the nature and purpose of the only statutory curriculum subject; 2) an institutional structure for the development and dissemination of advice and guidance affecting professional knowledge, standards and expertise; and 3) a local forum in which collegial

occupational relations and mutual support might contribute to the development of all professionals involved.

(Parker et al. 2016: 220)

What is notable in the context of the present chapter is recognition that many different parties were involved in 'professionalising' religious education.

However, there are some caveats. Immediately following the above section it is stated that SACREs and ASCs had the effect of 'limiting teachers' freedom to determine their own professional knowledge, standards and expertise'. Commenting on the West Riding syllabus of 1922 the authors state:

> Eminent scholars from across a range of denominations filled agreed syllabus committees . . . . This diverse membership provides an example of the constraints upon RI/RE teacher self-regulation and the limits of their autonomy to determine professional knowledge, standards and expertise in the area they profess.
>
> (Parker et al. 2016: 209)

Here it is scholars who are regarded as limiting the (self-) professionalisation of teachers.

A similar concern is raised in a related paper of the same year. In relation to Germany where religious education is largely denominationally based, it is reported that the law governing religious education 'does not only limit the possibilities for independent professional development of teachers in a specific manner but also structurally shapes initial as well as continuing professional development' (Freathy et al. 2016: 118). In relation to England the legal arrangements mean that 'certain questions are raised about the professionalism, professional identity and professionalisation of RE teachers that are quite unlike those asked of teachers in other subjects' (Freathy et al. 2016: 119).

To summarise: the status of religious education as a profession and therefore its practitioners as professionals are questioned by some scholars. Others argue that the concept may be clarified and have suggested a straightforward definition that provides a lens through which to study what is termed the 'professionalisation' of religious education. However, the process of 'professionalisation' as described above presents some anomalies; the implication being that professionalisation will not be achieved until religious education teachers have control, free from outside influences. If so, then religious education in England (and Germany) has yet to attain to the status of a (fully fledged) profession. Yet these scholars are able to identify the distinguishing marks of a profession in religious education over a long period of time. Perhaps the word professional does obfuscate more than it reveals. I now turn to the use of the word professional in the CoRE report.

How does CoRE use the word professional?

In what sense does CoRE use the word professional? The first of Regelski's definitions was that someone is a professional if they are paid for their services. This is certainly implied in several places where, for example, SACREs are unable to employ professional expertise because of lack of funding: 'Academisation and reductions in funding have reduced local authority support for RE via Standing Advisory Councils on Religious Education (SACREs) and professional advisers, to the point where such support is unsustainable in many areas and already disappearing in some' (CoRE 2018: 9; see also 54 and *passim*). Here professionals are those who are paid for their advice.

CoRE acknowledges that some professional advisers are linked with a particular religion or denomination: 'Church of England and Catholic dioceses as well as Jewish religious authorities offer specialist professional advice for RE to a much greater extent than local authorities or local teaching school structures are able to' (CoRE 2018: 23). Presumably such experts' professionalism is due in part at least to advisers' knowledge of and commitment to the particular religion or denomination appointing them. Others who are paid are of course teachers in school. School teachers are included in the list of the nine professionals to be appointed to write the programmes of study: 'Programmes of study should be developed by a national body of nine professionals, including serving teachers' (CoRE 2018: 14). Serving teachers are to be included. But who are the other professionals? This is clarified later as we shall see. The fact that it was felt necessary to specify that serving teachers were included may imply that there are grades of 'professionals' where advisers or consultants are of higher rank.

The second of Regelski's definitions is that a professional is someone with a calling or attraction to the profession in question. Teaching as a vocation has a long history but it does not appear in CoRE. Is this significant?

The third definition is that a professional is someone having specialist knowledge and skill in their chosen profession. CoRE certainly endorses this and much is said about the professional development of teachers and the need to provide this. For example: 'We note here that many SACREs and teachers have told us that where teachers are involved in the development of locally agreed syllabuses, this is important professional development for them and gives them a sense of ownership of the content' (CoRE 2018: 43). And:

> Most SACREs analyse examination results every year, and many also support RE in the following ways: . . . providing continuing professional development for teachers through conferences and workshops or contributing to teacher network days and INSET days. Many of these are led by professionals such as RE advisers or external consultants bought in by SACREs.
>
> *(CoRE 2018: 52)*

Clearly the religious education advisers and consultants are those within the profession with a level of knowledge and expertise that others within the profession can learn from (and perhaps lead to teachers becoming consultants).

To sum up: CORE understands a professional to be someone who earns their living through their knowledge and expertise, either as a classroom teacher or as an adviser or consultant; advisers and consultants being a notch higher up the religious education professional ladder. It is recognised that some professionals may be so because of their religious affiliation and that SACREs have an important role in furthering professionalisation.

Professional or religious?

CoRE reports in detail on both the organisations and individuals who responded to their consultation. Organisations were grouped according to whether they represented professions involved in religious education or religious groups (the latter included non-religious groups). The writers of the report had some difficulty in deciding which group/s should be called religious. The responses received by the Commission are listed:

> Fifty-six responses were from religious groups. Defining an organisation as a 'religious group' can be a subjective exercise. We have taken any organisation that includes a specific religious position as part of its identity as a 'religious group', e.g. the Association of Christian Teachers has been defined as a religious group, whereas the National Association of Teachers of RE (NATRE) has been defined as a professional body. This is not to deny that members of the Association of Christian Teachers are not themselves professionals, nor that the

personal religious position of members of NATRE will not have an impact on their professional work.

(CoRE 2018: 81)

One can see the problem. By separating responses into categories of religious and professional a divide is set up. It certainly caused the writers of CoRE pause for thought. One wonders whether the word professional causes more confusion than clarity as Regelski and Horn suggest. What if the report omitted the word, speaking simply of advisers, consultants, organisations and so on? Interestingly the Durham Commission, which issued a major report on religious education on behalf of the Church of England in 1970, did not categorise respondents, listing all organisations who responded in alphabetical order (*The Fourth R,* 289). It is arguable that this divide creates a tension which is difficult to resolve in the heart and mind of the religious education teacher. This tension is considered in some detail in the work of Judith Everington (2016). It is not a new problem and it is certainly not one solved by CoRE.

Nevertheless, it was undoubtedly a useful exercise to report on the identity of the organisations that responded:

> Of these religious groups, 44 were Christian. There were 3 Hindu groups, 2 Jewish groups, 2 Jain groups, 1 Muslim group, 1 Buddhist group, and 1 Baha'i group. In addition, there was 1 response from an organisation representing nonreligious views. Nine SACREs submitted evidence, along with evidence from the National Association of SACREs (NASACRE). Six further professional bodies submitted evidence including NATRE, NAHT and the Federation of RE Centres.
>
> *(CoRE 2018: 81)*

Fifty-six religious groups, 16 professional groups and 1 non-religious organisation responded to the consultation. The number of religious groups is remarkable, particularly the 44 Christian groups. In view of CoRE's recommendation to include worldviews in both the title of the subject and the content of the curriculum it needs to be noted that no worldview groups are listed and only one non-religious group. Also to be noted is that SACREs and NASACRE are listed as professional bodies. This might have given pause for thought too, since SACREs, as presently constituted, are made up of 50% religious representatives.

I move on now to consider the plan for developing programmes of study which at present in schools without a religious character (community schools) is the responsibility of an Agreed Syllabus Conference. This is where the definition of professional used by CoRE becomes particularly significant.

Programmes of study

Although Programmes of Study (PoS) will be non-statutory they are to mirror those developed for History and Geography in the National Curriculum in both detail and in that they are to be developed at a national level. The local networks (see below) may develop their own PoS, which rather lessens the authority of the national ones. However, what concerns me here is the matter of who is to write them and what their qualifications are. They are to be developed by a national body of 'a maximum of nine professionals, including serving teachers' (CoRE 2018: 14). This body could 'choose to take advice from other organisations as relevant' (ibid.). The body is to be appointed by the Department for Education (DfE) on the basis of recommendations from the RE Council, following an open application process. The professionals are to be selected on the basis of commitment to the Religion and Worldviews approach and proven expertise in some or all of four areas. These are:

(i) Specialist knowledge of Religion and Worldviews with both research and classroom experience
(ii) Curriculum development, within or beyond Religion and Worldviews
(iii) Initial teacher education or continuing professional development of teachers
(iv) Current or recent classroom experience in either primary or secondary phases.

All nine professionals are to be classroom teachers, advisers or those employed to teach courses of education in university. Our nine professionals may or may not be members of a religious group but if they are it is not why they have been selected. The body chosen may consult 'other organisations as relevant' so religious groups (and non-religious groups) may be invited to advise but not to determine the outcome. What this means is that control of the programmes of study is vested in the educational profession alone and further confirms the use of the word professional as outlined in the previous section. No places are reserved for those sponsoring schools with a religious character, free schools or academies yet these schools are to be required 'to provide Religion and Worldviews in accordance with the National Entitlement' alongside their own programmes of religious education (CoRE Recommendation 2), nor for theologians or members of religious groups.

Local Advisory Networks for religion and worldviews

Research by the Commission had shown that SACREs were often highly valued and performed an important role in supporting teachers. SACREs are to be reconstituted as Local Advisory Networks for Religion and Worldviews (LANs) and to be established in every local authority, funded through the Central Schools Services Block (CSSB) provided to local authorities. The LANs

> must facilitate the implementation of the National Entitlement to the study of Religion and Worldviews in all schools within the local authority boundaries by providing information about sources of support available and must connect schools with local faith and belief communities and other groups that support the study of Religion and Worldviews in schools.
>
> *(CoRE 2018: 16)*

They must also submit an annual report to the DfE and the local authority. These are their statutory duties. CoRE suggests a number of things that these bodies may do, such as provide CPD support, develop programmes of study in line with the National Entitlement, organise prizes and give advice. Interestingly all these activities apart from that related to the National Entitlement are already carried out by SACREs. There are to be five groups, as follows:

(i) Teachers of Religion and Worldviews from all phases including higher education
(ii) School leaders and governors
(iii) ITE and/or CPD providers
(iv) School providers including the local authority (LA) and Multi Academy Trust (MAT), dioceses etc.
(v) Religion, belief and other groups that support religious education in schools or wish to do so (this might include local museums and galleries as well as religion and belief groups).

This represents a significant change from the existing situation where SACREs are constituted of four committees. On Committee A are representatives of religions present in the area, including Christian denominations other than the Church of England; Committee B is the Church of England; C is teachers; and D is the local authority. At present committees A and B have a significant role, 50% of the whole (and each has a veto when it comes to agreeing a syllabus), but in CoRE's plan they are to take a place (along with libraries and museums) on one of five groups. This is startling. The recommendations of CoRE remove the responsibility of religious groups to contribute both to creating and to advising on the syllabus for local authority schools. Surely this needs explanation and justification?

But it is not just the religious voice which is affected. The proposal effectively removes a meaningful role from all participants. The statutory role of the new bodies is to 'facilitate an approach' whereas the current role of a SACRE is to 'give advice'. The new body is to facilitate an approach that has been decided elsewhere, in this case by a national body; the SACRE advises on which approach or approaches to take. The SACRE is an authoritative body able to advise, in the case of the ASC (to be rescinded under CoRE) to determine the religious education curriculum. LANs have the subsidiary role of carrying out the will of others. The existing structure therefore possesses a certain weight and authority that the proposed one does not. The fact that nothing is said about voting within the groups of a LAN suggests that there will be nothing important to vote on.

Initial Teacher Education and Continuous Professional Development

Detailed consideration is given by CoRE to Initial Teacher Education (ITE) and Continuous Professional Development (CPD). The latter is to be provided over a five-year period and is intended to provide training to all teachers of the subject. Two new modules for Religion and Worldviews should be developed for primary education students and made available for CPD. Funding from central government will be expected at both primary and secondary level to assist delivery of the new non-statutory programmes of study once they are ready, sufficient to provide online courses, curriculum materials and guidance. It is expected that partnerships of schools and teachers in higher education will apply for funding to provide this training along with local hubs. All this work is to be under the supervision of the nine professionals appointed by the RE Council to write programmes of study. This amounts to a retraining of all serving teachers who will be required to teach under the direction laid down in the National Entitlement. There is no mention of religious groups being invited to assist in this massive undertaking.

Collective worship

A further issue is the matter of collective worship (CW). CoRE states that it does not discuss this as its brief was for religious education only. At present SACREs have a statutory a role to give advice on CW in local authority schools. In my own authority, Liverpool, this duty is taken seriously. Advice is given and training put on regularly, much appreciated by the schools who take part. Nothing is stated about LANs taking on this role. This means that a further diminution of the role of local bodies is envisaged and it also means that collective worship would be left out on a limb with no support. The RE Council should have made recommendations to remedy this perhaps unintended consequence of CoRE's proposals.

Promoting a particular view

It was stated earlier that professions may use their power to exclude voices that do not conform to a particular view. The present legal structures allow a wide variety of approaches to religious education and a wide variety of professionals. CoRE's proposals turn this situation on its head. It gives authority to nine selected professionals of whom most are likely to be teaching at university level though they may have had experience in the classroom. So not only is responsibility taken away from the churches and politicians but also from classroom teachers. These nine professionals are selected on the basis of their commitment to the new approach. This is so not only for schools without a religious character. It is also to be required in all publicly funded schools. The form of religious education that is to be adopted must be that decided by CoRE and given expression in this report as a National Entitlement, and although the programmes of study to be produced by the nine professionals are not compulsory, the approach is. This represents a dramatic narrowing down of those considered competent (professional?) to determine what is taught in religious education and actively suppresses new approaches. In voluntary aided schools CoRE recommends that while they should continue to offer RE according to their Trust Deed they must also provide RE in accordance with the National Entitlement (CoRE 2018: 44, 33). This will pose quite a challenge as there may be considerable divergence in approach between the two requirements.

The restriction of the term 'professional' to teachers and educational experts is not unique to CoRE and goes back at least to the early 1970s. It may be that the writers of CoRE have simply taken it for granted that everyone now thinks that religious bodies and politicians should have no role in determining religious education and not felt it necessary to argue the case. Certainly, there has been little interest in recent years in researching the topic. Paul Smalley, until recently Chair of the National Association of SACREs (NASACRE), has pointed out how little research has been done into the work of SACREs in recent years (Smalley 2020: 265). I now consider attempts made in the 1970s to bring in a national prescription for religious education and to exclude a role for the churches.

The professionalisation of religious education in the 1970s

In the early 1970s there was a concerted effort on the part of both individuals and associations to remove control of religious education from the churches (see Thompson 2004: 74–85). A brief summary of the arguments follows here.

John Hull, editor of the Journal *Learning for Living*, devoted his editorial in the summer of 1973 to arguing that the longstanding control of the churches over religious education must now be surrendered. In a vivid turn of phrase he wrote: 'when for centuries you have had power to bind and loose it is very humiliating to be told that you are only a very interesting object of study' (quoted in Thompson 2004: 76). The problem was, in his opinion, that religious bodies would always use religious education to promote their own particular point of view. Peter Lefroy Owen, Chair of the Association of Religious Education (ARE), went further. He told the churches to refrain altogether from making statements on religious education. Religious education must stand apart from confessional bodies and to be seen to be promoting educational concerns. In his view the Church of England should be granted associate membership of the RE Council, not full membership. Hull recommended abandoning agreed syllabuses and replacing them with teams of teachers who could take advice (if they so wished) from the churches and other bodies. Others followed his example, Jean Holm, an influential lecturer at Homerton College and Alan Loosemore, adviser to West Riding, being two examples. Owen Cole called for a new act that would end the partnership between the church and school. Allan Wainwright thought the agreed syllabuses needed to go because they allowed teachers to continue with the old approach. ARE recommended the creation of 'National Guidelines' which could then be taken up and implemented by local groups of teachers and suggested that the local education authority should be given the right to convene such groups.

This debate culminated in the publication by the RE Council in 1975 of a document entitled 'What future for the Agreed Syllabus?' It argued that a new definition of the subject was needed and that compulsory national guidelines be drawn up by a legally constituted body. The task could not be entrusted to teachers since they had not been trained in the new ways of doing religious education. This body should be entirely independent of the faith communities although they could submit suggestions. However, at a meeting of the full RE Council it became clear that the document would not be accepted. Edwin Cox was charged with writing a further paper which was submitted to Shirley Williams, Secretary of State for Education, as a contribution to debate not a policy document. Williams took no action. She did not approve of a national religious education advisory group: 'In the circumstances I think it would be open to misunderstanding to consider the establishment of a national religious education advisory group' (quoted in Thompson 2004: 80). She went on to quote the law as it related to the agreed syllabus system.

The RE Council did not give up easily. In 1978 the RE Council sponsored a report into the supply and training of religious education teachers. In the final paragraph it was argued that a national impetus

> would need the support and involvement of HMIs, who would need to be brought together at national level with representatives from LEAs, colleges and teachers. Such a group would have the necessary professional status for its guidelines to carry weight in local situations.
> *(quoted in Thompson 2004: 79)*

Note the use of the word professional. Guidelines were to be drawn up without reference to churches or religious groups or the SACREs whose responsibility it was to determine religious education locally.

In 1975 the Birmingham Agreed Syllabus reflected some of the changes the RE Council wanted. It became clear that the agreed syllabus system was flexible enough to accommodate the change the profession was arguing for and gradually the attempt to change the law was abandoned.

Similarities between the CoRE proposals and those put forward in the 1970s

There are remarkable similarities between CoRE and attempts to reform religious education in the 1970s, not least the fact that the REC sponsored a report for change to the structures in both periods.

- Both argue for a new definition of the subject. CoRE introduces a new name, Religion and Worldviews, whereas in the 1970s the subject was not renamed but to be defined as 'open' and 'educational'.

- Both argue for new structures which would rely on 'professional' input from the universities, local authority RE advisers (and sometimes teachers) and not on the churches or religious groups.
- Both argue for the abandonment of the existing agreed syllabus conferences.
- Both recommend national compulsory guidelines.
- Both are chary of giving the task to classroom teachers who are untrained in the new approaches.
- Both expect any contribution of the churches and religious groups to be advisory only.

Some of the arguments put forward and their weaknesses will now be considered.

Supporting arguments and their weaknesses

In the 1970s

In the 1970s the argument centred on the need for religious education to be 'open' and 'educational' as stated above. This implied that religious education at this point was 'closed' and 'anti-educational' and the word 'indoctrinatory' was often employed to describe the sort of religious education that needed to be abandoned. But was this the case? The Durham Report, *The Fourth R*, was published by a commission set up by the National Society of the Church of England in 1967. It pointed out that all the reports on religious education in the years leading up to the 1970s assumed that an educational approach should be taken to the subject in contrast to any attempt to win converts to Christianity (Durham Commission 1970: 98–99).

The Fourth R agreed that RE should be 'open' but that it should not result in an 'orgy of relativism where the teacher pretends that any opinion is as good as any other' (Durham Commission 1970: 115). Rather it should mean that 'RE is conducted in the form of an exploration, that no one viewpoint is considered automatically or regarded as invariably correct' (1970: 116) and the whole matter was carefully considered in Appendix B, 'Indoctrination', contributed by Professor Basil Mitchell. It was disingenuous to argue that a new 'educational' approach was needed. The need for an educational approach (however defined) had been recognised and justified both by contemporary and earlier reports.

In addition, the Durham Report explicitly stated not only that religious education should be 'open' but that teachers should not press for commitment: 'To press for acceptance of a particular faith or belief system is . . .

not the task of a teacher in a county school' (Durham Commission 1970: 103). The Durham Report has often been criticised for its emphasis on one religion but its reasoning was entirely educational. It was believed to be educationally unrealistic that pupils should study 'the Bible and, *as well*, the Qur'an, the *Bhagavadgita*, the *Upanisads*, and the Buddhist scriptures' (1970: 213, italics in the original).

It was also inaccurate to argue that control of religious education needed to be taken from the churches. The structure of agreed syllabus conferences (and SACREs) was carefully set up to avoid control by any one of the four committees. Even if the two church committees teamed up they would only have 50% of the vote. And when it came to agreeing a syllabus all four committees had to agree before a syllabus could be adopted. In other words, the churches had a powerful influence but not overall control.

CoRE

The report begins with the heading: 'Introduction: the case for change'. It states that religious education has not kept pace with academisation and the school-led system and that this 'confirms the need identified in many previous reports for a change to the structures' (CoRE 2018: 4). The 2013 REC Report, *A Review of Religious Education in England*, lists seven reasons for change and this will be one of the reports to which CoRE is referring. Reasons cover such matters as the growth of academies, fewer schools being run by the local authority, less money being made available by LAs for training and supporting SACREs and lack of monitoring of both SACREs and agreed syllabuses. CoRE reiterates some of these reasons. CoRE's argument in relation to removing the requirement to set up an ASC refers to academisation and the fact that reduction in funding means that local authorities are often unable to fund the writing of a good syllabus.

These arguments are not convincing. Paul Smalley refers to charges that SACREs are 'barely functioning' and that the agreed syllabus system is 'collapsing because of academisation' and points out that 'there is no published empirical evidence to either support or refute these assertions' (Smalley 2020: 265). Academies without a religious character are required to adopt an Agreed Syllabus (which need not be the one in their local area) or write their own in accordance with the same requirements set out for religious education that agreed syllabuses have to meet and could have representation on an ASC to help with a review. Reduction of funding is a real issue, but some authorities do find the necessary funding while others buy in a syllabus. A survey of SACREs conducted recently found that of the 35 SACREs who replied, 21 had written their own syllabus or adapted an existing one from another authority, 11 had written a syllabus jointly with other authorities and 3 had bought in from a commercial provider (Smalley 2020: 267). If the money needed for implementing the CoRE recommendations were directed to SACREs the funding issue would be greatly eased.

In a brief section on the history of religious education, CoRE states that one of the reasons behind the need for change is 'a gradual shift towards the belief that it was wrong for the state to proselytise' (CoRE 2018: 30). Such a statement can only be made by those who have forgotten the 19th century debates about the inclusion of religion in the Board schools set up following the Forster Education Act of 1870. Religious instruction (as it was then called) was only included in the new state-funded Board schools because of a last-minute inclusion of the Cowper Temple clause forbidding the teaching of denominational formularies. The big issue then was proselytism. However, this is not the same as arguing that the state has no responsibility in relation to the character of the religious education provided in the schools that it funds. The aim of education in this country requires teachers to pay attention (amongst other matters) to the spiritual development of pupils. A recent requirement to inculcate British values through compulsory education is a further reminder that the state is not averse to certain forms of proselytism.

A further argument for change put forward by CoRE is the poor state of religious education in schools not having a religious character: 'If something is not done urgently to re-establish the subject there is a real risk that it could disappear from schools without a religious character' (CoRE 2018: 8). Much of this information on the state of religious education is useful. For example, it is instructive to learn that in comparison with History teachers at secondary level almost three times as many religious education lessons are taught by non-specialists. Fifty-three per cent of RE teachers have no post-A level qualification in religious education compared with 25.3% of History teachers. However, this disparity cannot be solved by either changing the structure of the subject nor by changing the definition. Nor is it a new issue. The problem of finding qualified teachers for religious education is longstanding and is highlighted in all 20th-century reports on religious education.

A survey of School Workforce Data sponsored by NATRE in 2015 and 2016 compared the number of schools offering no religious education at KS3 and KS4 (see CoRE 2018: 7–11). Overall at KS3 the number of schools not offering religious education increased from 20.5% to 23.1%

and at KS4 a more significant increase from 22.1% to 33.4%. Interestingly the number of academies without a religious character showed a *reduction* in the number of schools not offering religious education, from 34.1% to 29.6%. At KS4 the number of academies offering religious education fell by 3%. Without comparing figures over a longer period it is difficult to know how significant these figures are but the important question is again, will new structures increase the number of schools offering religious education? In my own area of Liverpool we have become aware on SACRE of a small number of high schools failing to offer religious education. Perhaps it was only a matter of time before head teachers, finding that they could get away with not complying with the law on collective worship, thought they could get away with not offering religious education. However, once Ofsted becomes involved[2] it is remarkable how quickly a school will reinstate religious education, and we have seen this happen in Liverpool.

Further evidence of the decline in religious education is shown in a study by CoRE of numbers of GCSE entries between 2010 and 2018. The steepest decline is in those taking the short course; from 255,000 in 2010 to 26,000 in 2018. This is most likely the result of government intervention ruling out the counting of short courses in school performance tables, as CoRE states (2018: 10). Interestingly although the number of entries for the full course declined from a peak of 272,000 entries in 2015 and 2016 to 229,000 in 2018, this figure is still a significant increase on 2010 when the numbers were 171,000. NATRE reported in 2020 that entries were holding firm, there being only a 1% drop in entries between 2019 and 2020.

CoRE states that at primary level 30% of schools responding in 2016 to a NATRE survey offered less than 45 minutes a week to their pupils. This means that 70% of schools responding offered 45 minutes a week, which is satisfactory. Much of CoRE is at pains to quote from respondents whose words illustrate that religious education is in good health, in some places anyway. So the situation is not all one sided.

What CoRE has not done is to argue a convincing case for change. There are weaknesses in religious education although it is easy to overstate them. CoRE argues for a new name and a new approach to religious education, but it is difficult to see how the problems identified will be solved by changing the name and approach. Possibly CoRE hopes that a change in law will bring greater compliance and more resources for the subject, although it is not clear that schools who break the law now will comply with a different one in the future. In the view of some, the proposals do not address the real problems of religious education and therefore will not solve them (see Barnes 2020: 9–23, *et passim*).

Conclusion

This chapter has asked the question: Who are the professionals in religious education? And a related question: Should religions have a voice in determining the subject? Historically this was a non-question before the 1970s. It was obvious to all that a joint effort of teachers, academics and religious bodies was needed, along with representatives from the local authorities whose responsibility it was to provide the service. The work of Freathy and Parker demonstrates that professionalisation was operative throughout the period from the early 1930s to at least the 1970s, that embraced collegial determination of religious education. Despite concerns since the 1970s about the link with religious and political bodies, the work of SACREs and ASCs has continued to the present day. CoRE's proposals, if implemented, would represent a break with tradition. The break proposed is so radical that religious education teachers would have to be retrained, their professional judgement realigned as they relearn their task. The careful work done by SACREs and ASCs, to say nothing of the National Association of SACREs, is to be called to a halt. The contribution of theologians, imams, rabbis and others to a nuanced and rich understanding of their faiths may be heard but not as determining factors. Where previously there were many voices contributing to what constitutes good religious education, CoRE advocates a small group of selected 'professionals' who are to expedite a particular approach. The current system may have its drawbacks but it has proved able to develop creative new forms of religious education. The Birmingham Agreed Syllabuses of 2007 and 2020 are examples. CoRE resists alternative points of view and narrows down the field of those considered competent to determine religious education to a group of nine, that are appointed on the basis of their commitment to the new approach. By contrast, current legislation opens up the field. It gives a voice to religious communities and politicians and to teachers of religious education up and down the country. It recognises that debate is a good thing.

This chapter has pointed out the problematic use of the word professional as it relates to religious education. What if we just asked the question 'Who are the best people to advise on the nature and purpose of RE?' It is likely that a mixture of primary and secondary practising teachers would come high on our list; they could advise on the educational suitability of a syllabus and what CPD is needed. It would be a good idea to appoint a range of representatives of the major religions in the country to test out the religious sense of the syllabus and offer the help of those within their communities with insight and the ability to offer training. Anglicans have a long history of involvement in education and offer the viewpoint and resources of a national church. Politicians from the local authority with knowledge of the needs of the local community and overall responsibility for education have a contribution to make too. SACREs might just be the answer.

Notes

1 For (c), see the work of Judith Everington (2016).
2 Recent changes to the inspection protocol stress a 'deep dive' where inspectors may look in depth at individual subjects including RE. If a school is not complying with the law on RE it will be picked up.

References

Barnes, L. P. (2020) *Crisis, Controversy and the Future of Religious Education*. London: Routledge.
Commission on Religious Education (CoRE) (2018) *Final Report: Religions and Worldviews: The way forward*. London: RE Council. Available online: www.commissiononre.org.uk/wp-content/uploads/2018/09/Final-Report-of-the-Commission-on-RE.pdf (accessed 6 December 2020).
Conroy, J. C. (2016) 'Religious education and religious literacy: A professional aspiration?' *British Journal of Religious Education* 38(2): 163–176. Doi.org/10.1080/01416200.2016.1139891.
Durham Commission (1970) *The Fourth R*. London: SPCK.
Everington, J. (2016) '"Being Professional": RE teachers' understandings of professionalism 1997–2014', *British Journal of Religious Education* 38(2): 177–188. Doi.org/10.1080/01416200.2016.1139892.
Freathy, R., Parker, S. G., Schweitzer, F. and Simojoki, H. (2014) 'Towards international comparative research on the professionalisation of religious education', *Journal of Beliefs & Values* 35(2): 225–241.
Freathy, R., Parker, S. G., Schweitzer, F. and Simojoki, H. (2016) 'Conceptualising and researching the professionalisation of religious education teachers: Historical and international perspectives', *British Journal of Religious Education* 38(2): 114–129. Doi.org/10.1080/13617672.2014.976953.
Horn, K.-P. (2016.) 'Profession, professionalisation, professionality, professionalism: Historical and systematic remarks using the example of German teacher education', *British Journal of Religious Education* 3(2): 130–140. Doi.org/10.1080/01416200.2016.1139888.
Parker, S. G., Freathy, R. and Doney, J. (2016) 'The professionalisation of non-denominational religious education in England: Politics, organisation and

knowledge', *Journal of Beliefs & Values* 37(2): 201–238. Doi.org/10.1080/136 17672.2016.1183906.

Regelski, T. (2008) 'The ethics of music teaching as profession and praxis'. Available online: www.researchgate.net/publication/267990844.

Religious Education Council (1975) *What Future for the Agreed Syllabus?* London: RE Council.

Religious Education Council of England and Wales (2013) *Review of Religious Education in England*. London: REC.

Smalley, P. (2020) 'A critical policy analysis of local religious education in England', *British Journal of Religious Education* 42(3): 263–274. Doi.org/10.1080/0141620 0.2019.1566114.

Thompson, P. (2004) *Whatever Happened to Religious Education?* Cambridge: Lutterworth Press.

4
DOES THE WORLDVIEWS APPROACH PROVIDE A NEW PARADIGM FOR RELIGIOUS EDUCATION?

L. Philip Barnes

In his Foreword to the Commission on Religious Education's (CoRE) *Final Report, Religion and Worldviews: The way forward: A national plan for RE* (2018), which was established by the Religious Education Council of England and Wales, the Very Revd Dr Stuart Hall comments that it offers 'a new vision' for religious education: 'The subject should explore the important role that religious and non-religious worldviews play in all human life.' The Report itself speaks frequently of its proposals as providing a 'new vision' (10 times in fact and the term 'new' as a qualifying adjective for CoRE's proposals is used over 60 times in 78 pages). Later supporting materials repeat the idea of studying 'religion and worldviews' as a new vision, then more characteristically as a 'new approach' and then finally and consistently as a 'new paradigm' for religious education (Benoit et al. 2020; Tharani 2020a). This interpretation is endorsed by Professor Trevor Cooling (2020), Chairperson of the Religious Education Council, who is widely quoted as having 'challenged the [then newly appointed] religious education commissioners to produce a "game-changer"'; for him '[a] more academic way of talking about a game change is to refer to it as a paradigm change' (Tharani 2020b: 39–40; Cooling et al. 2020: 20), that is, in the context of religious education, the adoption of a new belief framework with its attendant assumptions that will guide pedagogy, practice and the production of resources. 'CoRE's advocacy of worldview,' according to Cooling, 'represents a new paradigm' (Cooling et al. 2020: 13; Cooling 2021: 15).

The idea of a worldviews curriculum as a new paradigm of religious education has gradually come to characterise and to give unified form to CoRE's proposals. Such usage connects to ongoing debates about how best to describe and interpret the history of developments in religious education (see Barnes 2014: 5–6 and 232–244; Gearon 2014); it also sets religious education in a wider intellectual context where the language of 'theoretical models,' 'paradigms,' 'paradigm shifts' and 'revolutions' is used by various disciplines to describe the emergence and development of new disciplinary frameworks; and it is one such that CoRE believes it is initiating in religious education. Such terms go back to Thomas Kuhn (1922–1996), and his study of the nature of science and of scientific 'progress' in *The Structure of Scientific Revolutions* (1962; enlarged 2nd edition, 1970). Kuhn's terminology and his underlying ideas have been influential with those associated with developing a new worldviews paradigm of religious education. In the article by Cooling (2020), supporting and commending the proposals of CoRE, to which we have already referred, he speaks approvingly of Kuhn's idea about 'paradigm shifts' and how he views the emergence of a worldviews paradigm as something analogous to Kuhn's account of how one scientific paradigm 'replaces' (Kuhn's term, rather than 'follows') another.

The opinion that a shift to a worldviews approach constitutes a new paradigm for religious education is central to CoRE's case for its adoption. Both descriptive terms, *new* and *paradigm* are important, given that current theory and practice in religious education is widely recognised as bringing the subject to its present 'lamentable state' (Myatt 2020: 11). It is obviously important to distance proposals for reform from what has gone before, lest the accusation be made that little is new and consequently little will change for the better. The claim that CoRE's proposals constitute a new *paradigm* is also important, for not only is this designation, with its mainly positive intellectual and scientific associations, meant to rebut the suggestion that what is new is fragmentary, *ad hoc* and simply adding additional epicycles to the existing framework. A new paradigm must offer a comprehensive and integrated vision of beliefs and values to direct religious education while being sufficiently distinctive from what has gone before to offer hope that it will overcome current weaknesses.

The aspects of CoRE that have been noted will largely dictate the structure and content of what follows. A consideration of Kuhn's understanding of paradigms and paradigm shifts provides an introductory orientation to our discussion. The focus will be on the broad features of his position that can be usefully applied to other disciplines and fields of study, such as religious education. The overview of Kuhn's position is preparatory to an account of its use by Cooling and others to support the proposals of CoRE and the implementation of a new worldviews paradigm to replace, what CoRE calls, the world religions paradigm. This appropriation naturally raises critical questions, not mainly about faithfulness to Kuhn's particular interpretation, but about whether a worldviews approach to religious education is properly designated as both *new* and a *paradigm* in its own right.

Thomas Kuhn on paradigms and the scientific enterprise

Our interest is to extract from Kuhn the broad parameters of a plausible account of the nature of a paradigm that will illuminate its applicability and appropriateness to religious education. This aim, I believe, faithfully reflects that of Cooling and those supportive of the proposals of CoRE.

Kuhn was a historian and philosopher of science who reached the conclusion that the familiar picture of scientific progress moving along a linear trajectory of increasing objectivity, as the natural world disclosed its secrets to the ever-closer scrutiny of reason, as directed by a rigidly empiricist methodology (requiring verification or falsification), was fundamentally mistaken. According to him in *The Structure of Scientific Revolutions* (1970) science operates according to a commonly assumed network of commitments – 'conceptual, theoretical, instrumental, and methodological' (Kuhn 1970: 42) – that operationalises its practice, adjudicates its research priorities and successes, and so on. He (1970: 23–34) refers to this as 'normal' science (1970: 23–34): science pursued according to a common framework, which is normatively exemplified in certain experiments that illustrate the 'problem-solving' nature of the framework, i.e. those successful scientific experiments typically cited in scientific textbooks to illustrate the nature of the disciple or sub-discipline (1970: 35–42). This common network of commitments along with its exemplification in certain 'past [scientific] achievements' (Kuhn 1970: 175) constitute a paradigm.

During a period of normal science there is no attempt to test or falsify the accepted research paradigm. The paradigm (model) is not questioned. It sets the standard for rationality and hence determines scientific 'knowledge.' Knowledge production is a human activity and knowledge within a scientific paradigm attains its status within a community of scientists and accredited experts (an observation that Kuhn believes he insufficiently stressed in the 1st 1962 edition). Communities of scientists are 'the producers and validators of scientific knowledge. Paradigms are something shared by the members of such groups' (Kuhn 1970: 178), for the scientific community 'constructs' knowledge. According to Kuhn (1970: 150) 'the proponents of competing paradigms practice their trades in different worlds.' Paradigms determine what problems are significant and provide the tools for their solution, for normal science is a 'puzzle-solving' activity. The function of a paradigm is to supply puzzles for scientists to solve and so the 'fruitfulness' of the paradigm is illustrated and exemplified. The resolution of puzzles adds 'to the scope and precision with which the paradigm can be applied' (Kuhn 1970: 36). Yet puzzles can take a more challenging form when research findings do not fully conform to predictions generated by the paradigm or when novel findings emerge from new sources of evidence or from new scientific instruments for testing; as a consequence accommodation and a shift of meaning or significance elsewhere in the network of assumptions constitutive of the paradigm may be required. There is a point, however, which though difficult to determine, when, according to Kuhn, puzzles become 'anomalies,' that is when there is 'recognition that nature has somehow violated the paradigm-induced expectations that govern normal science' (Kuhn 1970: 52–53). A 'crisis' is admitted when there is an appreciation of the existence of a major anomaly or a group of anomalies that appears to undermine the credibility of the ruling paradigm. Crisis is a semi-technical term for Kuhn that denotes the increasing awareness by scientists working within existing scientific parameters that the paradigm guiding research is incapable of resolving anomalies.

A state of crisis initiates the search by some scientists for a new paradigm that can overcome identified anomalies. Kuhn (1970: 77) notes that faced with a crisis, 'novel theories' emerge and 'alternatives' to the prevailing paradigm are considered. He reserves the term paradigm for historically successful theoretical frameworks, whereas an unsuccessful framework of beliefs and values that fails to gain the support of the scientific community does not, in his terminology, attain 'the status of [a] paradigm' (Kuhn 1970: 77). Unsuccessful frameworks do not overcome identified anomalies as their proponents claim or perhaps what is proclaimed as a new framework is insufficiently novel and preserves too many assumptions and values from the existing paradigm. In time, however, a framework may emerge with the capacity to resolve the serious challenges that beset the old paradigm. If this is the case, the new 'paradigm,' though viewed as a rival by supporters of the old paradigm, will gradually come to replace it. Kuhn (1970: 6) refers to the replacement of one paradigm by another as a 'scientific revolution': 'The extraordinary episodes in which . . . [a] shift of professional commitments occurs are the ones known . . . as scientific revolutions. They are the tradition-shattering complements to the tradition-bound activity of normal science.' An example of a scientific revolution is the Copernican revolution in cosmology and the shift from Ptolemy's geocentric view, with its increasing number of postulated epicycles, to the heliocentric view of the solar system; other examples include Darwin's theory of evolution by natural selection and more recently Einsteinian physics replacing Newtonian physics. The revolution and the shift to a new paradigm will eliminate (at least) the most pressing anomalies and optimally provide a solution to many of the outstanding, unsolved puzzles associated with the old paradigm. Once accepted by the scientific community, what was once a new paradigm becomes the ruling paradigm, which now determines the reconfigured structure of normal science. The revolution is over and 'normality' returns.

Many commentators maintain that in *The Structure of Scientific Revolutions* (particularly in the 1st 1962 edition), Kuhn espoused a subjective, non-realist view of science, which denies the existence of objective truth and scientific knowledge, and which entails a strong form of relativism (Trigg 1973: 99–118; Chambers 2013: 115–119; Palermos and Pritchard 2018: 10–13). This is the interpretation typically accredit to him, even though it is not one of which he approves.[1] In a Postscript to the second enlarged edition he insisted that a subjective reading of his account of the scientific enterprise is based on 'misunderstandings' (1970: 174) and does not faithfully reflect his expressed position. Nevertheless, his endorsement of the view that scientists who follow different paradigms inhabit different worlds (hence the incommensurability thesis) undermines his positive (re)interpretation and leaves him open to the charge of inconsistency in his defence of the rationality of scientific 'knowledge,' or to put the matter equally bluntly, it is difficult to reconcile his belief that successive paradigms do not bring us any 'closer to the truth' (Kuhn 1970: 170 and 175) with his affirmation of the existence of scientific 'knowledge' (Chambers 2013: 115). How can there be scientific knowledge but not scientific truth? Whatever the deficiencies of the tripartite concept of knowledge (I am thinking of the Gettier Problems here, 1963), at least it incorporates a reference to both truth and knowledge: *knowledge* is justified *true* belief.

Our concern has been to extract from Kuhn the broad outline of the nature of a paradigm that will illuminate its applicability and appropriateness to religious education. Our account has been mainly descriptive, though (on a responsible reading) his separation of 'knowledge' from truth and his account of how knowledge is 'constructed' by experts is philosophically problematic, and arguably has been influential over CoRE (see below).

CoRE, institutional worldviews and personal worldviews

To determine whether CoRE's proposals collectively constitute a new paradigm or not, it is necessary to acquaint ourselves with its main features. CoRE proposes that religions should be reconceptualised as worldviews, that a range of non-religious worldviews should be included in the curriculum and studied to the same depth as religious worldviews at all key stages, that internal diversity within worldviews should be stressed, and finally, that the emphasis of the subject should be moved from that of religions (and institutional worldviews) to that of the personal worldviews of pupils. Some criticisms will be noted alongside analysis and commentary before attention is given (in the following section) to identifying just how novel these features are in English religious education.

Professor Cooling has commented that '[a] key feature of the [CoRE] report was its focus on "worldview"' (Cooling et al. 2020: 15).

> A worldview is a person's way of understanding, experiencing and responding to the world. It can be described as a philosophy of life or an approach to life. This includes how a person understands the nature of reality and their own place in the world. A person's worldview is likely to influence and be influenced by their beliefs, values, behaviours, experiences, identities and commitments.
>
> *(CoRE 2018: 4)*

This is not a dissimilar definition to that of Ninian Smart's, writing in *Working Paper 36*, in 1971 (Schools Council 1971: 47–52). He divided his influential six-fold dimensional account of religion into two parts: the first three, the doctrinal, mythological and ethical comprise a worldview; the addition of the ritual, experiential and the social dimensions constitute a religion. This distinction between a worldview, which is concerned with the intellectual side of religion, and a religion, which shows how the intellectual side comes to life in experience and practice, still captures the meaning attributed to both by most philosophers and scholars of religion (Bartholomew and Goheen 2013: 12–27; Moreland and Craig 2017). On this understanding a religious worldview is a narrower concept than that of religion. Incidentally, if the concept of a worldview covers the same content as a religion then there is nothing gained educationally or pedagogically by reconfiguring religious education around the former and not the latter, unless of course we add the study of a range worldviews to that of the study of a range of religions.

CoRE distinguishes two senses or uses of the term worldviews, that of institutional worldviews and that of personal worldviews.

> We use the term 'institutional worldview' to describe organised worldviews shared among particular groups and sometimes embedded in institutions. These include what we describe as religions as well

as non-religious worldviews such as Humanism, Secularism or Atheism. We use the term 'personal worldview' for an individual's own way of understanding and living in the world, which may or may not draw from one, or many, institutional worldviews.

(CoRE 2018: 4)

Twenty-four different examples of different religious and non-religious institutional worldviews are listed as appropriate for study in schools by CoRE, though the examples are not meant to be exhaustive (CoRE 2018: 18):

[Programmes of study] may draw from a range of religious, philosophical, spiritual and other approaches to life including different traditions within Christianity, Buddhism, Hinduism, Islam, Judaism and Sikhism, non-religious worldviews and concepts including Humanism, secularism, atheism and agnosticism, and other relevant worldviews within and beyond the traditions listed above, including worldviews of local significance where appropriate.

(CoRE 2018: 13)

In order to understand the full diversity of religious or non-religious worldviews, pupils may also benefit from awareness of a broader range of worldviews. . . . These may include ancient (and still living) traditions from China (e.g. Daoism, Confucianism), Japan (e.g. Shinto), Africa, Australia and New Zealand, and the Americas as well as Zoroastrianism and Jainism. . . . Historical and contemporary paganism in the UK may also be included, as this is both growing and influential beyond those who identify as Pagans. The range of worldviews may also include groups formed more recently that pupils may meet or belong to themselves, including Baha'i, Latter Day Saints (Mormons), Jehovah's Witnesses and Rastafari.

(CoRE 2018: 75)

Mentioned elsewhere as 'appropriate for study' is existentialism, whereas global capitalism, communism (presumably Marxism as well) and nationalism, are designated as inappropriate because they do not qualify as worldviews (2018: 75). When one looks closely at the 24 examples of worldviews provided by CoRE only four are properly non-religious worldviews (existentialism is a complicating case for there are both religious and non-religious existentialists). Controversially Paganism is recommended for inclusion in the curriculum.

The triumvirate of Humanism, secularism and atheism are always listed together throughout the Report (2018: 4, 26 and 28); in some cases agnosticism is added (2018: 13, 35 and 75). As presented, the option is there for pupils to study all four. Has serious attention been given by CoRE to the distinctions between these worldviews? It is a moot point how atheism and agnosticism *as worldviews* are to be distinguished for educational purposes and whether a study of the latter would add much to a serious study of the former. There will be an obvious duplication of content. The distinction often employed by philosophers (Rowe 2005) that atheism affirms the non-existence of God whereas agnosticism is the view that human reason is incapable of knowing whether God exists or not is for most people otiose; and certainly is for most pupils in schools. Both denote religious unbelief. A plausible case can be made for regarding atheism, agnosticism and Humanism, not as constituting independent and separate worldviews, but instances of the broader category of a naturalistic worldview – a relationship of tokens to type, in philosophical parlance. Furthermore, by definition, a Humanist will be a secularist and either an atheist or an agnostic (the number of Humanists in England is one seventh of one percent of the population). Citing secularism, alongside agnosticism, atheism and Humanism as a worldview is also controversial, as it is typically characterised as the view that public and political institutions should be independent of religion. It does not constitute a worldview as such, only that there should be strict limits to the public role of religions in society and that the state should be neutral between alternative religions and beliefs.

The deconstruction of religions

CoRE (2018: 5) recommends that religious education should attend to the 'diverse and plural nature [of institutional worldviews] and the ways that they have changed over time'; moreover, there should be recognition of diversity that goes far beyond 'crude differences between denominations.' Cooling endorses this recommendation and calls for attention to be given to the 'huge diversity' of 'adherents' experiences and perspectives' (2020: 408). But how credible is use of the concept of *institutional* worldviews to express internal diversity within religions? The reason for using the term *institutional* worldview is to refer to the set of beliefs and commitments that characterises a worldview and its adherents. A worldview refers to the basic beliefs that are foundational to some specific religion (what Smart calls the beliefs that characterise a 'religious system') that is sufficiently shared among adherents for it to take *institutional* form. (How many institutional worldviews can a religion have? – 4, 8, 12 or more!) If beliefs are not widely shared and endorsed, and given communal public expression in rituals and practices, it does not make sense referring to institutional worldviews. It is the distinctive beliefs of a religion, typically derived from acknowledged sources of authority, that distinguish it from other religions and give a specific religious identity to its adherents. A Muslim worldview, for example, acknowledges the revelation vouchsafed to Muhammad in the Qur'an, and accepts its teaching about the oneness of God, belief in angels and holy books, belief in God's messengers, and belief in the decrees of God (including predestination) and in the last judgement. If these foundational beliefs are discounted in what sense is a Muslim worldview described? When institutional worldviews (or religions) are differentiated into smaller and smaller units of meaning (below existing institutional, denominational, cultic or regional divisions), as recommended by CoRE, they effectively become personal worldviews and the study of institutional worldviews becomes insignificant and even redundant. Christianity, for example, does not denote the familiar doctrines and practices of traditional Christian faith but instead is the beliefs and practices of all those who think of themselves as Christian, whether they be cultural Christians or nominal Christians or committed Christians: religious understanding is gained by reflection on the results of empirical studies of what those identified as Christians, by whatever means, believe and practice. Individuals construct their personal versions of Christianity. This emphasis on personal constructions of religious identity is a prominent feature of CoRE's proposals for religious education and a central characteristic of its worldviews paradigm. Religious education is to be orientated to the diversity that results from individuals 'making sense of and giving coherence and meaning to the world and to their own experience and behaviour' (26). CoRE refers to this form of diversity as a 'personal worldview' (whether it deserves the accolade of a worldview is a moot point).

The question for educators is whether diverse and possibly idiosyncratic personal worldviews are worthy of serious and sustained study, as CoRE proposes. What is contributed to the aims of religious education and to the personal development of pupils by focusing on the study of the frequently eclectic, unsystematic and unreflective beliefs and practices of those who eschew formal religious identity? CoRE speaks of young people 'com[ing] to a more refined understanding of their own worldview' as one of the 'core tasks of education' (2018: 8): but is it? What does refining your worldview mean and what does it achieve educationally? CoRE misunderstands the relevance of personal worldviews to religious education (much less so Cooling, who by contrast adopts a hermeneutical approach, while professing to explain and support CoRE's position).[2] Where personal worldviews become relevant to religion education (and to education generally) is not as a subject in its own right (which is the view CoRE takes) but as 'shorthand' for the beliefs, values or presuppositions that one brings to the study of religions and religious phenomena and religious practices. Karlo Meyer (2021: 45–50), drawing on the hermeneutical tradition within European philosophy, has written recently about 'the conditionality of understanding' and of 'the pre-conditioning of our viewpoints' about religions: 'Religious phenomena can never be viewed purely "objectively"' (2021: 45). One's perspective on religions and religious phenomena is always conditioned by what one already believes. The initial beliefs that are brought to 'the hermeneutical task are variously described by philosophers as 'presuppositions,' 'assumptions' (*Voraussetzungen*, see Bultmann 1964), or following Heidegger (1962), as one's 'preliminary understanding' (*vorläufiges Vorverständnis*). These presuppositions can on occasions be corrected, revised, and even rejected in the interpretive encounter with the different aspects of religion and with religious phenomena (often referred to collectively as 'texts'). Secondary level pupils should be directed to identify and to reflect upon the nature and character of their presuppositions and the framework that they bring to the study of religion, not in order to 'refine' what they already believe but in order to recognise the ways in which their interpretations and encounters with religious phenomena and with religious individuals are conditioned by prior beliefs.

Furthermore, referring to personal worldviews may also not be as helpful a designation as CoRE believes. The issue is not whether everyone has beliefs, values, experiences and commitments, it is whether it is helpful to think of these collectively as a personal *worldview*. Can we talk about a worldview embraced by only a single person? People can hold a range of beliefs and values, not always consistent with each other or with some of their experiences or even with their professed self-identity: referring to a personal worldview may give the impression that what we believe and how we act possess a greater degree of coherence and unity than is the case for many. Individuals are often not reflective or consistent in their beliefs. Whereas many will have an opinion about God and his existence and nature, few will have thought seriously or at length about this and about what constitutes human nature, the meaning of life and of human history, whether knowledge is available to us and how we distinguish what is morally right from what is morally wrong, and so on; and it is answers to these that philosophers tell us constitute a worldview (Werther and Linville 2012). Many adults and particularly the young and non-religious people do not espouse a personal *worldview*: they do not have a reflective philosophical view of the nature of reality, of the kind that is properly described as a worldview.

How *new* is the proposed worldviews paradigm?

In a recent article intended for teachers of religious education, Trevor Cooling (2021) asked the question whether CoRE's proposals represent a 'Paradigm shift or [the] shuffling of content?' Predictably, as then chairperson of the RE Council that established the Commission, as the person accredited with inspiring the worldviews approach (Tharani 2020b: 39) and as the person who pioneered the description of the findings of the Commission as a 'paradigm shift' (incidentally, the language of paradigm and paradigm shift are not used in the Final Report), Cooling (2021: 55) concludes that CoRE is not 'just another shuffling of curriculum.' But is CoRE's proposed worldviews paradigm truly new? Acquaintance with the genealogical history of post-confessional religious education seriously questions the claim to newness. Cooling (2020: 408), with commendable candour, acknowledges 'that CoRE . . . draw[s] heavily on the insights developed by Robert Jackson (1997) through his work on the contribution of ethnography to phenomenological RE.' Just how heavily CoRE's proposals draw on the work of Robert Jackson is worth briefly exploring.

Robert Jackson's interpretive approach has been one of the most discussed pedagogical approaches in Britain and internationally in the last 25 years, at least by academics (for extended discussion and criticism, see Barnes 2014: 180–217). In his article 'Religious Education's representations of "Religions" and "Cultures,"' which was written in 1995, and gave programmatic form to interpretive religious education, Jackson (1995: 277) distinguished his approach from what he explicitly referred to as '[t]he "world religions" movement in British RE.' This is an interesting comment, for it indicates that during the period when CoRE maintains that a world religions paradigm dominated English religious education (according to it from the early 1970s to the present), one of the most influential movements, through its originator, specifically distinguished his 'new' pedagogy from a world religions approach. Positively, Jackson acknowledged that the world religions movement, inspired by Ninian Smart, endeavoured 'to empathise with those being studied' and that '[g]reat sensitivity was shown to the adherents of the "religions" and their practices and beliefs' (1995: 278).

> Nevertheless, the 'religions' were represented in terms governed by a powerful western intellectual tradition which, in the eighteenth and nineteenth centuries, had defined them. The idea of a 'world religion' is an extension of the eighteenth century idea of a 'religion' and, arguably, still presents 'other religions' as structured on a parallel with

> Christianity. Although the term 'world religions' is sometimes used as a synonym for 'religions of the world,' they are sometimes perceived as having a universal message and a doctrine of salvation potentially available to people in different cultural contexts (thus distinguishing them from primal religions, for example). They also have scriptures, a class of special interpreters and appeal to large numbers of people (Fitzgerald, 1990, 104). Many educational books and school resources operate with this idea of a religion . . .
>
> *(Jackson 1995: 278)*

(Contrary to what Jackson believes, Christians and Muslims almost unanimously claim that their respective religions do have 'a universal message and a doctrine of salvation potentially available to people in different cultural contexts.')

The same themes and observations (as above) are developed more fully in his first book length treatment of interpretive religious education, *Religious Education: An interpretive approach* (1997). Here Jackson expresses the view that 'religious wholes' are 'artificial constructions from the experiences of individuals' (1997: 45) and 'should be recognised as abstractions or reifications' (1997: 127). This interpretation is intended to support his (controversial) contention that religions are not 'in competition with each other' (Jackson, 1997: 127, and 1995: 277). He also questions usage of the concepts of 'religion,' 'world religions' and the names of the different religions, Hinduism and Buddhism, for example, because they are 'constructed' by 'powerful outsiders' (Jackson 1995: 283). These names, he believes, serve to reinforce and perpetuate false representations of 'religious traditions' (Jackson, 1995: 284, and 1997: 108–110), his preferred term for religions; though it is difficult to see how this term is any less susceptible to (what he believes to be) the charges of essentialising and reifying than use of the terms he criticises – all are common nouns! The inevitable result of this is to move the focus of religious education away from what he regards as essentialised and discrete religions to personal appropriations of religious traditions as mediated through internal membership groups. Individuals 'construct' their distinctive religious identities in dialogue with traditions, cultural ideas, the beliefs of their peer group and so on. Different insiders and outsiders construct their own personal versions of a religious tradition (1997: 64).

This short review of the interpretive approach clearly illustrates how influential it has been over CoRE's proposals. Its emphases on the problematic character of the concept of 'religion,' and of religions as separate and distinct and in competition with each other, and most importantly, the diverse and plural nature of worldviews are all indebted to it (see CoRE, 2018: 5 and 36; Benoit et al. 2020: 7–8). But there is another important, unacknowledged source that CoRE draws upon. CoRE and Cooling both refer to 'personal worldviews,' which is not a concept derived from Jackson, even though it is consistent with his position. The language and concept of personal worldviews is indebted to the 'narrative pedagogy' of Clive Erricker (2000; Erricker & Erricker 2000). At the same time as Jackson was developing and refining his interpretive pedagogy in the late 1990s, Erricker, like Jackson, was deconstructing the idea of distinguishable religions with characteristic beliefs and practices, but instead of Jackson's focus on personal appropriations of religious traditions, Erricker focused on the liberative potential of pupils constructing their own *worldviews* from a broader range of sources than the religions; in fact, for him, preferably without reference to religions and their ideological superstructures. CoRE in acknowledging that personal worldviews are often 'constructed' without recourse to religious beliefs and practices, *and that these should be the object of study*, follows Erricker rather than Jackson. Hence the concern that the beliefs and practices of the religions will be marginalised under a worldviews approach. Giving primary attention to the importance of personally constructed worldviews also marginalises the role of considerations of truth in religious education, for the impression is given by CoRE that everyone can have their own interpretation of the world and of religion, and that everyone's subjectively constructed attribution of meaning to religion is equally true: truth is what we take it to be true, not truth that is there to be discovered and which remains true regardless of our attitude to it (one can hear echoes of Kuhn here).

Interestingly, alongside Cooling's admission that CoRE draws heavily on interpretative religious education, he also (2020: 405) admits that 'Worldview is not a new idea for RE.' He refers to Ninian Smart's reference to worldviews in *Working Paper 36* (Schools Council 1971) and to Stopes-Roe's (1976) use of the term 'life-stance,' which carries broadly the same meaning. Both these references go back to the 1970s. He also refers to recent discussions of worldviews by continental and North American educators (e.g. van der Kooij, de Ruyter and Miedema 2013; Miedema 2014; Taves 2020). Cooling could have noted, and what we have noted, is that the concept of a personal worldview, which figures prominently in CoRE's revisioning of religious education, was central to Clive Erricker's self-confessed postmodern approach to religious education (for criticism, see Wright 2001). He should have been able to identify this influence, for he contributed a not entirely positive review of Erricker et al.'s *The Education of the Whole Child* (1997), the book in which Erricker developed the concept of 'personal worldview,' to the *Journal of Education and Christian Belief* in 1999.

Our review and analysis show that there are good reasons for concluding that CoRE's proposed worldviews paradigm does not constitute a *new* disciplinary framework, significantly different from what has been influential in religious education since the late 1990s: it relies too heavily on existing approaches and perpetuates many of the assumptions that have distracted and frustrated the contribution of religious education to the entirely legitimate aims of liberal education. In most respects it duplicates the assumptions and commitments of interpretive religious education, augmented by Erricker's concept of personal worldviews. CoRE's proposals are best interpreted as a version of postmodern religious education that combines features from both Jackson's and Erricker's positions, which despite their differences, clearly illustrate postmodern emphases (see Barnes 2014: 180–197). The big difference, however, is that CoRE seeks legal support to have its approach followed by all schools, as opposed to being but one of many possible approaches that teachers of religious education may choose to adopt.

Paradigms, revolutions and anomalies

A new paradigm must offer a comprehensive and integrated vision of beliefs and values to direct religious education and it must have the resources (or at least indicate its potential) to overcome current weaknesses.

The title of Kuhn's *The Structure of Scientific Revolutions* (1962 and 1970) indicates that his chief interest in the history of science was how one paradigm 'replaces' another, i.e. the nature of the process by which this happens. Central to Kuhn's understanding of why a 'paradigm shift' occurs is (1972: 6) its ability to overcome the anomalies that have accumulated under the existing dominant paradigm. If there are no anomalies, there is no need to seek a new disciplinary framework and if, according to Kuhn, any proposed disciplinary framework is to be regarded as a new paradigm, it must be capable of resolving the anomalies. The logic is straightforward: weaknesses ('anomalies') bring a subject into a 'crisis state'; responses are proposed and if there is convincing evidence in their favour a 'revolution' occurs and a new paradigm that overcomes the weaknesses assumes dominance, and 'normal' practice resumes. Translating these features into religious education: the identification of (intractable) weaknesses in religious education provides the stimulus to seek a new paradigm, and its plausibility, in turn, depends on its capacity to overcome current weaknesses.

CoRE gives superficial attention to these essential requirements, even though the concepts of 'paradigms' and 'paradigm shift' have been made central to its supporting material and its campaign to have a worldviews approach instituted in all schools, both faith and non-faith schools. The cause of the 'crisis' in religious education, which CoRE and the RE Council admit, and which occasioned the setting up of CoRE, is largely confined to (formal) issues, such as limited Continuing Professional Development, scarcity of resources, inadequate support for SACREs, the number of non-specialist teachers of religious education (CoRE 2018: 8), and so on, most of which can be resolved by extra funding and do not require a new paradigm to be in place.

The religious landscape

One theme in CoRE that is mentioned, though never developed, is the increasing secularisation of society and the emergence of 'new social realities' (2018: 5): a new paradigm is needed for a new situation. Note how this view neatly sidesteps the issue of what is currently wrong with religious education and what has caused its crisis. We might say it is the 'no-fault option.' Here is CoRE's (2018: 6) longest reflection on the changing contours of the religious landscape in Britain (in its Report).

> Non-religious worldviews have also become increasingly salient in Britain and Western Europe. According to the most recent British Social Attitudes survey, over 50% of adults identify as not belonging to a religion, with 41% identifying as Christian. The proportion of adults identifying as not belonging to a religion has increased from 31% in 1983 and has remained fairly stable around 50% since. While some of these individuals may identify with non-religious worldviews such as Humanism, many have looser patterns of identification or do not identify with any institutional worldviews.

Would it have been a good idea to take account of a wider, global perspective on religion, where the percentage of Muslims in the world is rising fastest and the unaffiliated are shrinking as a share of the world's population (see Pew Research Centre 2015)?

The changing religious landscape of Britain, however, is much more complex than CoRE acknowledges. It is unlikely that the concept of individuals constructing their own personal worldviews is uniformly common in all communities across society or even that it is a new phenomenon: it is something social commentators have been acknowledging since the 'counter-culture movement' of the 1960s (Roszak 1995) and the increasing secularisation of society from then onwards. Nevertheless, alongside evidence that formal membership of Christian churches is declined is evidence of continuing high levels of religious participation and even doctrinal uniformity among Muslim communities in Britain (Field 2010; Casey 2016: 123–131; Policy Exchange 2016; Ipsos MORI 2018). There is also evidence (as noted above) that the proportion of adults identifying as not belonging to a religion has remained fairly stable at around 50% for the last 40 years; added to this is survey evidence that shows that many of those without religious affiliation (the 'nones,' for example) often believe in spirits, in angels, in life after death or reincarnation; many occasionally pray or believe in the existence of some 'higher power,' many even believe in God, etc. (see Bullivant 2008; Madge and Hemming 2017).

An important issue is how far the changing religious landscape in Britain ought to be reflected in religious education, even assuming that we know in what ways the landscape is changing and can agree on the aspects of change that are most relevant to education. Some might argue that emerging patterns of religious unbelief and improvised forms of religious beliefs indicate increasing lack of knowledge about religions and understanding of their role in historical or modern societies and therefore that religious education should focus on overcoming religious illiteracy. The problem for CoRE is that recognition of the same religious and cultural shifts can be used to support radically different policies and practices. In any case it is unduly optimistic to believe that taking account of the religious landscape in which religious education is practised and of the lifeworld of pupils somehow justifies a worldviews model of religious education. All post-confessional models of religious education attend to these in some form.

The weaknesses of post-confessional British religious education

The chief weaknesses of post-confessional British religious education cannot be confined to its failure to keep pace with demographic and social change. Moreover, the strategy of refocusing religious education on personal worldviews because the religions are believed to hold limited interest for students, whom CoRE believes to be increasingly irreligious, can be interpreted as relinquishing the educational challenge of relating religious material to the lifeworld of pupils, a challenge that all subject specialists in different disciplines and areas of study have to address. The problem is that the fundamental weaknesses of British religious education, which most objective commentators acknowledge are systemic and historically extended, are overlooked by CoRE, yet the issue of what is wrong and why religious education is in such a poor state have to be addressed.

In the early 1990s Stephen Orchard (1991 and 1993), then General Secretary of the Christian Education Movement, conducted two reviews of HMI reports on religious education, from 1985 to 1988 and from 1989 to 1991 respectively. His conclusions were largely negative: 'poor teaching and unbalanced content'; 'Pupils are given unimaginative and repetitive lessons, with no attempt at development of the subject or to differentiate content and method according to the ability of the pupils.' There are no further reviews of inspection reports of this nature available from the 1990s from which to draw conclusions. Between 2007 and 2013 the Office for Standards in Education (Ofsted) produced three informative and authoritative reports (2007, 2010 and 2013) that evaluated the strengths and weaknesses of religious education in primary and secondary schools. On occasions improvements were noted but serious weaknesses were acknowledged in all three reports. The 2013 report helpfully identified 'eight major areas of concern' (2013: 40): low standards, weak teaching, problems in developing a curriculum for religious education, confusion about the purpose of religious education, weak leadership and management, weaknesses in examination provision at Key Stage 4, gaps in training, and finally the impact of recent changes in education policy. The teaching of Christianity was a particular cause of concern in all three reports. The following comments are typical: 'Many primary and secondary schools . . . did not pay sufficient attention to the progressive and systematic investigation of the core beliefs of Christianity'; 'teaching about Christianity [is] one of the weakest aspects of RE provision.' More generally, 'Many pupils leave school with scant subject knowledge and understanding. Moreover, RE teaching often fails to challenge and extend pupils' ability to explore fundamental questions about human life, religion and belief.' One limitation of the reports is that they are constrained by the inspection schedule and criteria and consequently provide a narrow perspective on religious education. They do not consider the importance and effect of historically extended influences over religious education or ascertain the role that different theoretical understandings (paradigms) play in conditioning/determining the success of learning and teaching and the extent to which they facilitate or frustrate the fulfilment of the aims of the subject.

A more recent and wide-ranging source of information about the 'workings' of religious education in the classroom are the findings of the 'Does Religious Education Work?' project (Conroy et al. 2013), based on research conducted at the same time as the crisis within the subject was beginning to demand wider attention. A fuller summary of the findings has been presented elsewhere (Barnes 2020: 18–20); consequently, the following are recorded to illustrate the seriousness of identified weaknesses and make no claim to comprehensiveness:

- Teachers observed in classroom situations often felt uneasy talking about the transcendent aspects or 'other-worldly' aspects of religions: 'Steeped as many appear to be in the discourse of secular relativism' (Conroy et al. 2013: 37–39; quoting from 39).
- There was a strong tendency for teachers to stress the ethical aspects of religions over their religious aspects (2013: 40).
- Teacher's interpretations of the theological and doctrinal claims of a particular religion or tradition appear sometimes to have little connection to official explanations or to the interpretations and explanations upheld by those communities themselves.
- Despite claims to the contrary there was little evidence of a critical element in religious education (2013: 48–49).
- Religious education is 'colluding in its own secularization' (2013: 88).
- Responses by students to the question, 'Do you believe your school has helped you get along better with members of other religious groups?' showed that students in denominational schools were 'significantly more likely' to respond positively than students in 'diverse schools' (2013: 208).
- Students seem to be invited to construct their own version of religion that embraces their spirituality while little attention is paid 'to the linguistic and conceptual demands of the geneaologically (*sic*) rich traditions of religious systems, and the otherness that they embody' (2013: 226).[3]

Not to address major weaknesses that are identified in a range of relevant sources effectively undermines CoRE's claim to be developing a new paradigm, for not only is it not new, it also lacks the central distinguishing feature of a paradigm, which requires that attention is given to the weaknesses of an existing paradigm and a convincing case made by reference to argument and evidence that these weaknesses will be overcome in any proposed new paradigm.

Conclusions

The main focus of this essay has been to answer the question whether a worldviews approach provides a new paradigm for religious education. The question is straightforward and the answer is equally straightforward. Our analysis has shown that a worldviews approach is heavily dependent on earlier approaches. CoRE's proposals 'rehearse' ideas and commitments that have been influential in religious education from the 1990s onwards. To use Cooling's language (quoted earlier), it is precisely 'the shuffling of content' and not as he believes a new paradigm. The further claim that the proposals of CoRE collectively constitute a paradigm is also difficult to maintain. Significantly, there isn't any reference to 'anomalies,' in the context of religious education, that is, to the *weaknesses* that beset contemporary religious education, and to the reasons for its failure to fulfil (in this case) the entirely appropriate aims of liberal education. CoRE recognises that there is a crisis in religious education, but chooses not to analyse the true causes and nature of the crisis, and thus effectively undermines its (own) claim to be developing a paradigm, for what is constitutive of a paradigm, namely recognition of and attention to current weaknesses, is missing.

That the proposals of CoRE cannot be characterised as a new paradigm may seem to some an innocuous conclusion, of no great moment, for the hope could be entertained that the proposals might still work. But this would be to fail to appreciate the force of the argument developed here. The reason why the proposals of CoRE cannot be regarded as a paradigm is because the true weaknesses of contemporary religious education (which are well documented, as summarised above) are overlooked, and therefore they will continue to undermine any positive contribution the subject could have. This conclusion is reinforced by recognition that what is advertised as new is not new but the republication and realignment of earlier beliefs and commitments (albeit with much pomp and ceremony), which have in all probability contributed to the current crisis (see Barnes 2014); even on an overtly optimistic reading they have failed to alleviate the crisis. Religious educators should look to other approaches and to other commitments if the subject is to fulfil its educational potential.

Notes

1 John Horgan (2012) records an interview with Kuhn in February 1991 which records Kuhn's deep annoyance at what he felt were misrepresentations of his work.
2 Cooling (2020) emphasises the hermeneutical relevance of personal worldviews to the study of religions, whereas CoRE emphasises the content of personal worldviews as appropriate for study.

3 Cooling is undoubtedly aware of these criticisms, as he refers to some of them in his (2015) review of the 'Does Religious Education Work?' project.

References

Barnes, L. P. (2014) *Education, Religion and Diversity: Developing a new model of religious education*. London: Routledge.

Barnes, L. P. (2020) *Crisis, Controversy and the Future of Religious Education*. London: Routledge.

Bartholomew, C. G. and Goheen, M. W. (2013) *Christian Philosophy: A systematic and narrative introduction*. Grand Rapids, MI: Baker Academic.

Benoit, C., Hutchings, T., and Shillitoe, R. (2020) *Worldview: A multidisciplinary report*. Religious Education Council of England and Wales. Available online: religiouseducationcouncil.org.uk/wp-content/uploads/2020/10/20-19438-REC-Worldview-Report-A4-v2.pdf (accessed 6 December 2021).

Bullivant, S. (2008) 'Research note: Sociology and the study of atheism,' *Journal of Contemporary Religion* 23(3): 363–368. Doi.org/10.1080/13537900802373114.

Bultmann, R. (1964) 'Is exegesis with presuppositions possible?' In *Existence and Faith: Shorter writings of Rudolf Bultmann*, 342–251. London: Collins Fontana.

Casey, Dame L. (2016) *The Casey Review: A review into opportunity and integration*. London: Department for Communities and Local Government.

Chambers, A. (2013) *What Is This Thing Called Science?* 4th edition. Berkshire: Open University Press.

Commission on Religious Education (CoRE) (2018) *Final Report: Religions and worldviews: the way forward*. Available online: commissiononre.org.uk/wp-content/uploads/2018/09/Final-Report-of-the-Commission-on-RE.pdf (accessed 6 December 2021).

Conroy, J. C., Lundie, D., Davis, R. A., Baumfield, V., Barnes, L. P., Gallagher, T., Lowden, K., Bourque, N., and Wenell, K. (2013) *Does Religious Education Work? A multi-dimensional investigation*. London: Bloomsbury.

Cooling, T. (1999) 'Review of Clive Erricker, Jane Erricker, Cathy Ota, Danny Sullivan & Mandy Fletcher, *The Education of the Whole Child*,' *Journal of Education and Christian Belief* 3(1): 64–66. Doi.org/10.1177/205699719900300113.

Cooling, T. (2015) 'Review of *Does Religious Education Work? A multi-dimensional investigation*,' *Journal of Beliefs & Values* 36(1): 115–117. Doi.org/10.1080/13617672.2015.1013819.

Cooling, T. (2020) 'Worldview in religious education: Autobiographical reflections on *The Commission on Religious Education in England: Final report*,' *British Journal of Religious Education* 42(4): 403–414. Doi:10.1080/01416200.2020.1764497.

Cooling, T. (2021) 'Paradigm shift or shuffling the content?' *REtoday* 38(2): 53–55.

Cooling, T., with Bowie, B. and Panjwani, F. (cited as Cooling et al., 2020). *Theos Report: Worldviews in religious education*. London: Theos. Available online: theosthinktank.co.uk/cmsfiles/Worldview-in-Religious-Education-FINAL-PDF-merged.pdf (accessed 6 December 2021).

Erricker, C. (2000) *Reconstructing Religious, Spiritual and Moral Education*. London: RoutledgeFalmer.

Erricker, C., Erricker, J., Sullivan, D., Ota, C. and Fletcher, M. (1997) *The Education of the Whole Child*. London: Continuum.

Erricker, C. and Erricker, J. (2000) 'The children and worldviews project: A narrative pedagogy of religious education.' In *Pedagogies of Religious Education*, edited by Michael Grimmitt (188–206). Great Wakering, Essex: McCrimmons.

Field, C. D. (2010) *Muslim Opinions and Opinions of Muslims: British experiences*. Manchester: Institute for Social Change, University of Manchester.

Gearon, L. (2014) *On Holy Ground: The theory and practice of religious education*. London: Routledge.

Gettier, E. L. (1963) 'Is justified true belief knowledge?' *Analysis* 23(6): 121–123. Doi:10.2307/3326922.

Heidegger, M. (1962) *Being and Time*. Oxford: Blackwell.

Horgan, J. (23 May 2012) 'What Thomas Kuhn really thought about scientific "truth,"' *Scientific American*. Available online: https://blogs.scientificamerican.com/cross-check/what-thomas-kuhn-really-thought-about-scientific-truth/ (accessed 6 December 2021).

Ipsos MORI (2018) *A Review of Survey Research on Muslims in Britain*. London: Ipsos MORI Social Research Institute.

Jackson, R. (1995) 'Religious education's representation of "religions" and "cultures,"' *British Journal of Educational Studies* 43(3): 272–89. Doi.org/10.1080/00071005.1995.9974037.

Jackson, R. (1997) *Religious Education: An interpretive approach*. London: Hodder and Stoughton.

Kooij, J. C. van der, de Ruyter, D. J. and Miedema, S. (2013) 'Worldview: The meaning of the concept and the impact on religious education,' *Religious Education* 108(2): 210–228. Doi:10.1080/00344087.2013.767685.

Kuhn, T. S. (1970 [1962]) *The Structure of Scientific Revolutions*. 2nd edition, enlarged. Chicago: University of Chicago Press.

Madge, N. and Hemming, Peter J. (2017) 'Young British religious "nones": Findings from the Youth on Religion study,' *Journal of Youth Studies* 20(7): 872–888. Doi.org/10.1080/13676261.2016.1273518.

Meyer, K. (2021) *Religion, Interreligious Learning and Education*. Berlin: Peter Lang.

Miedema, S. (2014) 'From religious education to worldview education and beyond: The strength of a transformative pedagogical paradigm,' *Journal for the Study of Religion* 27(1): 82–103.

Moreland, J. P. and Craig, W. L. (2017) *Philosophical Foundations for a Christian Worldview*. 2nd edition. Downers Grove, IL: IVP Academic.

Myatt, M. (2020) 'Foreword: Reforming RE.' In *Reforming RE: Power and knowledge in a worldviews curriculum*, edited by Mark Chater (11–14). Melton, Woodbridge: John Catt.

Ofsted (2007) *Making Sense of Religion: A report on religious education in schools and the impact of locally agreed syllabuses*. Manchester: Ofsted. Available online: dera.ioe.ac.uk/id/eprint/11105 (accessed 6 December 2021).

Ofsted (2010) *Transforming Religious Education*. Manchester: Ofsted. Available online: webarchive.nationalarchives.gov.uk/ukgwa/20141107041843/http://www.ofsted.gov.uk/resources/transforming-religious-education (accessed 6 December 2021).

Ofsted (2013) *Religious Education: Realising the potential.* Manchester: Ofsted. Available online: gov.uk/government/publications/religious-education-realising-the-potential (accessed 6 December 2021).

Orchard, S. (1991) 'What was wrong with religious education? An analysis of HMI reports 1985–1988,' *British Journal of Religious Education* 14(1): 15–21. Doi.org/10.1080/0141620910140104.

Orchard, S. (1993) 'A further analysis of HMI reports on religious education: 1989–91,' *British Journal of Religious Education* 16(1): 21–27. Doi.org/10.1080/0141620930160104.

Palermos, O. S. and Pritchard, D. (2018) 'How do scientific claims relate to truth?' In *Philosophy, Science and Religion for Everyone*, edited by Mark Harris and Duncan Pritchard (4–15). Abingdon: Routledge.

Pew Research Centre (2015) *The Future of World Religions: Population growth projections, 2010–2050.* Available online: pewforum.org/2015/04/02/religious-projections-2010-2050/ (accessed 6 December 2021).

Policy Exchange. (2016) *'What Muslims Want': A survey of British Muslims by ICM on behalf of Policy Exchange.* London: Policy Exchange/ICM Unlimited.

Roszak, T. (1995) *The Making of a Counter Culture.* Berkeley: University of California Press.

Rowe, W. L. (2005) 'Agnosticism,' in E. Craig (ed.) *The Shorter Routledge Encyclopedia of Philosophy* (10). London: Routledge.

Schools Council (1971) *Working Paper 36: Religious education in the secondary school.* London: Evans/Methuen.

Stopes-Roe, H. (1976) 'The concept of a "life stance" in education,' *Learning for Living* 16(1): 25–28. Doi.org/10.1080/00239707608556927.

Taves, A. (2020) 'From religious studies to worldview studies,' *Religion* 50(1): 137–147. Doi.org/10.1080/0048721X.2019.1681124.

Tharani, A. (2020a) *The Worldview Project: Draft discussion papers.* London: Religious Education Council of England and Wales.

Tharani, A. (2020b) 'The Commission and its recommendations.' In *Reforming RE: Power and knowledge*, edited by Mark Chater (37–44). Woodbridge: John Catt.

Trigg, Roger (1973) *Reason and Commitment.* Cambridge: Cambridge University Press.

Werther, D. and Linville, M. D. (eds) (2012) *Philosophy and the Christian Worldview: Analysis, assessment and development.* London: Bloomsbury.

Wright, A. (1994) *Religious Education in the Secondary School: Prospects for religious literacy.* London: David Fulton.

Wright, A. (2001) 'Dancing in the fire: A deconstruction of Clive Erricker's postmodern spiritual pedagogy,' *Religious Education* 96(1): 120–135. Doi.org/10.1080/00344080121331.

5
THE WORLD IS NOT ENOUGH

Religious education beyond worldview perspectivism

Gert Biesta and Patricia Hannam

The report from the Commission on Religious Education (CoRE 2018) makes an interesting intervention in the discussion about religious education and its future. Although the report was written within the context of religious education in England and Wales, similar discussions are taking place in many other countries (see, for example, Moyaert 2018; Bråten 2021). In this regard, then, the ideas put forward in the report potentially have a much wider significance. The CoRE report grew out of concerns about the state of religious education (see, for example, Clarke and Woodhead 2015; Butler-Sloss Report 2015) and makes a proposal for a new 'National Plan for RE.' The ambition of this plans is to ensure "that learning in this area remains academically rigorous and a knowledge-rich preparation for life in a world of great religion and belief diversity" (CoRE 2018: Foreword).

Perhaps the most striking aspect of the report is the proposal to rename 'Religious Education' as 'Religion and Worldviews.' This is not just a matter of rebadging a particular curricular area which, in itself, may be relatively uncontroversial. Cush and Robinson (2021) explain that the CoRE report very deliberately spoke of 'Religion and Worldviews' and not only of 'worldviews.' This was both to 'clarify the main emphasis of the field of study, and also the need to draw attention to the need to problematise the concept of "religion". . . .' (Cush and Robinson 2021: 66). However, it seems likely that the CoRE report has assumed that religion is as now being discussed in the religious education community as a kind of worldview (see Appendix 2 of the CoRE report, 2018: 72–75); subsequent commissioned reports affirm this position (see Benoit et al. 2020).

By seeing religion as a worldview and, more specifically, as a worldview amongst other worldviews, the report therefore not only takes a very specific approach to the question of what religion is, but also takes a very specific approach to the question of how we might understand the way in which human beings exist 'in' the world. Moreover, by suggesting that central to religious education should be the study of worldviews in order to promote the formation of students' individual worldviews, the report also takes a very specific approach to the question of education itself. The shift from 'Religious Education' to 'Religion and Worldviews' thus raises important philosophical, theological and educational questions that all have to do with the idea of a worldview.

The suggestion to capture the essence of RE in terms of the idea of worldviews has already generated a significant amount of discussion (see, for example, Cooling with Bowie and Panjawi 2020; Cooling 2020, 2021; Barnes 2022). While Cooling has pointed out that there is the question 'whether the term worldview captures the full potential of CoRE's proposed game-change' and acknowledges that the term may have 'too many unhelpful associations,' he nonetheless concludes that 'worldview is possibly the best term currently available' (Cooling 2020: 412). He therefore argues that the task now is 'to interpret this term in academically rigorous, pedagogically sophisticated teacher-usable ways,' adding that this is needed so as to 'promote pupils' academic, personal and civic development as flourishing human beings' (Cooling 2020: 412).

In this chapter we take up the challenge as to whether worldview is 'the best term available.' We do so on the assumption that 'worldview' is actually a very accurate notion for articulating what the Commission on Religious Education is after in their proposals, so that in this regard it seems unwise to look for another term. The main point we seek to make, however, is that precisely by seeing religion as a worldview, and turning religious education into the study of worldviews with the ambition to encourage children and young people to develop their own personal worldviews, the report is proposing a future for religious education that is problematic for philosophical, religious and educational reasons. While we do think that the CoRE report has provided an important stimulus to the discussion about the future of religious education, we wish to argue that conceiving of it as a form of worldview education would neither serve the religious nor the educational dimension of religious education. In this chapter we present our main concerns and articulate an outline of a different future for religious education.

Religion and worldviews education

The final report from the Commission on Religious Education (CoRE 2018) makes a convincing case for the need for action. Religious education in England is currently not part of the National Curriculum for schools but determined locally by each local authority. This does of course leave religious education open to many interpretations. The investigations made by the Commission show fairly conclusively that provision of religious education in England and Wales is patchy, and whilst there are some examples of good practice around the country, this is frequently also not the case. The report spells out how the situation for religious education has been undermined by a number of government initiatives, including academisation[1] (which particularly has contributed to the erosion of the local infrastructure for religious education) and changes to accountability and performance measures (such as the EBacc, which has significantly contributed to the marginalisation of religious education in the secondary school curriculum).[2] The report also shows that provision for initial teacher education for RE in primary schools is non-existent or at best minimal. Against this background, the report makes 11 recommendations which are intended to 'enable all pupils in all schools to receive a high-quality education in Religion and Worldviews' and to 'support and strengthen the subject for the foreseeable future (CoRE 2018: 10). This is in large part done through the proposal for a 'national entitlement' understood as a 'set of organising principles which form the basis for developing programmes of study' (CoRE 2018: 32).

As mentioned, the first recommendation of the report is that the name of the subject should be changed from 'Religious Education' to 'Religion and Worldviews,' and that this change should be reflected in subsequent legislation and guidance. This proposal puts religion in the wider context of worldviews, and thus potentially offers a broader 'framing' for the subject than an exclusive focus on religion would do. An important question, however, is what the adoption of the idea of worldview exactly entails. In the introduction, a worldview is described as 'a person's way of understanding, experiencing and responding to the world,' and also as 'a philosophy of life or an approach to life (which) includes how a person understands the nature of reality and their own place in the world.' And: 'A person's worldview is likely to influence and be influenced by their beliefs, values, behaviours, experiences, identities and commitments' (CoRE 2018: 4). The report does acknowledge that the notion of worldview is not perfect (see CoRE 2018: 31), but nonetheless is workable: 'the best fit (. . .) the best available catch-all term to describe both religious and non-religious approaches to life' (CoRE 2018: 31).

Although there is some acknowledgement that worldviews are about more than beliefs – reference is made to practices (see, for example, item 4 of the entitlement; CoRE 2018: 12), which means that worldviews are not entirely seen as cognitive belief-systems – it is also very clear that worldviews are basically understood as 'frames' for sense making. For example, in item 6 of the entitlement, we read: '[Pupils must be taught] how worldviews may offer responses to fundamental questions of meaning and purpose raised by human experience, and the different roles that worldviews play in providing people with *ways of making sense of their lives*' (CoRE 2018: 12; emphasis added). If this is, in a sense, a meta-perspective for education – the suggestion here is that pupils must be taught how worldviews 'work' – there is also a much bolder claim in the report with regard to this, namely that 'it is one of the core tasks of education to enable each pupil to understand, reflect on and develop *their own personal worldview*' (CoRE 2018: 5; emphasis added).

The report thus relies on a distinction between so-called 'institutional worldviews' and 'individual worldviews'. Institutional worldviews are defined as 'organised worldviews shared among particular groups and sometimes embedded in institutions [which] includes what we describe as religions as well as non-religious worldviews such as Humanism, Secularism or Atheism' (CoRE 2018: 4). The report uses the expression 'personal worldview' for 'an individual's own way of understanding and living in the world, which may or may not draw from one, or many, institutional worldviews' (CoRE 2018: 4). While, at first sight, this distinction and the definitions given, may look relatively clear and uncontroversial, Barnes (2022) has shown – convincingly in our view – that it's actually far from clear from the report what actually constitutes an institutional worldview, and also which worldviews are to be included in this category and which fall outside of it. He highlights that there are worldviews that do not take an institutional form (see Barnes 2022: 90), which means that the adjective 'institutional' may either be redundant or misleading, and also raises the question whether an 'agnostic worldview' should be characterised as a worldview, as one could argue that agnosticism 'is usually taken to express the view that all religious claims lack the status of knowledge' (Barnes 2022: 91). He also wonders on what grounds 'existentialism' is seen as a worldview that is 'appropriate for study,' whereas 'global capitalism, Communism . . . and nationalism are designated as inappropriate' (Barnes 2022: 92). And this, as he shows, is not just a question about which views fall under the category of 'worldview,' but also about the criteria used for selecting which (world)views should be part of the curriculum and which not (see also Barnes 2022: 92).

With regard to the idea of 'personal worldview' Barnes wonders whether this notion suggests 'more coherence and unity than is the case for many' (Barnes 2022: 90). He explains that the issue is not

> whether everyone has beliefs, values, experiences and commitments, [but] whether it is helpful to think of these collectively as *personal worldviews*, [as] people can hold a range of beliefs and values, not always consistent with each other or with some of their experiences or even with their professed self-identity.
> *(Barnes 20222: 90, emphasis in original)*

More strongly, he argues that many people, and 'particularly the young and non-religious do not espouse a worldview: they do not have a reflective philosophical view of the nature of reality, of the kind that is properly described as a worldview' (Barnes 2022: 90).

While it is clear, then, that the notions of institutional worldview and personal worldview are not unambiguous, we wish to highlight a number of further problems with the idea of worldviews and its role in religious education. The first problem is philosophical and has to do with the question whether it makes sense to think of our knowledge of the world in terms of particular perspectives with which we view the world. The second is theological and has to do with the question whether religion can be adequately captured as a particular view one has on an otherwise non- or a-religious world, or whether living religiously has something to do with the acknowledgement of the possibility of transcendence. And the third is educational and has to do with the question as to whether education is the kind of thing that can be limited to 'understanding' worldviews or indeed anything else.

The problem with 'worldviews' (1): philosophy

The first issue we wish to highlight has to do with the suggestion that a worldview constitutes a particular *perspective* one has or can have on the world. It is clear from the CoRE report that 'worldview' is not understood as an epistemological category – the issues at stake in worldviews are not, or not only, about cognition and belief, about truth and falsity, but also about values and attitudes – but the notion of a worldview nonetheless seems to suggest that a worldview is a perspective with which one 'approaches' the world, so to speak. Such approaches can either be 'personal,' and it does make sense to assume that we all 'approach' the world in a different ways. They can also be collective, standing for ways in which groups may have shared ways of 'approaching' the world. The philosophical problem we wish to highlight here has to do with the question whether we can meaningfully distinguish between the world and our view of it or perspective on it.

Perhaps the most convincing case against this idea can be found in the philosophy of perception, where it has been argued that we never perceive something 'in itself,' so to speak, in order then to apply a particular perspective on it. We immediately see chairs, dogs, lampposts, clouds, human beings, and so on. So it is not that we see 'something' which we then interpret as 'a dog' – the dog is immediately perceived and in its totality. This idea, which is also a central insight from Gestalt psychology, at the very least suggests that any perspective we may have is not applied to some 'empty' sensory content, but is actually on the 'inside' of our perception and therefore not applied at will. This does not immediately exclude that we can talk meaningfully about different perspectives, but these are not to be found at the level of perception.

In 20th-century analytical philosophy the issue has been discussed in relation to the question whether we can meaningfully distinguish between 'conceptual schemes' and the 'content' to which such schemes are supposedly applied. Donald Davidson, in his landmark paper 'On the very idea of a conceptual scheme' (Davidson 1973) has argued, convincingly in our view, against the idea of 'scheme–content dualism,' which he has identified as the 'third dogma' of empiricism, that is the third untenable assumption of the logical positivist view of (scientific) knowledge. (At this point Davidson refers to Quine's paper on the 'Two dogmas of empiricism'; see Quine 1951.)

The point we wish to make here is that what is misleading about the very idea of a worldview, is that it suggests that we are spectators of a world outside of us, and that we view this world through different 'lenses' or 'perspectives' and, moreover, that we can change our perspective at will. We can of course talk differently about what we perceive, and we can also value differently what we perceive, and we can even have different attitudes to what we perceive, but we are much more 'thrown into' the perceptual world than that we stand on the outside with a set of different schemes, lenses, or spectacles at our disposal. There is, to put it differently, little to 'view,' therefore, and also little to choose.

The problem with 'worldviews' (2): theology

The second problem we see with the idea of worldviews is of a theological nature and has to do with the question whether it makes sense to think of religions as worldviews and also to think of religions as worldviews amongst *other* – that is non-religious and perhaps even anti-religious – worldviews. One concern, which follows from the epistemological point we've made above, is whether it makes sense to think of the world as, in itself, secular or agnostic, and of religion as a particular kind of view on and/or attitude towards this world. That might be a way to position religion somewhere in a 'safe corner,' so to speak, where it can add something to an otherwise 'neutral' reality but doesn't 'touch' or 'affect' this reality itself. But such a view amounts to trying to give religion a place in a secular – which often means: modern or scientific or Western or *entzauberte* (Weber) – world, thereby accepting the hegemony of the latter and, in that sense, not taking religion seriously *in* its own terms and *on* its own terms. The 'debate' between 'science' and 'religion' is, of course, not yet concluded, which is one important reason why the idea of religions as worldviews may be problematic, at least from the position of religion.

A further issue here, has to do with the question how one might conceive religion or, in more practical or existential terms, how one might conceive what it might mean to try to be religious or try to live a religious life. One distinctive characteristic of the religious life, so we wish to suggest, is that of trying to live one's life with an acknowledgement of the possibility of transcendence. This can be, for example, an acknowledgement of the possibility of revelation or, in less biblical terms, of the possibility of givenness. To try to live one's life religiously, to put it differently, is out of an acknowledgement that much in life, including life itself, is given rather than produced, constructed, or taken. This rather 'minimal' – one could also say rather 'formal' – way of conceiving of the religious life, suggests that it is anything but a view one has on the world, as this would put the self 'before' the world, both in space and in time, but precisely highlights the opposite, that is, where what is 'beyond' the self comes first, so to speak, and where this 'beyond' cannot be 'reined in' or controlled by the self, and thus can go 'all the way up,' so to speak.

Linked with this, and noted by Ramon Panikkar in his Gifford Lectures of 1989 (published in 2010 as *The Rhythm of Being*), is how western sensibilities have tended since the late 19th century and through the 20th century to move away from conversations about the ultimate and of mystery, and instead sought clear distinctions between religion and what is named non-religion. There has been emphasis on human beings as being solely rational and self-understanding as something that can only come from within. Panikkar's work brings another layer of interest theologically, since it is informed not only by his scholarship as Catholic theologian and scientist, but also as scholar of 'The Dharmic traditions.' For example, he suggests, 'the notion of *dhivani* of classical indic aesthetics' (Panikkar 2010: 278), as well as notions of Kosmos enable recognition of emphasis of human existence in relational terms as being present across both Dharmic and Abrahamic traditions. This is in contrast to the positioning of humanity as observer emerging from scientific inquiry. Again, in referring to these things, we are not suggesting that talking about worldviews makes no sense, but we are highlighting that religion may actually be the very opposite of what can be found in the idea of a worldview and that, in that regard, subsuming religion under the category of 'worldviews' may miss the very 'point' of what religion and the religious life may be about.

The problem with 'worldviews' (3): education

The third set of problems we wish to highlight is educational and has to do with the two suggestions in the CoRE report, one being that religion and worldviews education should focus on understanding what worldviews are and how worldviews 'work' so to speak. As mentioned above: '[Pupils must be taught] how worldviews may offer responses to fundamental questions of meaning and purpose raised by human experience, and the different roles that worldviews play in providing people with ways of making sense of their lives' (CoRE 2018: 12). The other is the suggestion that 'it is one of the core tasks of education to enable each pupil to understand, reflect on and develop their own personal worldview' (CoRE 2018: 5).

The first suggestion makes sense to the extent to which the very idea of worldview makes sense, so we might say, but as soon as we acknowledge some of the problems with the very idea of 'the world' as something 'to view,' there is already the question how meaningful this idea is for education. While one could argue that the study of worldviews, but perhaps better the study of the very idea of worldview and all the problems related to it, might be an interesting topic for the curriculum, it not obvious that such a topic should be part of the curriculum for religious education – it would be much better at home in a philosophy curriculum or, perhaps, a social studies curriculum. But here it is already important to add that to think of the world as something that can be viewed or can come into view in particular ways, is only one of the ways in which we can think of the relationship between human beings and the world. Thinking of this relationship in terms of views of the world or perspectives on the world, puts the perceiving and knowing self first and things of the world, natural and social, as an object of interpretation and sense-making. Such a 'hermeneutical worldview' (see Biesta 2016; Hannam and Biesta 2019) is possible, but it is only one of the ways in which we can think of the relationship between human beings and the world. There is at the very least a 'gesture' that goes in the opposite direction, where the guiding question is not 'How can I understand or make sense of the world?' but where the first question is 'What is the world asking of me?' (see Biesta 2017). Such a world-centred approach (Biesta 2021) highlights that 'the world' is precisely not something for me to 'view,' but rather something that appeals to me, poses questions to me, and even puts me *in question*. This provides an altogether different starting point for education than what is entailed in the idea of worldviews (including the study of worldviews).

The leading idea of the CoRE report, so we wish to suggest, is that the study of worldviews is not an end in itself, but that religion and worldviews education should ultimately 'enable each pupil to understand, reflect on and develop their own personal worldview' (CoRE 2018: 5). Does this suggestion make educational sense? While it may sound attractive, liberal and pupil-friendly, the problem with suggestions such as these – which are far from uncommon in contemporary educational thinking – is that they lack a sense of limits and limitations. The suggestion is that it is up to each individual to develop his or her own personal worldview, but if this is all that is suggested, the question which worldviews are 'ok' and which worldviews are 'not ok,' to put it in simple terms, remains remarkably absent. While one could argue that education needs provide space, time and opportunities for children and young people to meet themselves, to meet the world, and to meet their own life in relation to the world, this is not just a question of developing one's own personal worldview, one's own personal set of beliefs and preferences. Rather, the task of education is allow for children and young people to give their emerging views and values a 'reality check,' so to speak, in order to begin to figure out which views, beliefs and preferences are going to help in leaving a worthwhile life, with others, on a planet that has limited capacity for sustaining all life projects, and which views, beliefs and preference are going to hinder. The answers are not absolutely clear – this is, in a sense, a lifelong challenge. But this challenge needs to be on the educational agenda in order to prevent an 'anything goes' situation where any worldview is simply 'ok' because it is the individual's worldview.

And here again, we wish to highlight, that the 'reality check' needed is precisely one where children and young people can come into 'dialogue' with the world, natural and social, in order to discover not just what they may want from 'the world,' but even more so what the world may want from them. This has very little to do with sense making, and even less so with construction, but is perhaps much closer to an experience of transcendence or revelation – an experience that something is coming *to* children and young people, to put it briefly (see Biesta 2011).

Introducing a different outlook

In this section, we offer an alternative proposal. This is one seeking to offer a different way of responding to concerns raised about religious education in recent years, recognising there is a strong case for change. In what has preceded this section we have shown a 'turn' to worldviews to resolve matters raises other philosophical, theological and education problems. We therefore question whether 're-staking out' the field of study by introducing the concept of worldviews will be sufficient remedy for religious education's troubles. In the proposal outlined here we therefore take a different starting point. We begin instead by setting out what it is that we intend religious education to achieve, drawing on theory which addresses what education *is* and what is desirable for it to *do* at this point in history. From here our proposal moves to take another look at religion, and what it is to live a religious life, conceptualising this beyond belief and practice. The next step is to set out how such purpose can be brought into reality. Here we take up a discussion of what teachers, through their teaching, would do to make it possible for religious *education* to happen. Nothing here rules out bringing what might be termed 'non-religious ways' of existing in the world to the religious education classroom. This proposal does not necessarily limit what is encountered and studied, but what is different is that religion and existing religiously in the world is presented *in* and *on* its own terms. Religion here is taken seriously and not in relation to another category outside of itself; that is to say as just another worldview. This proposal also seeks to take education seriously and not therefore limit what religious education should do only to the study of worldviews and in particular to the development of a child's personal worldview.

Religious education as part of education in the public sphere

Our proposal begins with a statement of intent for religious education exemplified here as being about making it possible for children to encounter 'what a religious way of existing in the world might offer in leading one's life, individually and collectively' in order to 'play an educative part in the lives of children and young people as they come to speak and think and act in the world' (see for example Living Difference III 2016, Living Difference IV 2021 purpose statements, Hampshire County Council 2016, 2021). This means we open with a discussion about education, what this is and what it should do, allowing for the possibility that an encounter with and study of religion might offer something of value into the educational context. Regarding education, in brief, we would hold to the view that education has at least three 'domains of educational purpose': qualification, socialisation, and subjectification (see for example Biesta 2020 and 2014). Qualification is concerned with the presentation and acquisition of knowledge and skills, so children and young people are able to act in the world in knowledgeable and skilful ways. Socialisation is the concern to introduce children and young people to different traditions and practices giving them a sense of orientation in the world and invites them to find their own place also. The educational domain of subjectification encourages children and young people to become the subjects of their own life and to engage with their own freedom in meaningful and responsible ways. All domains are equally important and give a way of checking also what religious education should and can achieve.

Another point to make at this stage however, is that the religious education we are discussing is that which takes place in the public sphere and therefore has particular responsibilities in relation to public life, and not only to the individual experiencing education. This means consideration must be given to both freedom and plurality. What is important in our proposal here is that freedom is seen as a matter of being in relationship with the wider social and natural world. This is relationship with all that is, comprising the world and even the cosmos beyond, rather than solely as an individual's right to do what they want to do. The teacher's responsibility therefore is to seek a subtle and sensitive balance between concern for each individual's uniqueness, and for the web of plurality within which we live our lives. At the heart of all this lies both attentiveness and discernment. Although all this is of broad educational significance, in the present discussion and for the proposal we make here it is of particular importance to bring it into the light. This is because attention to broader educational questions will help the teacher make better choices in the way they make curriculum as well as gain clarity over what it is they should do, practically, in the classroom to achieve the intended purpose.

A brief word here about attentiveness and discernment before they are woven into the discussion further below. In practical terms we would say both are required for education to occur. That is to say where freedom and plurality count for something, for without attentiveness there may be no realisation that there is anything new or different from what I am already familiar with to bring my interest to. Discernment is also essential since it is in this way a I am able to work out what matters for me and for the world. Both attentiveness and discernment could be seen as being significant markers distinguishing education from other kinds of things such as instruction, indoctrination or coercion (see Hannam 2018). Importantly, and in terms of the discussion here, it will be seen that discernment is something quite different, qualitatively, from 'developing my own personal worldview' (CoRE 2018: 5).

What is it to live a religious life?

Having begun to explore educational questions here, we turn back to religion. It seems common-sense to highlight that what it is to live a religious life is not one thing. However, in our view this is far too infrequently emphasised in practice in the religious education classroom. What is rather more common is for religion to be aligned directly with belief (see for example, the Equalities Act 2010 and Article 18 of the European Convention on Human Rights). We want to point out that while this may be the case for some who identify with a religious life, is not the case for all. Instead, in this proposal we broaden the way that leading one's life with a religious orientation is conceptualised, by proposing that what this might mean can be answered in several, qualitatively different ways. These would include the idea that to live a religious life can mean to subscribe to certain beliefs, where they are understood in propositional terms, as well as adherence to certain practices. However, beliefs and practices are not all there is, since for many, what it is to live a religious life is closer to a way of 'being in and with the world: with a particular kind of awareness of and faith in the world and other human beings' (see for example Living Difference III, Living Difference IV purpose statements (Hampshire County Council 2016, 2021), and for a longer discussion see Hannam 2018). Conceptualising religion and what it might mean to live a religious life in this way makes the discussion wider, influencing not only what it is that can be brought to the classroom for the children and young people to encounter and study. More than this, broadening the way religion is conceptualised will require teachers to consider carefully how religious education is taught, that is in such a way for religion to be taken seriously in its own terms.

Beginning this proposal by making a response to educational concerns about for example plurality, means that there are immediately implications that require the classroom to be understood to be a place where great value is placed on children and young people's uniqueness. This is as well as ensuring there is emphasis placed on the concern for the common world, the world we all live in and are dependent upon, which is a world of plurality. The significance of beginning a proposal by discussing what education should achieve turns things around. The focus is no longer on the re-arranging of the material to brought to the classroom but to where the uniqueness of each child and value of all that is in the wider social and natural world we all share, becomes of central concern. In this way religious education cannot be seen as merely cultivating a 'view' on the world. To do so would be to imply a separateness as if there were many worlds, and our common world risks being lost.

Teaching religious education

So, what is it that teachers can do? We would describe this in three 'steps' (from Weil 1965) which in a school context, with children or young people of any age, would be spread over a period of allocated teaching time or sequence of lessons. These three steps would be repeated as a carefully made spiral curriculum unfolds. In this way curriculum making and practical classroom teaching are inextricably bound together.

The first step we would suggest is for the teacher to bring the child to attend (see Hannam 2018 for a more extended discussion). What this means is that the teacher through various sensitive activities cultivates the classroom in such a way as to make it possible for the child to bring their attention to the matters that are at hand. This is not something that can be 'paid' (Weil 1965: 68) or forced; it is the opposite of coercion and in no way resembles instruction. It is something the child has to do for themselves, and perhaps continues to be familiar to the teacher in the nursery school but a less familiar part of teaching for teachers of older children in contemporary school contexts.

The teacher's role here is to make the conditions possible where attention, the child's attentiveness can happen. Practically, the teacher may begin the first 'moments' of a sequence of lessons where the child or young person can become attentive to certain aspects of their own experience or where an experience is evoked in some way in the classroom. Perhaps in year 1 this may be the experience of 'special' where the quality of 'specialness' is created in some way in the classroom. Weil has noted that this quality of attention or attentiveness, is essential if the next educational moment is to be possible. Weil describes this as intellectual humility, but it can also be appreciated as a kind of intellectual open-mindedness which it is not difficult to see is fundamental to, or even a prerequisite for, the seriousness of study. Here in practical terms with children in the infant school, the teacher might introduce further the idea of there being some places that are special, leading into the study of special places for those of different religious or other traditions.

What is important here is that where the child's attention has not been brought to their own experience of special or specialness, or where the experience has not been identified and not named perhaps; there is no way the child could recognise what it would mean for someone, for example in the Jewish tradition with regard to Torah, as special or holy. The child will be able to bring their attention to their experience and so perhaps also begin to recognise in the fullest sense, what it means to be in and with the world, where there are others also experiencing. This will include bringing their attention to how the world may appeal to us as human beings in different ways, to how the world might 'speak' to and call us and even insist at times on certain ways of being. How attending to these things may also lead to a kind of regard to the immensity of all that is, and that at times this may or will also bring limits to us in what we can or can't do in the way we live. All this does not yet require formal study. This comes next.

From this point, comes what we would term the intellectual moment in a sequence of lessons. The child or young person is more open to receive substantial materials the teacher chooses and selects to introduce into the classroom. Weil terms this 'intellectual humility' or a kind of intellectual open-mindedness, recognising that to study new material requires attention and focus. There are two significant things to note at this point. The first is that this proposal would place teachers' professional judgements and action at the very heart of education. And the second is to note the importance of recognising what it is to live a religious life is not one thing. This proposal is therefore an approach to teaching religious education that takes religion seriously and doesn't reduce it to a 'view' on 'the world.' If the teacher has responsibilities in relation to the three domains of educational purpose and in relation to uniqueness, freedom and plurality, it is clear this cannot be operationalised or understood solely in terms of delivery of parcels of knowledge. That is as knowledge simply to be remembered and repeated on another occasion. Clearly teachers have professional responsibilities for selecting the activities and the materials for the children and young people to engage with and study; helpful further reading in relation this this would include Biesta 2017 and Lewin 2021. However, first the teacher has to find ways to make it possible for the child or young person to bring their attention and interest and curiosity to the matters at hand.

The final step in the process of teaching we would call the discernment step. This is where the teacher brings the child or young person, over time, to come to discernment about how what they have encountered may matter for their own lives as well as for all that is, including all other beings existing in this time and even in the future. The important thing here is that this discernment is not the same as developing one's one personal worldview, one's own set of beliefs or practices or other preferences. This is precisely the moment in a sequence of lessons practically where children and young people have the opportunity to give their emerging views, values and preferences a 'reality check' as discussed earlier in this chapter. This is the space where children and young people have the opportunity to discern value and to work out which of their views and preferences are likely to help secure the common world upon which we are all dependent and which might hinder or even destroy the future. This is not a matter of the child choosing what they want, and it is little concerned with 'making meaning' at least not in individualistic terms. What is at stake here is not only the unique child or young person and their personal view on the world, but the possibility of a common world for us all, at all.

Conclusion

A key point we want to make before setting out in this concluding section of our chapter, is that beginning by 're-staking out' or reorganising the material to be brought to the classroom by introducing the notion of 'worldviews' is likely to be an insufficient response to the problems facing religious education. Additional philosophical, theological and educational problems emerge and some have been explored in the first half of this chapter. We have proposed an alternative, which begins with stating what it is that can be achieved educationally in bringing children and young people get a glimpse of what it might be to live with a religious orientation on life; knowing that this is not one thing. Here religion is not reduced to another view among many on the world. Rather, it is seen in terms at times, of being a matter of holding belief, or as adhering to traditions, or as a way of existing in the world and in all that is in the cosmos. This proposal, rather than making the 'turn' to worldviews, returns to religion. It seeks to ensure that religion can be taken seriously in religious education, on its own terms.

As a consequence of this, religious education lends itself to being taught in what we have from Weil (1965) identified in terms of three 'steps,' or 'moments'; taking place over a sequence of lessons or time allocated for teaching particular materials. We discuss this first in terms of a proper experiential 'moment' where the child or young person can come to attend to their own experience, in the fullest sense, of what it means to be in and with the world. Attentiveness to what is new will be a prerequisite for the second 'moment,' that is for full intellectual engagement with texts, with history, anthropological ethnographies, or theology, or whatever else the teacher brings. However, this kind of intellectual engagement can never be one that is content with mere reproduction or memorisation. Therefore, the teacher's role cannot be reduced to mere 'delivery,' and the curriculum to something to be 'delivered.' Rather the teacher's role here is to make possible for the child or young person to engage fully with intellectual humility (see Weil 1965 and Hannam 2018), including an engagement with all the scholarship around religion and the religious relevant to a particular course of study. This cannot be an end in itself, however, which is why we articulate from Weil a final 'step' or 'moment' of discernment.

All that has gone before, the experiential and intellectual 'moments,' is there in order to encourage children and young people to come to discernment. The opportunity to work out what may be of value for my own life and for the life of the world. We have sought to articulate why this is precisely not the same as 'developing your personal worldview.' Instead this is about having the opportunity to encounter and study before discerning what any of this may have to offer.

A brief word about curriculum making. Suffice to say that this proposal would see making curriculum as a multidimensional activity where the teacher, whose judgement would be trusted here to make the curriculum relevant in the context of the children and young people in her care, takes a number of factors into account. The first will be what it is that is sought to be achieved – educational considerations. Therefore, and in order to fulfil the multi-dimensional nature of educational purpose, it is likely that the curriculum is best thought of as a 'spiral' rather than entirely linear. Progress through time, over several years will also be thought of in terms of a spiral and so a curriculum needs to be planned in such a way that experiences and some content can be revisited at each and every age in different ways and in different contexts. There will be elements of this that we hope children progress with, that will not be measurable. This is either not at all or for sure not in the same way. However, this does not mean such elements are not equally important. The three 'moments' in the way of teaching discussed here will support the revisiting of materials over time so that all, and especially discernment, can be broadened and deepened over time.

This is therefore a proposal that takes religion seriously, not reducing it to a view on the world, and a proposal that takes education seriously, not reducing it only to the study of worldviews and development of a child's personal worldview.

Finally, why indeed might all this matter? Why might it matter that religious education is not reduced to a kind of 'perspectivism'? It matters not only because this limits what it is possible for religion to bring to the classroom, as well as because it would limit the ambition for what education can achieve. Most importantly it matters at this point in history because the idea of humanity being at the centre of their own separate universe is already an old and problematic way of seeing our human-beingness in the world. As already noted earlier in this chapter, it brings a tacit acceptance of a secular position which sees religion as a kind of optional 'extra' possibility. It limits what religion is in itself. As Panikkar notes (2010: xxviii) the influence of such a technocratic way of seeing has had a great impact on everything, including education, all over the world. One such impact he sees has been to demand that little time is spent on what he calls '*truly* philosophical studies' (our emphasis), perhaps interpreted as we propose here.

Our proposal is one that seeks to bring these things together, to link again the study of religion as and for itself into educational contexts. Our audacious proposal is that perhaps this will be critical for the re-emergence of a common world. One where the child and young person's attention is brought to their experience of our common world, before studying with intellectual humility and then to discern what is of value in order to live together, in such a way by which we may care enough to ensure the world, and all that we are dependent upon, is not destroyed.

Notes

1 In England, since the 1944 Education Act, school buildings have been owned by, and the education has taken place in, publicly funded institutions under the oversight of local authorities. However increasingly in the last 15 years legislation has enabled schools to function in all respects independently from the local authority and be known as 'academies.' Further, various 'Multi Academy Trusts' (MATs) have emerged, functioning as chains of schools with particular ethos and sometimes shared curriculum. These schools do not have to follow either the National Curriculum or the Locally Agreed Syllabus for religious education, and have therefore led to further complexity of what passes for religious education in England.
2 Religious education is statutory in all publicly funded schools in England, for children up until the age of 18. Young people sit external examinations in many subjects at 16, in an examination known as the General Certificate of Secondary Education (GCSE). Enabling young people to study GCSE in Religious Studies was a way many schools sought to meet their statutory obligation to teach religious education to older secondary age students. However, this has been compromised by RS GCSE not being included in a performance measure for schools introduced by national government in 2010, known as the English Baccalaureate (EBacc). This caused many schools to limit access to GCSE RS, resulting in a decline in examination entries. This has further compromised provision for religious education for young people in the later secondary years.

References

Barnes, L. P. (2022) 'The Commission on Religious Education, worldviews and the future of religious education,' *British Journal of Educational Studies* 70(1): 87–102. Doi.org/10.1080/00071005.2021.1871590.

Benoit, C., Hutchings, T. and Shillitoe, R. (2020) *Worldview: A multidisciplinary report*. Religious Education Council of England and Wales. Available online: religiouseducationcouncil.org.uk/wp-content/uploads/2020/10/20-19438-REC-Worldview-Report-A4-v2.pdf (accessed 6 December 2021).

Biesta, G. (2011) 'Transcendence, revelation and the constructivist classroom; or: In praise of teaching.' In R. Kunzman (ed.) *Philosophy of Education 2011* (358–365). Urbana–Champaign, IL: Philosophy of Education Society. Available online: educationjournal.web.illinois.edu/archive/index.php/pes/article/view/3305.pdf (accessed 7 December 2021).

Biesta. G. (2014) *The Beautiful Risk of Education*. Boulder, CO: Paradigm Publishers.

Biesta, G. (2016) 'The rediscovery of teaching: On robot vacuum cleaners, non-egological education and the limits of the hermeneutical world view,' *Educational Philosophy and Theory* 48(4): 374–392. Doi.org/10.1080/00131857.2015.1041442.

Biesta, G. (2017) *Letting Art Teach: Art education after Joseph Beuys*. Arnhem: ArtEZ Press.

Biesta, G. (2020) 'Education, education, education: Reflections on a missing dimension.' In G. Biesta and P. Hannam (eds), *Religion and Education: The forgotten dimensions of religious education?* (8–19). Leiden: Brill.

Biesta, G. (2021) *World-centred Education*. London/New York: Routledge.

Biesta, G. and Hannam P. (eds) (2020) *Religion and Education: The forgotten dimensions of religious education?* Leiden: Brill.

Bråten, O. M. H. (2021) 'Non-binary worldviews in education,' *British Journal of Religious Education*, 1–11. Doi.org/10.1080/01416200.2021.1901653.

Butler-Sloss Report (2015) *Living with Difference: Report of the Commission on Religion and Belief in Public Life*. Cambridge: The Woolf Institute.

Clarke, C. and Woodhead, L. (2015) *A New Settlement: Religion and belief in schools* (Westminster Faith Debates). Available online: faithdebates.org.uk/wp-content/uploads/2015/06/A-New-Settlement-for-Religion-and-Belief-in-schools.pdf (accessed 7 December 2021).

Commission on Religious Education (CoRE) (2018) *Final Report: Religions and worldviews: the way forward*. Available online: commissiononre.org.uk/wp-content/uploads/2018/09/Final-Report-of-the-Commission-on-RE.pdf (accessed 7 December 2021).

Cooling, T. (2020) 'Worldview in religious education: Autobiographical reflections on *The Commission on Religious Education in England: Final report*,' *British Journal of Religious Education* 42(4): 403–414. Doi:10.1080/01416200.2020.1764497.

Cooling, T. (2021) 'The Commission on Religious Education: A response to L. Philip Barnes,' *British Journal of Educational Studies*, 1–16. Doi.org/10.1080/00071005.2021.1954142.

Cooling, T. with Bowie, B. and Panjwani, F. (2020) 'Worldviews in religious education.' THEOS. Available online: https://www.theosthinktank.co.uk/research/2020/10/21/worldviews-in-religious-education (accessed 7 December 2021).

Cush, D. and Robinson, C. (2021) '"Buddhism is not a religion, but paganism is." The applicability of the concept of "religion" to Dharmic and nature-based traditions, and the implications for religious education,' in G. Biesta and P. Hannam (eds) *Religion and Education: The forgotten dimensions of religious education?* Leiden: Brill.

Davidson, D. (1973) 'On the very idea of a conceptual scheme,' *Proceedings and Addresses of the American Philosophical Association* 47: 5–20. Doi:10.1093/01992 46297.001.0001.

Hampshire County Council (2016) *Living Difference III.*

Hampshire County Council (2021) *Living Difference IV.*

Hannam, P. (2018) *Religious Education and the Public Sphere.* London: Routledge.

Hannam, P. and Biesta, G. J. J. (2019) 'Religious education: A matter of understanding? Reflections on the final report of the Commission on Religious Education,' *Journal of Beliefs & Values* 40(1): 55–63. Doi.org/10.1080/1361767 2.2018.1554330.

Lewin, D. (2021) 'Religion, reductionism and pedagogical reduction,' in G. Biesta and P. Hannam (eds) *Religion and Education: The forgotten dimensions of religious education?* Leiden: Brill.

Moyaert, M. (2018) 'Inter-worldview education and the re-production of good religion,' *Education Sciences* 8(4): 156. Doi.org/10.3390/educsci8040156.

Panikkar, R. (2010) *The Rhythm of Being: The Gifford Lectures.* New York: Orbis Books.

Quine, W. V. O. (1951) 'Two dogmas of empiricism,' *The Philosophical Review* 60(1): 20–43.

Weil, S. (1965) *Waiting on God.* London: Fontana Books.

6
THE PHILOSOPHY OF 'WORLDVIEWS'

Roger Trigg

The basic purpose of 'worldview' education is to inject more life into religious education as a subject in schools when it has lost its way. Yet with an unfocused subject matter, there is no possibility of deciding what good teaching in the area might be. The idea of worldview education becomes vacuous if worldviews are merely the fleeting fancies of rootless individuals without even a common heritage. Such autonomy is unconstrained by the character of the world in which we are set, by human nature, or any particular heritage. Cut off even from traditional religion, the idea of 'worldviews' leads us to the abyss of nihilism.

The challenge of science

The Commission on Religious Education (CoRE) of 2018 made 'worldviews' the focus of religious education alongside religion. It informed us that the term is a translation of the German *Weltenshauung*. The very artificiality of the term to English ears should warn us that it could carry with it philosophical assumptions, not always made clear. It could itself be a product of what the Germans term *zeitgeist*, the spirit of the age. Fashionable theory, particularly in education, can act as a front for the deeper philosophical and social trends which affect educationalists as much as anyone else. It takes time for the philosophy of an earlier generation to have an impact on contemporary thinking. What was once radical can appear 'common sense'. Education then simply expresses the views of the age, without making the subject available to rational critique, or providing any form of distinctive leadership for the next generation.

As someone involved in professional philosophy since the 1960s, with a particular concern for the philosophy of religion, I have been an interested spectator of the development of the philosophy of education, and the way in which different philosophical theories influence the way in which religion is regarded and taught in schools. As a boy, I was taught 'Scripture', but the teaching of Christianity, and religion more generally, has gone through several phases since then, often marked by change of title. From 'Religious Instruction', to 'Religious Knowledge', to 'Religious Studies', the subject has been influenced by changing assumptions. At sixth form level it has often become just the philosophy of religion and ethics. It is now being challenged to make another change. From a secure Christian base, or even the more general teaching of world religions, we are faced with a clear discomfort that the focus should be on religion at all. Whilst nods are made in the direction of religious belief, religion is for the most part being gathered under the seemingly anodyne concept of 'worldviews'. This reflects a trend in law away from the explicit protection of religion as such. It is still explicitly championed in the United States, being specifically mentioned in the First Amendment to the U.S. Constitution. Yet in various Declarations of Human Rights, the phrase freedom of religion or belief' is now normally used. Article 9 of the European Convention on Human Rights (a document of the Council of Europe) refers to 'religion or belief' rather than to just religion. Courts welcome this, as they do not have to spend time arguing about what counts as a religion, itself a contested concept.

Widening the scope of protection has in practice made it more difficult to decide which beliefs deserve protection and which do not. The more the phrase 'religion or belief' covers, the less purchase it can have on the need for respect and toleration. If everybody's beliefs have to be protected, none can be unless societies to break down into anarchy. An immediate reaction to the idea of worldviews must be similar. If anything can count as one, just because someone thinks something important, perhaps nothing should. We cannot respect worldviews as a particular category if it includes everything including a belief in the importance of Manchester United FC. We must therefore look at the philosophical presuppositions that lead some to think that it can be a useful category.

When I first studied academic philosophy, I was surrounded by the influence and effects of logical positivism. It was a science-based philosophy, explicitly preaching a 'scientific world conception', and the product of the Vienna Circle, which met just before the Second World War in Vienna. Its members and adherents were scattered by the war and were to influence Anglo-American philosophy profoundly. The leading British exponent was A. J. Ayer, a Fellow of my own Oxford college, New College. He had attended meetings of the Circle and later taught me when he was Professor of Logic. His famous book *Language, Truth and Logic* (1946) had an immense influence after the war. It held that not only truth, but meaning, was to be determined by what is accessible to science. What cannot be verified scientifically, including religious and moral statements, could not be true. They were meaningless strings of words. This set in train a science-based philosophy, which eventually took leave of verificationism, but settled for a more general materialism, physicalism, or 'naturalism'. All agreed that what lay beyond the ambit of science could be dismissed as groundless metaphysics. Much can be said against all this (Trigg 2015), but the fact remains that the orientation to science in much philosophy has lived on, and poses problems for the status of philosophical subjects which have a focus outside science. The philosophy of religion is now a vigorous subject in its own right in universities, but it was shellshocked by the depredations of logical positivism throughout most of the twentieth century. Even now, the shadow of the challenge of science ensures that in schools today many pupils still just take it for granted that science and religion have to be opposed to each other.

If science determines what is true, what are we to say about religion? Science, it seems, can be safely taught as knowledge in schools, but educationalists have often felt that they could no longer in good conscience teach religious 'knowledge'. Religious belief may be a major factor in societies, with wide political and social effects, but its content has been seen by successive generations as problematic. Even if many people had religious beliefs, their content could not appear to be taught as if it had equal status with physics. Indeed, if the content of religious belief was as meaningless as the verification principle of meaning would have us believe, there would seem to be nothing to teach, or indeed to understand.

The philosophy of religion in the 1950s was beleaguered. The philosopher Antony Flew, in a famous symposium published in 1955, told the parable of a garden, where there was allegedly an invisible gardener who could not be detected: Flew asked (in Mitchell 1971: 13): 'Just how does what you call an invisible, intangible, eternally elusive gardener differ from an imaginary gardener, or even no gardener at all?' Flew (who towards the end of his life turned back to theism) then pursued an atheist agenda by drawing an analogy between the elusive gardener and a God who created the world. He asked what could count for the believer against the possibility of God's existence. If nothing could, that might suggest the belief gains no purchase on the real world. The influence of the verification theory is clear, since the idea of evidence tended to coalesce about what scientists would accept. For the strict verificationist, the idea of 'eschatological verification' by a divine experience in the life to come, a view put forward by the philosopher of religion John Hick (1989: 178), would be totally ruled out as itself unverifiable.

These debates posed serious questions of religious believers as to how their belief might be rationally justifiable. The temptation is always to rely on faith as subjective, a magic, personal, ingredient that has no need of reason (Trigg 2022). Yet that yields ground to the scientific naturalist. Instead of science, with its rigorous method being seen as one superb expression of human rationality, its methods become the defining feature of everything rational. The sombre influence of the Vienna Circle continues, even though physics itself now readily talks of unobservable particles, and multiple universes that we can never access. Science may now deal with realities that transcend the limits of human knowledge, but many still take a narrow view of science to mark the boundaries of human rationality.

The retreat to worldviews

Given the onslaught from science in the 1950s, the immediate reaction of some philosophers was to take a path that has been well trodden since. The contribution to Flew's symposium, immediately following his challenge about the gardener, was by the Oxford philosopher, R. M. Hare, one of the leading exponents of moral philosophy in the mid-twentieth century (Mitchell 1971: 15). He suggested that when someone allows nothing to count against the theory, it asserts nothing. The verification theory looms large. He points out, nevertheless, that there was still a basic difference in outlook between people. Hare coined the word *bliks* to describe individual differences of outlook to the same facts. He follows the eighteenth-century empiricist, David Hume, in alleging that our whole commerce with the world depends on our prior expectations. Hare suggest that the difference between these expectations or *bliks* cannot be settled by observation of what happens in the world, but maintains that theism is not like some kind of scientific explanation. It is, he alleges, by our *bliks* that we decide what is or is not an explanation. Truth is left to science, so that all we are left are subjective attitudes. *Bliks* seem to be the property of individuals not groups, and encapsulate each person's outlook on the world, and are clearly a forerunner of the idea of a personal worldview. One tension is already inherent in Hare's account. He seems to want to talk of not just Christianity but 'religion', and his examples are resolutely individual. This individualist idea of a *blik*, like that of a worldview, seems ill-equipped to deal with beliefs that are collectively held and taught with standards of what is and is not true.

Another tension appears in his willingness to rule out some *bliks* as insane. He gives the example of someone with the irrational belief that harmless people around him want to murder him. Yet if a *blik* sets the standards for what is to count as an explanation, and there can be no facts to disprove this, who are we to say that someone else's *blik* is mad or insane? We may not share it, but once any universal standard of truth has been jettisoned, nothing can count against an individual's outlook, because it is just different from other people's. In the end, Hare's *bliks* provide the ultimate standard for each person. The only reason for dismissing one as insane is because it goes against majority opinion, and it remains unclear why that should be influential.

Once truth is reserved for science, all else is a matter of subjective reaction. That was the message of verificationism, not just for religion but for morality. At the extreme, the emotive theory of ethics held that the moral judgements were mere expressions of emotion, just like saying 'Boo!' to burglary. Hare himself was famous for producing an elaborate theory of reason and morality (Hare 1952). Neo-Kantian in form, it nevertheless showed the influence of the verification theory in that it refused to accept that morality concerned objective good or evil. It was based on subjective reactions, or arbitrary 'decisions of principle'. Richard Dawkins still exemplifies the continuing influence of logical positivism in his attacks on religion, when he calmly assumes that the only 'evidence' is what science can accept as such (2006: 282). Science and scientific theories are then validated in their own terms in what inevitably becomes a circular argument. Since Dawkins and A. J. Ayer were for some years colleagues in New College, Ayer was an obvious philosophical influence.

Empiricism, as exemplified in logical positivism, results in a stress on the subject of the experience, rather than on the nature of what is experienced. Experience is human experience, and the result is to make reality anthropocentric, reflecting whatever we think we know. Yet since I cannot have other people's experience, even my knowledge of other minds can then become problematic to a sceptic. How can I even know that other people have similar experiences to mine? The result of this process of thinking is to drive people in on themselves, so that at the philosophical extreme, we are assumed to live in a solipsistic world, a world of our own great individual creation. We become individuals unconstrained by anything outside ourselves. Once we lose our collective grasp on the world, it becomes merely a personal projection, so that even your existence would only be a part of my constructed world. The whole story lapses into absurdity, illustrated by the tale of the woman who approached the famous philosopher Bertrand Russell, early in the twentieth century, to say that she was very convinced by solipsism. The only trouble she had, she confessed, was that she could not understand why other people did not agree with her.

Yet we all do live in the same world, whatever our experience of it, and whatever our understanding of other people. It has its own character, and is far from malleable to our own individual wishes. Reality is objective, and while it is the focus of our attempts to obtain knowledge, it often outstrips them. The idea of progress in empirical science depends on the notion that there is much that we do not know, and indeed much that we do not realise we do not know. What reality is like and how we, whoever we may be, understand it, are logically distinct (Trigg 1989). That is the position of the philosophical realist, but it is also that of common sense. We cannot restrict reality to what science at the present is capable of unravelling. That makes reality dependent on the present capabilities of scientists, rather than providing space for developments in our understanding.

In a similar way the emphasis on worldviews, at whatever level, whether that of a child or Nobel prize-winner, redirects focus from what is possibly the case to the particular circumstances of individuals. We look not at the world we live in but the view we have of it, and then the question arises as to who 'we' are. One possibility is that we are autonomous, isolated individuals, and much that is written about worldviews seems to start from that assumption. It is an approach in tune with a 'liberal' political philosophy that repudiates the relevance of ideas of heritage and community. Each person, it seems, is different and must come to separate conclusions. The Commission (CoRE) writes in its report (2018: 5) that 'it is one of the core tasks of education to enable each pupil to understand and reflect on and develop their own personal worldview'. There lies the path to a cynicism that suggests that we each construct our own world. As a general observation about people in general this is already incoherent, accepting, as it seems to, that different people can have independent existences. Perhaps that is to be seen as just the worldview of other individuals. At root, however, is an idea of an autonomy so radical and individual that we cannot be assumed to have common ground. Educationalists themselves have nowhere to stand and nothing to teach, because they retreat from any idea of a real world independent of us all.

Paradigms and relativism

Logical positivism provoked reactions against it even from within the philosophy of science. A notable figure was that of T. S. Kuhn. In his

Structure of Scientific Revolutions (1962) he stressed the priority of the theory, and introduces the idea of 'paradigms'. As I said in my *Reason and Commitment* (1973), when I attacked his views at a time when they had not reached much beyond the philosophy of science, his position challenges the idea that scientific theories could aspire to any form of objectivity. Paradigms govern how the world is seen, and the transition from say, classical and quantum physics illustrates that the 'scientific revolution is a displacement of the conceptual network, through which scientists view the world' (Kuhn 1962: 101). The priority of theory over the raw data of the empiricists meant that different theories, or paradigms, could not all appeal to the same independent evidence. What counted as relevant information in one theory might be ignored by another. They each inhabited a different world, since each paradigm or theory makes fundamentally different claims about the kind of world it inhabits. For Kuhn, 'successive paradigms tell us different things about the population of the universe and about that population's behaviour' (Kuhn 1962: 102). They literally construct not just different pictures of *the* world but different worlds. As with empiricism, the stress remains on the nature of the construction, which this time is social and shared rather than individual. There is no place for some independent reality to which all potentially have access. Instead the stress is on major scientific changes or 'revolutions', which Kuhn explicitly names in a chapter heading as 'changes in world view' so that 'after a revolution scientists are responding to a different world' (1962: 110).

The relativist tendencies of Kuhn's work were evident in the 1970s, when I criticised them, and they are evident now. Whether one talks about paradigms or scientific theories, the focus is on the scientists holding a paradigm, and not what it purports to be about. One sees the world through the lens of a particular worldview, or has no view at all. The idea of one world can have no content independent of a particular theory. That means, as Kuhn argues, (Lakatos and Musgrave 1970: 266). that different theories are incommensurable, and cannot be rationally compared, or mutually translated. As I suggested in 1973, this leads to a pernicious conceptual relativism. Just as meaning and truth were elided in the verification theory, relativism about truth can also become a relativism of meaning. The holders of different paradigms, theories, forms of life or whatever, have no means of understanding those who inhabit alien ones. There is, by definition, no common ground, no single reality. Human rationality has to be parcelled in different self-contained apartments, with no means of mutual communication. My view of others' views of the world can never be more than my view. Where subjectivism tends to stress the individual as the source of understanding and meaning, a typical relativist will appeal to the shared standards or values of a particular group or society. Both however will reach a point when the 'other' that they imagine they see can only be a projection of their own assumptions.

Kuhn's critique of positivist notions of raw data was salutary. The 'bucket theory of the mind', according to which we are passive recipients of information, cannot tell us the whole story. Human minds actively search, and just as the searchlight picks up some things with clarity, and leaves much in total darkness, a scientific theory will be selective in what it deems relevant and important. Even today many, including politicians, have a naïve view of science, thinking it provides 'facts' so that policy can be 'data-driven' by 'evidence'. Yet what is counted as a relevant fact or piece of evidence depends on what one is looking for, and deems significant. Blithely relying on science as if there was always an agreed and assured body of appropriate knowledge to hand is naïve. Science, particularly when confronting the unknown, as in the spread of a new virus in a pandemic, must proceed cautiously. It is provisional and fallible, unlikely at first to provide any properly grounded certainty. Yet that does not mean that there is no truth to be discovered. A healthy acknowledgement of human limitations should not encourage a cynical disregard for the pursuit of knowledge. The temptation, however, is to use the selectivity of our attention to suggest that all truth is out of reach or a figment of our imagination. It is to switch our concern to the social context of scientists, or even their individual psychology. We wonder why people believe something instead of examining the content of what they believe. Theories, or paradigms, become self-contained, and, as Kuhn says (1962: 108), different scientific schools will disagree even about what the problems are and will 'inevitably talk through each other when debating the relative merits of their respective paradigms'.

The emphasis on paradigms in science, and elsewhere, inevitably strikes at the root of any idea of scientific rationality. Science breaks up into warring factions. Kuhn uses the image of scientific revolutions knowingly. Like a political revolution, for him a scientific revolution has everything to do with power, and little to do with rational persuasion. Imre Lakatos was an influential philosopher of science at the London School of Economics in the late 1960s and was much bruised by the student unrest there in 1968: he saw connections between mob rule and Kuhn's view of science. He pointed out that in science there is then apparently 'no other way of judging the theory but by assessing the number, faith and vocal energy of its supporters (Lakatos and Musgrave 1970: 93). That meant in turn, he said, that 'truth lies in power'. Those words, written half a century ago, apply today when it is often taken for granted by many that the identity and social position of the person is far more relevant than the content of what they might say. The idea of a neutral rationality that all humans share is thereby repudiated. Power is all, and the oppressed have to fight back. That is dangerous as a political creed in democracies, and it proves fatal for science. It encouraged many to take up the so-called 'sociology of knowledge', to call attention to the social context of scientists. Science became Western science and could then sometimes be dismissed as just another example of the use of Western imperialist power.

Whilst a reaction against the empirical certainties of positivism, and the glorification of science, was due, this was achieved by dismissing science as a source of knowledge at all. Yet without any access to common ground, in this case an objective reality to be investigated, everything could be reduced to squabbling sects within and beyond the physical sciences, each unable to understand the other. Similar reasoning in the social sciences, particularly in social anthropology, brought difficulties for the idea of understanding alien societies. (Trigg 2001: 80). Anthropologists might go native and live with remote tribes, following alien customs. Yet their own theories about them forbade them to compare such societies with their own or others', let alone suggest that any tribe's beliefs were mistaken or their practices somehow misguided. The splintering of areas of understanding becomes inevitable.

Saying that the world is as science says is anthropocentric, switching attention from reality to the way humans may experience it. Empiricism can be accused of denying any idea of the real world in favour of looking simply at how it is experienced. That changes the subject from ontology, the theory of what there is, to epistemology – how we can know it. Yet concentrating on knowledge, while ignoring the fact that there is something to know, inevitably leads to concentration on who knows and what their situation might be. Positivism led to a reaction against the concentration on science, but the result was a loss of grip on the idea of humans being placed in an objective world confronting them.

Is everything 'interpretation'?

The shift from a narrow science-based view of the world to an uneasy amalgam of subjectivism and relativism has inevitably influenced education, and religious education in particular. At first, it had to justify itself against frontal attacks on the idea of religion, and withdrew from claims about truth to the safer ground of different people believing different things. Teaching Christianity became transformed into just an attempt to understand different religions, a task which a relativist would say was impossible for the nonparticipant. Because of the intense difficulty of mutually uncomprehending groups facing each other, religious education became more and more co-opted into a task of social engineering, so as to promote the much trumpeted ideals of equality and diversity. Intriguingly these various phases of religious education have been portrayed by Trevor Cooling as themselves paradigm changes, a deliberate echo of Kuhn's views. In effect, the anti-rational, relativist approach to science has been duplicated at the different level of educational theory about the role of religious education.

Different approaches to the subject have been dubbed 'paradigms', even perhaps themselves worldviews that determine how all else should be seen. Cooling (2020: 25) suggests that 'the paradigm changes in RE that I have described were responses to changing social contexts'. This might indicate a rational approach to changing social conditions and needs, but Kuhn's idea of paradigms was more radical. Even in science, they expressed a change in social attitudes that was actually to determine how things were to be assessed, what was to count as evidence, and indeed what was a suitable focus of investigation. Common sense, and the assumptions involved in the use of language, tell us that we should be investigating something, and that there is a world to be discovered, not projected from our own intellectual frameworks. It is thus impossible for relativists, let alone subjectivists, to state their assumptions coherently in public language. It makes no sense to say that there is no such thing as truth, because that itself is a statement that claims to be truth. If there is no world, but only individual or collective beliefs about 'it', there must at least be a world that contains such beliefs. The whole basis of human thought and language assumes some shared world.

Trevor Cooling, and others advocating the worldviews approach, would deny they are merely trying to convert others to their own arbitrarily held worldview. Cooling seems to think that he himself can espouse what he terms 'critical realism'. That, he maintains, accepts that there is a truth 'out there' to which all human beings are accountable. The bite, though, comes in his qualification that 'human knowing is inevitably worldview formed, so must always be an interpretation of reality'. Does that mean, as Nietzsche thought (Trigg 1999: 140) that everything is interpretation? Nietzsche had the grace to add that even that remark was an interpretation. If we make any reality inaccessible, by definition it ultimately drops out of sight as irrelevant. We can then only negotiate between different interpretations, assuming we can compare them in the first place. Yet if truth is not at stake, why listen to others, when I am content with my own opinion and interpretation? Any negotiation would only be a struggle for power not truth.

For the worldview approach to education, the whole point seems to be a negotiation between different views. That might seem to coalesce with current concerns about social cohesion, and respecting diversity and equality. Mutual understanding is made to seem important. Yet at this point, we may wonder again what can make such understanding possible. The proposals encapsulate assumptions that comparison of different views is problematic. They cannot be attempts to decipher the same world, but inhabit different ones. Cooling suggests (2020: 46) that 'everyone inhabits a worldview', stressing 'the tacit influence that is associated with worldviews'. We can see the world through a different lens without realising it. What we see may literally differ from person to person. Yet the Commission (2018: 26) wrote that 'a worldview is a person's way of understanding, expressing and responding to the world'. That trades on the idea that there is a world to be discovered, whilst simultaneously suggesting that it all depends on personal interpretation.

Cooling is drawn to hermeneutics, which arose originally from the discipline of biblical interpretation. Yet whatever the role of interpretation, texts must still bring something to readers and not just reflect their prejudices. Cooling (2020: 59) defines hermeneutics as 'the theory that everything is a matter of interpretation'. That coheres with the wider claims of post-modernist philosophy, decrying the notion of a universal rationality. In such philosophy there is often talk of different readings, different understandings, of the same text without any idea that there is any way of resolving the differences. There is nothing beyond the encounter of reader with a text, and each encounter has to be different. There could then be then no question of one interpretation being better than another.

The fact of interpretation can be, and is, seen from both individual and collective perspectives. Cooling alleges that it is important to introduce pupils to 'interpretation and perspective'. Each is rooted in particular worldviews, and Cooling says (2020: 62) that 'we have to make judgements about the validity of each other's interpretations on the basis of evidence'. He considers this to be a clear example of the hermeneutical approach. Yet this idea of evidence implicitly harks back to empiricists' idea of raw data accessible to everyone. It suggests that different worldviews do have a common base in the information that is provided. Yet at the same time Cooling says that pupils learn that there is no worldview-free answer to the question 'Who is Jesus?'. If that is the case, and we are all imprisoned in our own perspectives, interpretations, worldviews or whatever, there can be no evidence we can appeal to that is not already question begging. If we try to answer the question about Jesus, for instance, by appealing to the Resurrection, we will be told that that is already a mere article of faith within a Christian worldview. The apparatus of relativistic hermeneutics forbids us looking at any so-called historical facts.

Cooling (2020: 54) takes the German philosopher H-G. Gadamer as his inspiration in talking about hermeneutics. Gadamer followed in the tradition of philosophers such as Husserl and Heidegger, and provided an antidote to an exclusively science-based philosophy. With its emphasis on human beings and their consciousness, hermeneutics reacted against this, as did the later Wittgenstein. Gadamer, writing in the same era as Kuhn, stressed the historical differences between people, and by refusing to allow any notion of a common human nature, he removed any common ground between us. In a book written 40 years ago (Trigg 1982) I criticised the relativist tendencies of Gadamer's thought. He explicitly criticised forms of hermeneutics which took human nature as the 'unhistorical substratum' of its theory of understanding. We cannot be freed from our historical limitations, but have to look at everything from within the standpoint of our own 'historical horizon'. This created the familiar problem that we are all trapped within our particular horizons and cannot see beyond them. Everything is seen and interpreted within our own terms. Yet although we all have our own presuppositions and prejudices, it is a further step say that we cannot see historical events and people in their own terms, not just ours.

Diversity, plurality and nihilism

Repudiating any notion of human nature and suggesting that instead it is constructed out of different social and historical circumstances, makes humans shut-off from each other in different, and self-contained, compartments. Differing presuppositions and understandings will probably not coincide. At best, we may only see in them a reflection of ourselves. Gadamer tries to talk of the 'fusion of horizons'. According to Cooling (2020: 56) such understanding 'comes through dialogue with worldviews that are different from one's own'. He assumes it entails 'relational interaction between teacher, student and object of study'. Yet what philosophical understanding can make this feasible? The shadow of Kuhn's thesis of incommensurability falls over any such project. The later Wittgenstein's stress on the formative role of different 'forms of life' in the production of concepts makes cross-cultural understanding similarly problematic. The problem of understanding alien societies became acute, particularly for social anthropology (Trigg 2001: 64 ff). The more differences are stressed, the more possibilities of mutual understanding and dialogue are removed. There has, at least in principle, to be some common ground.

Postmodern philosophy, with its emphasis on multiple traditions, challenged the idea of the one world that we all confront, and also the assumption that humans share any common nature. Gadamer scoffed at 'connaturality'. When diversity rules and we are all the creatures of our particular histories, what hope can there be that we can begin to understand people who live in very different circumstances, and are the product of different histories? How can we compare our languages with those of people who are said to be living in a different world? The postmodern negation of universal rationality is radical, and its obsession with diversity influences much contemporary thinking. It is very different from the basic moral view that we are all human, and that our common human nature makes us more similar than different. That also underpins our assumption that human languages are inter-translatable.

It is even uncertain how different traditions or perspectives are to be identified. When I myself wrote criticising the views of Gadamer some 40 years ago, I was doing so against the background of social circumstances that have already radically changed, not least through the influence of social media. Does that make a difference to the world we live in, and our perceptions of it? Are we now already living under a different tradition, or paradigm? Am I myself even a different person from the one who once criticised Gadamer? Perhaps his views, while pertinent in one context, no longer are. From a philosophical point of view these issues seem nonsensical. We seem to be treading a path to a solipsism that breaks down all communication.

The eighteenth-century Scottish philosopher David Hume took it for granted that, as he put it (Trigg 1999: 83): 'It is universally acknowledged that there is a great uniformity among the actions of men in all nations and ages, and that human nature remains still the same in its principles and operations'. An obsession with difference undermines the ability to understand other cultures and languages, and also removes the possibility of history itself. Hume himself trenchantly says: 'Would you know the sentiments, inclinations and course of life of the Greeks and Romans? Study well the temper and actions of the French and English?' Contemporary genetics assumes similarity across different kinds of humans with a shared human genome, that influences behaviour. That pits human biology, as presently understood, against contemporary thinking that prefers to concentrate on human diversity. The scientific study of human drives, needs and interests, regardless of history and culture, should be significant. It does however go against another philosophical current flowing through the advocacy of worldviews, that is the distrust of so-called essentialism, thinking that the idea of, say, humanity refers to a set of common characteristics so that any concept could have a 'fixed central meaning'. Cooling (2020: 44) talks of CoRE's concern that people 'engage with the complexity of organised worldviews rather than essentialist and often stereotypical portrayals of monolithic traditions'. Christianity, for instance, can therefore be dissolved into a myriad personal reactions by individuals. This raises again whether worldviews have a collective dimension or merely an individual one. In both cases, barriers are erected to understanding those who are different from us. In either case, however, it seems impossible to think any interpretations could be better or worse than any other. Yet Cooling (2020: 60) in his advocacy of hermeneutics, maintains that some interpretations are plainly wrong when learning about worldviews in religious education. Where does he himself stand to make such an observation? If he can see some interpretations are wrong, might that suggest that there is a reality to be discovered that ultimately constrains everybody's judgements? Yet the dismissal of an 'essentialised picture' of a worldview would suggest that worldviews are whatever different holders think they are. They cannot be a fixed body of understanding waiting to be taught. He gives the example of pupils in a Catholic secondary school, who maintained that all were Catholics, but some certainly did not believe in God. This he thinks goes to underline the fact that worldviews are not necessarily propositional in nature. It is then apparently not a joke to maintain the one can be a Catholic atheist. Nothing could illustrate more the way in which the idea of worldviews is so malleable as to lose all meaning. It rules out the function of reason. To suggest one can be a genuine Catholic, let alone a Christian, while espousing atheism, is to take leave of rationality and launch into a realm where one can believe anything with impunity. Nothing can count against a belief, even internal inconsistency. We are teetering on the edge of nihilism whereby the propensity to believe anything means I might just as well believe nothing. Ultimately all belief becomes pointless.

The Commission's original stress on the diverse and plural nature of worldviews, and the ways they have changed over time, might suggest that the whole notion dissolves into meaninglessness. Everyone has a worldview 'which is merely a person's way of understanding and experiencing and responding to the world'. We are also told that worldviews are not 'fixed, bounded entities' (CoRE 2018: 36). They are even not specifically religious. As above all they are 'fluid and dynamic'. It seems that any attitude at all can be a worldview.

Plato was once confronted by the views of the pre-Socratic philosopher Heraclitus, who believed that constant change, or flux, constituted the ultimate reality. Plato, in subtle philosophical arguments in the dialogue *Theaetetus*, pointed out that without some stability everything lapses into an extreme subjectivism which makes communication impossible. Transposing these views to contemporary education, one could observe that in a diverse, plural and changing world, the idea of a worldview itself, so far from being dynamic, degenerates into an anarchic chaos, where what anybody believes is right for them. Plato made great play of the fact that Sophists, such as Protagoras, who, (as perhaps the first explicit relativist) taught that there was no truth, could not in consistency ply their trade in education, because there was nothing to teach. They could not in all honesty claim any expertise with which to impart knowledge to others because, in a fluid, changing world where no one's judgement was fixed, there was no knowledge, because there was nothing to know.

Is this the position the advocacy of worldviews education gets driven to? We are told that the shift in language from 'religion' to 'worldview' signifies that greater attention needs to be given to 'individual lived experience' (CoRE 2018: 30). The Report of the Commission also stresses the plural and diverse nature of worldviews. Everyone has different experiences and will react differently. There then seems nothing left to teach.

Toleration and truth

One answer could be that schools ought to inculcate 'British' values of toleration, respect, justice and so on. Yet that might itself be the product of a distinct worldview, presented for political reasons. Why, too, are they British values? Why are they important? These are fundamental moral questions, and morality barely seems to surface as a subject of concern in the proposed teaching of worldviews. Yet one reason religion is important in any society is its close, even rational, connection with how we treat each other. Religion tells us what kind of people we as humans are, and something of the nature of reality in which we are placed. Without a firm grip on the idea of human nature, even the idea of human rights becomes meaningless. Being human then loses any significance. Moral questions are often based on metaphysical beliefs, but a worldview education is not interested in such pressing issues, any more than it deals with ideas about what might constitute a 'good society' or 'the common good'.

The basic purpose of worldview education is to inject new life into a religious education that seems to have lost its way. By making its subject matter so unfocused, it removes any possibility of anyone deciding what constitutes good teaching in the area. It is unclear what those preparing to teach the subject might have to know, since the very possibility of knowledge on the subject seems to have been removed. The peremptory dismissal of religion as meaningless in favour of science has been met more recently by seeming distaste for any truth to be discovered or searched for. That, as Plato once recognised, is the death of all education.

A relevant case (*Folgero v. Norway*) about religious education in 2007 in the European Court of Human Rights concerned the teaching in Norway of an education which aimed to help 'give pupils a Christian and moral upbringing'. Not surprisingly, given the secularism of contemporary Europe, the judges objected to this. What was perhaps more surprising was that the opinion divided the judges of the Grand Chamber by nine to eight. The Commission on Religious Education refers to this judgement (CoRE 2018: 65). The Court insisted that all beliefs were to be treated equally and that Christianity has to be taught in an 'objective, critical and pluralistic manner' (Trigg 2012: 60). That stems from a liberal view of the state as so morally neutral that it has no commitment to any belief, perhaps not even to the importance of such basic principles of equality, freedom and justice.

The judgement was controversial within and beyond Norway and raises unanswered questions as to what teaching in an 'objective' manner might require. Absolute indifference to the possibility of the truth of religious claims undermines the importance and relevance of any of them. Yet there is great confusion about the impact of the recognition that religions claim truth. Recognising that truth is at stake or that a particular religion claims it need not imply that intolerance of other beliefs is necessary. Christianity, for example, has taught the importance of freedom of choice, and a God-given freedom of the will. Forced worship or forced commitment is not genuine. Intolerance can itself be prohibited by the nature of the beliefs involved.

There are three levels of claims about truth. The first is the claim that truth is at stake and a subject is important. The second is that individuals, whether pupils or teachers, have specific knowledge of that truth. The religious teaching of the need for humility might warn us about thinking that we know more than we possibly can do. Third, there is the question whether even if we are confident in our knowledge, we still have a right to enforce it on others. Coerced religion is not sincere, and we should recognise that even claiming truth need not imply certain possession of knowledge, let alone the right to use power to force others to our point of view. The great fear of religious education, particularly in teaching Christianity, used to be indoctrination. The result appears to be that now all religions are regarded on a par with no way even in principle of choosing between them. It is hardly surprising that many young people just assume that they can all be equally dismissed as irrelevant. The pursuit of truth can no longer be seen as an exciting challenge in such areas.

The 'British values' that successive governments have advocated have not appeared from nowhere, but are themselves the result of a long history of mainly Christian influence. Whether they can long survive when such foundations are forgotten or removed is a crucial question. What should not be so problematic is that the role of the Christian religion and its association with the state, have been intertwined since Saxon times in England. It is part of an English, indeed British, education to understand what Christianity has stood for and its central position in the development of ideas, art, music, architecture, literature and much else. For good or ill, it has had a central role in social developments. Ignoring its role in the history of the British Isles is to ignore history.

A great contemporary problem is what has been called religious illiteracy. Even well-educated people in the United Kingdom often have little idea of what Christianity stands for or what the Bible says. They no longer recognise ordinary Biblical allusions. Given a lack of sympathy for religion as such, they then have little sympathy for, or comprehension of, the role of other religions, and that is often a problem for British diplomacy abroad. Is this perhaps the result of the last 60 years of religious education teaching? The fear of indoctrination, or of partiality towards religion in general, and Christianity in particular, has somehow cut students from their heritage. This is a failure of education, and is nothing to do with Christian proselytising. Even the atheist Richard Dawkins (2006: 344) says firmly that 'an atheistic worldview provides no justification for cutting the Bible, and other sacred books, out of an education'. He trenchantly says that 'we can give up belief in God while not losing touch with a treasured heritage'. The present teaching of religious education is undoubtedly unsatisfactory in many ways, but teaching worldviews seems a vacuous alternative when they are described as the varied and fleeting fancies of rootless individuals. Individuals are then unconstrained by their heritage, the character of the world in which they are set, or the needs of the human nature we all share. The abyss of nihilism beckons.

References

Commission on Religious Education (CoRE) (2018) *Final Report: Religions and worldviews: the way forward*. https://www.commissiononre.org.uk/wp-content/uploads/2018/09/Final-Report-of-the-Commission-on-RE.pdf.

Cooling, T. (with Bob Bowie and Farid Panjuvani) (2020) *Worldviews in Religious Education*. London: Theos.

Dawkins, R. (2006) *The God Delusion*. London: Bantam Press.

Folgero and others v Norway, ECHR, Application No. 15472/02, Judgment, Strasbourg, 29 June 2007.

Hare, R. M. (1952) *The Language of Morals*. Oxford: Oxford University Press.

Hick, J. (1989) *An Interpretation of Religion*. Basingstoke: Macmillan.

Kuhn, T. S. (1962) *The Structure of Scientific Revolutions*. Chicago: University of Chicago Press.

Lakatos, I. and Musgrave, A. (eds) (1970) *Criticism and the Growth of Knowledge*. Cambridge: Cambridge University Press.

Mitchell, B. (ed.) (1971) *The Philosophy of Religion*. Oxford: Oxford University Press.

Trigg, R. (1973) *Reason and Commitment*. Cambridge: Cambridge University Press.

Trigg, R. (1982) *The Shaping of Man*. Oxford: Basil Blackwell.

Trigg, R. (1989) *Reality at Risk: A defence of realism in philosophy and the sciences*. London: Simon and Schuster.

Trigg, R. (1999) *Ideas of Human Nature*, 2nd edition. Oxford: Basil Blackwell.

Trigg, R. (2001) *Understanding Social Science*, 2nd edition. Oxford: Basil Blackwell.

Trigg, R. (2012) *Equality, Freedom and Religion*. Oxford: Oxford University Press.

Trigg, R. (2015) *Beyond Matter: Why science needs metaphysics*. West Conshohocken, PA: Templeton Press.

Trigg, R. (2022) *Faith: A very short introduction*. Oxford: Oxford University Press.

7
'RELIGION', 'WORLDVIEWS' AND THE REAPPEARING PROBLEMS OF PEDAGOGY

Daniel Moulin-Stożek

In a widely influential book published at the turn of the millennium, Michael Grimmitt made the astute observation that the various pedagogical models of religious education advanced over the preceding 30 years had all sought to reconcile a tension between the secular norms of the English education system and the study of religion and religions (Grimmitt 2000). Recent calls for 'Religion and Worldviews Education' (RWE) have also been proposed to address this same problem. For example, the Final Report of the Commission on Religious Education (CoRE) suggests change is necessary because of the increase of 'non-religious worldviews' and the decline of Christian identification among the general population (CoRE 2018: 6). This chapter engages with some of the earlier models of religious education and considers how they have sought to address similar perceived challenges. This analysis offers the opportunity of a comparison between previous pedagogical models and the proposed RWE approach. This is a valuable exercise to undertake for those both inclined and disinclined towards RWE. First, there has yet to be a thorough exposition explaining exactly how RWE may differ from pre-existing theory and practice in religious education. Second, in the accounts of RWE currently available, with the exception of Cooling's (2020) passing reference to the human development approach of Grimmitt, little attempt has been made to draw upon the conceptual resources offered by earlier research in religious education – despite the overlooked but striking fact that the term 'worldview' has already been in use by religious educationists for over 40 years. (The first time 'worldview' was advocated as a key concept for RE pedagogy dates to Pearce 1979.)

If RWE is to be established as a new and distinct approach to religious education, engaging with previous research is necessary, and that would entail rectifying a current gap in the research literature by considering it in the context of previous pedagogical innovation. This chapter sets out to begin this constructive process. Given that recent literature advocating RWE is still developing, it is important to observe some caution about the dangers of setting up a 'straw man' when attempting to evaluate it. The definition given of the key concept underlying RWE, 'worldview', as a 'person's way of understanding, experiencing and responding to the world' (CoRE 2018: 4) offers ample scope for varying interpretations and therefore perhaps an indeterminate range of potential applications to teaching, learning and curriculum. Moreover, advocates of RWE have been swift in accusing interlocutors of misinterpretation and misrepresentation of their position (see Cooling 2021). Yet extant attempts to gain some conceptual purchase on RWE are limited in their engagement with research, particularly empirical research in religious education, and often take the form of polemics in the context of a supposed crisis (see Chater 2020). The multidisciplinary research review commissioned by the RE Council of England and Wales (Benoit et al. 2020) entertains the varying uses of the term 'worldview' across different academic disciplines, posing questions they may raise for education as opposed to addressing head-on how they have been, or may be, applied to religious education. Because of challenges of engaging with RWE as a relatively undeveloped approach, rather than attempting to state the RWE position and then critique it, this present chapter proceeds via a slightly different premise. It identifies three long-standing challenges facing religious education addressed in research literature. It then considers what the previous pedagogical models and RWE may have to offer in response to them.

The pedagogical models that have informed teacher training and practice in religious education over the last 50 years are included in Grimmitt's (2000) book which, in comprising concise chapters written by their advocates, perhaps remains the most appropriate resource to engage with them (below I also cite earlier expositions). The enduring influence of these 'classic pedagogies' – despite numerous critiques in academic literature – has recently been acknowledged by the *Ofsted Research Review Series: Religious Education* (2021). Perhaps the most pervasive have been the phenomenological or world religions model (Smart 1968) – represented in

Grimmitt's anthology by the Chichester Project (Brown 2000); the human development model (Grimmitt 1987); the critical realist or religious literacy model (Wright 1993); the concept-cracking model (Cooling 1994); the ethnographic or 'interpretive' approach (Everington 1996; Jackson 1997); and the 'deconstruction' model (Erricker et al. 1994). All these approaches have a considerable literature surrounding them spanning some years – each well worth survey and evaluation in their own right. It is neither possible nor necessary to attempt to summarise all these debates and developments here. Rather, given most of them rely on 'worldview' (or near-cognates) in their articulations, I identify some of the goals and pitfalls shared between the classic pedagogies and RWE by focusing on three principal and 're-appearing' problems: 'How can young people learn from religion if they do not believe in it?'; 'How can the reification of religious traditions be avoided?'; and 'How can teachers deal with conflicting truth claims in the classroom?' These issues, addressed in the following sections, commonly faced by any student or teacher of religious education, are not exhaustive of the problems that religious education faces or those its research base addresses. They have been selected because they represent salient conceptual and practical problems that are pertinent in general, and particularly so when considering the potential contribution of the concept of 'worldview' to religious education, and/or the prospect of RWE.

How can young people learn from religion if they do not believe in it?

A perennial problem of RE has long been considered to be the lack of relevance of 'religion' to young people in contemporary society – a concern dating to at least the 1960s when the epithet 'Cinderella subject' was first coined (Garforth 1961). The lack of value given to religious education by colleagues and pupils has been reported by teachers for some time, particularly by those in training (Sikes and Everington 2004). This is sometimes presumed to be a problem stemming from lack of religious affiliation – the 'silent majority' of pupils having little or no experience of a religion outside of religious education (Rudge 1998). On account of this demographic, White (2004) argues in a widely cited article that because England is becoming increasingly secular, it does not make sense for religious education to be a compulsory school subject. The same concern has been taken up by advocates of RWE. As non-religious worldviews are more widespread than before, the subject should change in its name and approach (CoRE 2018). This is perhaps a pervasive idea to be welcomed by those indifferent or hostile to 'religion' being promoted or included in public education. However, this is not a response to any recent sociological or intellectual development, nor is it based on an accurate appraisal of the subject, which – according to most of the classical pedagogical models of the last 50 years – has markedly *not* sought to cater for, or promote, any religious belief or practice, certainly not in particular, nor arguably even in general.

The idea that religions comprise dead myths unworthy of study is some centuries old. By the late eighteenth century, it was already a commonly held view among mainstream European intellectuals that 'religion' had been superseded at least as it had been traditionally understood. As the theologian Don Cupitt has argued, even Victorian enthusiasm for Christianity was a question of 'value-judgement' (Cupitt 2006: 3). This can be understood as a natural corollary and legacy of the Enlightenment critique of religion: the belief that the scientific method was the best means to knowledge, and vital to social amelioration; and the undermining of Christianity's claim to sole truth through increasing engagement with non-Christian religions. However, for religious education, rather than being new issues to address at the beginning of the third decade of the twenty-first century, these challenges and opportunities formed the intellectual background in which religious education, as we know it, was first articulated at the inception of universal education in the nineteenth century (Moran 2003).

One noteworthy and pithy response to these challenges, dating to 100 years before the 1988 Education Act that enshrined multi-faith religious education in England and Wales, was made by the Russian author and influential progressive educationist, Leo Tolstoy, who remarked: 'There are a thousand religions and they are all absurd, so why should we study them?' (Tolstoy 1934 [1887]: 25). It was in recognition and response to the critique of religion that enabled liberal Christians before the turn of the twentieth century to advocate a religious education free from the influence of denominational catechesis that could accommodate the intense competition of *fin de siècle* religious sectarianism by offering a religious education for all based on a moral and cultural consensus. In England, the limitations of such a venture were taken into account by a conscience clause. Yet the expansive opportunities arising from such a universal religious education free from any prescriptively rigid religious authority allowed it to apparently incorporate non-Christian religions with some ease in the future (Moulin-Stożek and Metcalfe 2020). For a further account of how these intellectual and cultural currents impacted religious education in England and Wales, see Barnes and Wright (2006). For the present argument it is germane to explain how the classical pedagogical models – as sixth or seventh generation inheritors of the Enlightenment critique of religion – sought to make religious education relevant not only to those uncommitted, but also to those unacquainted, with a religion, decades before the advent of RWE.

One essential ingredient of the classic pedagogical models is the flexibility to allow for pupils' individuated responses to any religious material included in the curriculum. Another has been the deliberate inclusion of diverse beliefs and values so as to present a range of perspectives. The classic pedagogies' commitment to both principles entails, to varying extents, the deployment of 'worldview' as a means to capture the nuanced processes of pupils' engagement with religions. Although having this in common, the classic pedagogies each attempt to create distinct pedagogical frameworks by which religious education and to some extent, religions, can become relevant and valued, regardless of pupils' own religious affiliations or the absence thereof.

The phenomenological approach appropriates a universal construct 'religion' through anthropological categories germane to both 'religious' and 'secular' practices, beliefs and institutions. It is for this reason that Smart (1989) was able to approach Soviet Marxism as a secular worldview through the familiar dimensions of doctrine, myth, ethics, rituals and organisation as he was 'world religions'. This universal applicability gives some affordance to the phenomenological approach to engage with the secular and thus remain relevant beyond the study of Christianity. It also provides a systematic structuring of knowledge that lends itself to curriculum and lesson design. Indeed, Smart's (1989: 560) interest in 'worldview analysis and the future of education', brought to fruition in his later works is perhaps one of the most important articulations of 'worldview education' to date. For despite the apparent rigidity of the earlier dimensions-of-religions hypothesis, in 'World Philosophies' (2000) Smart argued that 'worldview analysis' could be undertaken with the thinking of anyone, even outside of a given religious or philosophical system.

The classic pedagogies advanced in the years between the creation of the phenomenological approach and proposals for RWE sought to rectify the former's obvious deficiencies while retaining many of its assumptions. Identified problems included the reification and essentialisation of religions and the (questionable) perception that in proposing the possibility of an objective or neutral study of religion it drove a wedge between moral and spiritual education and religious education. Although useful in terms of presenting religious education as a non-confessional subject, the phenomenological model arguably made the study of religion less meaningful. On this proviso, Grimmitt's (1987) human development approach set out to modify it in order to make the case for religious education's contribution to pupils' personal, social and moral development. According to this view, all pupils, despite of their religious affiliation or interest, benefit from religious education by virtue of religious material being appropriate to profoundly engage with 'adolescent life-worlds'. For, in what has become a widely held dichotomy, not only can anyone learn 'about' a religion, but learning 'from' any given religious material involves the pupil in the construction of a personalised reflection in response to it. In other words, informing the development of their own worldview.

The interpretive or ethnographic approach invokes a similar individualised process of 'edification' – the impact of engaging in interpretive inquiry upon an individual's own thinking given the differences between one or another's ways of life. The study of religion as 'understanding the religious worldviews of others' (Jackson 2004: 88) can be undertaken on cultural grounds, necessary because of the multi-faith society and therefore relevant to all. Located in opposing conceptions, the concept of worldview is also pivotal in the pedagogies advanced by Erricker and Wright. Like proposals for RWE, the *Children and Worldviews Project* (Erricker et al. 1994) set out on the premise that the phenomenological and other models sought to include too much religious content when most learners had secular worldviews. It followed that to avoid marginalising learners, children's construction of their own worldviews should be supported by activities that aided this constructive process by means of telling their own, and listening to others', stories. In doing so, it was argued, children develop requisite skills inherent to what 'religious education' should be, such as: 'understanding why others do things', 'reflection on the emotions of others', or 'recognition of difference' (Erricker and Erricker 2000: 200). Wright (2015), on the other hand, employs 'worldview' to mean the structured and systematised ways of seeing the world, pre-existing the individual, that make religious education possible: 'The heuristic notion of "worldview" provides a means of identifying and explaining culturally grounded accounts of the ultimate order-of-things' (Wright 2015: 209). Rather than comprising a child's individuated negotiation of the world, worldviews are 'religious traditions and secular alternatives' 2015: 208) that can be explored through an undergirding framework based on the assumptions of critical realism.

The brief examination of classic pedagogies given in this section shows there is a long and rich tradition in religious education research literature of open ideas as to how young people can learn from religion if they do not believe in it. Research in religious education over the last half century has centred on demonstrating how the study of religion can be of value in a secular and plural context to those of all faiths and those of none. In sometimes quite opposing ways, the classic pedagogies utilise the idea of 'worldview' to do this. They do so in two ways: either in order to allow for pupils' individuated responses to the curriculum – to give opportunities for them to construct their own worldview; and/or, to expand the content of religious education beyond traditional religious beliefs and practices. As these principles are essential to all the major approaches to religious education of the last 30–50 years, in theory at least, it would seem impossible for any of the classic pedagogies or their advocates to dispense with the notion of 'worldview'. However, this often-overlooked point leaves open the question: given the longstanding influence of the classic pedagogies, what difference is there between RWE, as a new paradigm, and religious education as it has existed for some time? If proponents of RWE are correct that there is a 'crisis' in religious education which may be caused by outmoded and/or inappropriate pedagogical methods, how is restating a longstanding concept employed by them going to solve those problems? Indeed, why should we consider worldviews to be any more relevant to young people than religions? Surely, to paraphrase Tolstoy, 'there are a thousand worldviews and many of them are equally as absurd as religions. As they cannot all be true, why should we study them?' These questions are addressed in the subsequent sections in relation to some further of the 're-appearing' problems of religious education.

How can the reification of religious traditions be avoided?

To reify is to make an abstract idea more real than it should be. It is highlighted here as a reappearing problem in religious education for two principal reasons. First, in the context of the current movement to decolonise the curriculum, the propensity for religious education to harbour reified, colonial, representations of religions is an issue that any new initiative should be fit to counter. Second, it has been suggested that RWE, by incorporating 'worldviews' is better equipped to avoid the problem of essentialising religions than existing approaches. Arguably disingenuous, given that there have been several pedagogical models advanced since the phenomenological model, RWE is often presented as its immediate successor designed to avoid such reification. For example, on page 6 of the CoRE *Final Report*, it is argued that change to RWE is necessary because it seeks 'to move beyond an essentialised presentation of six major world faiths' (2018: 6). This is a somewhat misleading statement as the problem of essentialisation and reification has already been extensively addressed in religious education research literature over the preceding 20 years, most notably in the work of Everington (1996) and Jackson (1997; 2004).

The interpretive approach offers a set of sensitising concepts and methods by which to structure teaching and learning about religions in order to avoid reification and essentialisation: reflexivity, interpretation and representation. Each of these stages of inquiry encourages pupils and teachers to explore the fuzzy and dynamic nature of religion and culture, crucially with a self-criticality to their own methods of interpretation and representation. The emphasis on interpreting individuals' complex, occasional and varying personal relationships with their self-identified cultural traditions allows for greater nuance and range in the study of religion, which as Jackson acknowledged, went beyond commonplace but simplistic definitions of 'religion' and 'culture'. Indeed, even those categories are subject to reification, especially in the religious education curriculum. Jackson engaged with post-colonial scholarship decades before the decolonising the curriculum movement, observing how various stereotypes of Islam, Hinduism and Sikhism permeated religious education. It is important to note here that unlike any of the other pedagogical models – classic or contemporary – the interpretative approach has an empirical research and evidence base which has been applied and evaluated internationally (Jackson 2011). Engagement with the extensive work of the Warwick Religions and Education Research Unit, surprisingly absent in discussions about RWE, is therefore essential to the development of any new paradigm.

It is now worth considering RWE in regard to the problem of reification. One way of doing this is to consider the radically different uses of 'worldview' in the classic pedagogies. Jackson (2004) eschews the appropriation of religions as belief systems that can be reduced to propositions. For Jackson, 'worldview' is useful in that it captures the nuanced, not necessarily 'religious', possibilities available in a given interpretation or representation of culture. Wright (2015), on the other hand, sees it as valuable for opposing reasons. It offers the opportunity of the systematisation of non-religious truth-claims comparable to those of religions in order to make them amenable to public scrutiny through the conceptual apparatus of critical realism – an approach that leads Jackson to accuse Wright of falling into the trap of reification (Jackson 2004). We can compare these two perspectives with that of a third, Erricker and Erricker (2000), who suggest a more radical anti-realist epistemological position. The construction of children's worldviews is wholly subjective, only to be supported by an individual child's own narrative-making.

Because of the relative lack of engagement with classical pedagogical theory (compared with, for example, the peer-reviewed exchanges between Wright (2001) and Erricker (2001)), it is not exactly clear how the epistemological conceptions of worldview in classic pedagogies compare to those proposed by RWE. However, it would seem the use of the words 'Religion' *and* 'Worldviews' reflects some key assumptions of this proposed rebranding. This terminology could be interpreted as implying that there is a construct 'Religion' which is an object of study in some sense distinct to secular worldviews but incorporates a number of 'religions' that share common features. 'Worldviews', on the other hand, are also to be objects of study, categorically differently from 'Religion', but in comparison to it, are pluralised.

The first issue of note here is the susceptibility to reification offered by the category 'Religion'. This is understood by decolonial scholars to be a concept originating from a Christian perspective that when applied to other traditions, (including arguably some contemporary expressions of Christianity), results in a distorted, reified understanding, as argued about the creation of 'Hinduism', for example (Fitzgerald 2017). The second issue is that whereas in some of the previous pedagogical models, worldviews are often to be considered an emergent and individuated consequence of pupils' engagement, in RWE they are to be categorisable systems – only eligible for study if they meet certain standards (see CoRE 2018: 75). This move would seem to stifle advances made in religious education almost 50 years ago to allow and support pupils' autonomy in their thinking about religion. It would also seem – by overlooking the valuable research undertaken in the wake of the phenomenological approach – to present what could be considered a Smartian 'World Religions 2.0'. For the elevation of various non-institutionalised positionings into the constructs of 'worldviews' with defined characteristics reifies complex and nuanced personal perspectives into dubious, indeed, non-existent ontological entities. Such an approach is unlikely to be able to challenge some inherent colonial legacies of religious education. For while the interpretive approach includes a self-critical, reflexive process in engaging with cultural representations, RWE would seem to uncritically impose universal notions of 'Religion' and 'non-Religion' into the curriculum in the same manner phenomenology did with 'Christianity' and 'other religions'. Many indigenous values, beliefs and practices, indeed much of mainstream global contemporary culture, do not neatly fit into a 'Religion' and 'Worldviews' dichotomy, not least those examples given of non-religious worldviews by CoRE (2018: 75). 'Humanism, existentialism and Confucianism' are all examples of religious as well as non-religious worldviews – unless reified as otherwise.

How can teachers deal with conflicting truth claims in the classroom?

Religious plurality has been acknowledged as an important consideration for religious educationists since the 1970s (see Hardy 1976), presenting the issue of how, in the context of an array of competing and contested truth claims, religious or otherwise, can religious education take place? Considering RWE in the context of different approaches to plurality is necessary because providing a model for teachers and students to engage with different views is an important dimension of any approach to religious education conducted in a diverse society. One response to plurality, common among students, teachers and parents is a form of relativism – that since religious preferences and indeed, religious experience and knowledge are not objective, what is 'true' for one person does not need to be held as 'true' for another. While all classic pedagogies of religious education attempt to create teaching methods that allow individuals to construct or hold onto their own sincerely held views, the assumption that the subjectivity of the subject matter entails religious education should be founded on a form of relativism is problematic for several good reasons. Engaging with the classic pedagogies here may again inform our understanding of the pitfalls of such a view. The classic pedagogies take one of three broad strategies to engage with plurality. The first is to circumvent and/or diminish the role of truth claims by presenting an anthropological framework to explore beliefs and practices (the phenomenological, human development and interpretative models). The second is to address head-on the competing truth-claims of religious and non-religious worldviews through processes of comparison and critical judgement of their constituent beliefs and belief-systems (critical realist and concept cracking models). A final approach is to embrace a radical relativism accepting of truth claims as equally valid (as in the deconstruction model of Clive and Jane Erricker (2000).

The definition given by RWE of worldviews as any 'person's way of understanding, experiencing and responding to the world' (CoRE 2018: 4) would seem to lean towards an Erricksonian approach to plurality – perhaps one of the most controversial and challenging approaches advocated so far. The Errickers' argument rests on the position that no body of knowledge has a special status over the students' own 'true-for-me' knowledge. As there is no objective grounding to morality or religion, the curriculum cannot be based on any shared moral or spiritual understanding. Though attractive in its seeming openness to others' worldviews, the problem with such a position is that it comprises an objective theory in itself, thus resulting in paradox. If we assume relativism, we have no justification for a pedagogy, or for being professional educators – a point well made by Socrates of the Sophist Protagoras (Plato 2014 [c.368 BCE]). A relativist foundation to religious education struggles to give itself the epistemological legitimacy to assert itself. This has the effect of presenting serious problems for policy and practice such as, in the absence of any commitment to a form of realism, how to articulate a confident purpose for the subject or how to approach misconceptions and extremism among pupils (Moulin-Stożek 2020).

At this point it is worth considering again what connotations the term 'worldviews' may bring and how it may clash with at least some of the prevalent sincerely held beliefs that make up a religiously diverse society. For while plurality means there is more than one perspective, it does not entail that all those perspectives embrace a strong form theological or moral relativism. From the perspective of many 'insiders', what may be called 'worldviews', are more than a way to view the world. To a believer – of atheism, Islam or any faith – a true tradition gives the world in its fullness, not a merely a view of it. The Holy Qur'an does not give a view of the world, traditionally interpreted. It is the Revelation of the One God. Not comparable in terms of adherents' beliefs about the role of a text, but to an ardent atheist, Darwin's *Origin of the Species* is also not a mere 'view' – although it may now be somewhat outdated or improvable. To this 'Islamic' and 'scientific' worldview, there is an important criterion to add – that they are considered by their insiders to be true and demonstrably so. Importantly though, despite supposedly being distinct worldviews, they are not necessarily contradictory as advancing them as totalising 'worldviews' might suggest. These problems raise a difficult challenge for RWE as it would seem, in these cases at least, that to label a 'worldview' makes it liable to patronise the positions it appropriates, relativising them to the significance of just one view among many others, while at the same time reifying them into seemingly comprehensive positions that are mutually exclusive.

Conclusion

In this chapter we have considered three pertinent questions facing the development of any new approach to religious education: 'How can young people learn from religion if they do not believe in it?'; 'How can the reification of religious traditions be avoided?'; and 'How can teachers deal with conflicting truth claims in the classroom?' We have explored what RWE may have to offer in response to them alongside brief engagements with some of the strategies advocated in the articulations of 'classic pedagogies' advanced in the last 30–50 years. In regard to each of the questions considered, it would seem RWE gives little opportunity for new insight and, on several counts, falls foul of some previously identified problems, while also presenting some new ones. It does not provide any fresh means of giving relevance or motivation to those young people who may be disinclined to study religions or worldviews. Moreover, it arguably provides less opportunity, rationale or structure for pupils' free and nuanced engagement with religions when compared to those offered by the processes of 'learning from', 'edification', 'judgement' or 'narrative construction' detailed in the classic pedagogies.

RWE may also be open to increased risk of reification, including the perpetuation of an out-moded categorisation of 'religion' that harbours colonial and ethnocentric connotations and the equally discriminatory implication that religions may also only constitute views as opposed to paths to more absolute truths. Grimmitt (2000) was at pains to separate 'religion' from 'religions' in his commentary. The difference is crucial. One offers an overarching frame for the study of religions as 'religion', as though they share some common basis. The other offers greater prospects of understanding different traditions on their own terms without relating them back to a single category. Stressing 'religion', as opposed to 'religions' or 'traditions', in any rebranding of religious education invites the problems inherent with positing religion as a singular phenomenon. Perhaps worse is juxtaposing this with a pluralised construct, 'worldviews' as though they may be always separated. The conceptual benefits of advocating worldviews as a means of addressing plurality in the classroom for the above reasons do not provide a sounder method than some of those offered by the classic pedagogies. Rather, the relativising impact of suggesting that there are multiple opposing worldviews rather than one reality clashes with the sincerely held beliefs of many religious believers and atheists.

Aside from observing some a priori assumptions that are presumably inherent in its chosen terminology, this chapter has attempted to offer some ample leeway as to how RWE may be interpreted, noting that it is likely to be interpreted (or misinterpreted) in diverse ways. This is not just because it is a relative newcomer, and hence it is reasonable to assume it may be conceptually and practically underdetermined, but also because most pedagogical ideas are liable to modification (or distortion) when applied and interpreted by practitioners and pupils. A good example of this, and very relevant to conclude the argument of this chapter, is the very notion of a 'pedagogy of RE'. Inspired by Grimmitt's aforementioned (2000) book, the idea that there are 'pedagogies of RE' has informed classroom practice, teacher training and scholarly discourse. It has led to a common assumption that religious education should be understood or even practised in regard to one or other of the competing conceptions outlined in the book. In comparing RWE to the classic pedagogies and suggesting that it may be lacking in comparison, I have not meant to advance them, or one of them, as a complete and satisfactory model for religious education. My point has rather been to suggest they offer insights that should be taken into consideration when suggesting innovation in religious education.

All the classic pedagogical models harbour implicit or explicit ontological and epistemological assumptions concerning knowledge and inquiry in religious education. One key problematic that has spurred much debate since their development has been how they may distort 'religion' by appropriating it through one or another interpretative and often very reductive framework. It is for these reasons I have previously suggested that relying upon any one of the classic pedagogies reduces pupils' right to different interpretations of religions as they may present a mode of engagement with religions that clashes with a given pupil's religious or non-religious beliefs (Moulin 2009). The same would apply to RWE. By emphasising the concept of worldview as pivotal, RWE presents a framework that is no less spurious or discriminatory than its forebears.

The *Ofsted Research Review Series: Religious Education* (2021) points out that classic approaches to RE are not so much pedagogies as 'models' of religious education that incorporate 'aims, methods and methodology' (42) – somewhat distinct from the narrower, more usual use of the term 'pedagogy', to mean a particular method of teaching. (It is worth noting that Grimmitt himself observed this distinction, also favouring the term 'pedagogical model' to describe it (2000: 17).) Considering the discussion given in this chapter, one conclusion to draw in response to this astute point is to question whether conceptions of religious education, including RWE, should, or need to, set out to define ontological and epistemological conditions of teaching and learning so as to become a 'paradigm'. It is the epistemological assumptions of a pedagogical model where bias and distortion may lie, not just in its selection of subject-content. This is a significant issue for religious education as religious traditions usually offer their own onto-epistemologies. Approaching them through an epistemologically-driven pedagogical model is therefore likely to clash with representing them.

Given the inherent problems in advancing an approach, as all the models and RWE have done, that seeks to somehow squeeze 'religion' or 'worldviews' into a generic and secular model, it may be more advantageous to ask what may happen if such a project – common to RWE and the classic pedagogies – is abandoned and pedagogical innovation were to focus on the science of teaching and learning ('pedagogy' as it is usually understood). Do we need a general approach which is intended to make religious education of renewed relevance as it is suggested of RWE? For any such quest could not only be reductive and naively ambitious, but also unnecessary in terms of developing suitable methods of teaching for any given topic. Religions typically offer the means to understand their own set of onto-epistemological commitments on their own terms. I mean this in the sense that most given texts, practices, etc., sacred or otherwise, afford opportunity for an interpretation of themselves as well a contribution to an understanding of life or other things. It follows that there is opportunity for the development of bespoke pedagogical methods relevant and appropriate to any given topic. Notwithstanding the importance of educational theory, as 'finer grain' pedagogies such practices would be more amenable to evaluation through empirical research, making possible a more thorough, collaborative and evidenced exercise of pedagogical evaluation. This approach would perhaps move innovation and development in religious education away from potentially fruitless polemic and speculation.

References

Barnes, L. P. and Wright, A. (2006) 'Romanticism, representations of religion and critical religious education', *British Journal of Religious Education* 28(1): 65–77. Doi.org/10.1080/01416200500273695.

Benoit, C., Hutchings, T. and Shillitoe, R. (2020) *Worldview: A multidisciplinary report*. London: Religious Education Council of England and Wales. Available online: https://www.religiouseducationcouncil.org.uk/wp-content/uploads/2020/10/20-19438-REC-Worldview-Report-A4-v2.pdf (accessed 18 December 2021).

Brown, A. (2000) 'The Chichester Project: Teaching Christianity: a world religions approach', in M. Grimmitt (ed.) *Pedagogies of Religious Education: Case studies in the research and development of good pedagogic practice in RE* (53–69). Great Wakering: McCrimmons.

Chater, M. (ed.) (2020) *Reforming Religious Education: Power and knowledge in a worldviews curriculum*. John Catt Educational.

Commission on Religious Education (CoRE) (2018) *Final Report: Religion and worldviews: the way forward: a national plan for RE*. Available online: https://

www.commissiononre.org.uk/wp-content/uploads/2018/09/Final-Report-of-the-Commission-on-RE.pdf (accessed 18 December 2021).

Cooling, T. (1994) *Concept Cracking: Exploring Christian beliefs in school*. Stapleford Project.

Cooling, T. (2020) 'Worldview in religious education: Autobiographical reflections on the Commission on Religious Education in England final report', *British Journal of Religious Education* 42(4): 403–414. Doi.org/10.1080/01416200.2020.1764497.

Cooling, T. (2021) 'The Commission on Religious Education: A response to L. Philip Barnes', *British Journal of Educational Studies*. Doi.org/10.1080/00071005.2021.1954142.

Copley, T. (2005) *Indoctrination, Education, and God: The struggle for the mind*. United Kingdom: SPCK.

Cupitt, D. (2006) *The Old Creed and the New*. London: SCM.

Erricker, C. (2001) 'Shall we dance? Authority, representation, and voice: The place of spirituality in religious education', *Religious Education* 96(1): 20–35. Doi.org/10.1080/00344080120607.

Erricker, C. and Erricker, J. (2000) 'The Children and Worldviews Project: A narrative pedagogy of religious education', in M. Grimmitt (ed.) *Pedagogies of Religious Education: Case studies in the research and development of good pedagogic practice in RE* (188–206). Great Wakering: McCrimmons.

Erricker, C., Sullivan, D., Ota, C., Erricker, J. and Logan, J. (1994) 'The development of children's worldviews', *Journal of Beliefs & Values* 15(2): 3–6. Doi.org/10.1080/1361767940150201

Everington, J. (1996) 'A question of authenticity: The relationship between educators and practitioners in the representation of religious traditions', *British Journal of Religious Education* 18(2): 69–77. Doi.org/10.1080/0141620960180202.

Fitzgerald, T. (2017) 'Problems with "religion" as a category for understanding Hinduism', in *Defining Hinduism* (171–201). London: Routledge.

Garforth, F. W. (1961) 'Doubts about secondary school scripture', *Religion in Education* 28(2): 73–76. Doi.org/10.1080/6108555915.

Grimmitt, M. (1987) *Religious Education and Human Development: The relationship between studying religions and personal, social and moral education*. Great Wakering: McCrimmons.

Grimmitt, M. (2000) *Pedagogies of Religious Education: Case studies in the research and development of good pedagogic practice in RE*. Great Wakering: McCrimmons.

Hardy, D. W. (1976) 'The implications of pluralism for religious education', *Learning for Living* 16(2): 55–62. Doi.org/10.1080/00239707608556937.

Jackson, R. (1997) *Religious Education: An interpretive approach*. United Kingdom: Hodder & Stoughton.

Jackson, R. (2004) *Rethinking Religious Education and Plurality: Issues in diversity and pedagogy*. London: Routledge.

Jackson, R. (2011) 'The interpretive approach as a research tool: Inside the REDCo project', *British Journal of Religious Education* 33(2): 189–208. Doi.org/10.1080/01416200.2011.543602.

Moran, G. (2003) 'Religious education', in R. Curren (ed.) *A Companion to the Philosophy of Education* (323–341). Oxford: Blackwell.
Moulin, D. (2009) 'A too liberal religious education? A thought experiment for teachers and theorists', *British Journal of Religious Education* 31(2): 153–165. Doi.org/10.1080/01416200802661126.
Moulin-Stożek, D. (2020) 'Educating for the world or "religion and worldviews education?"' *Journal of Beliefs & Values* 41(4): 385–387. Doi.org/10.1080/13617672.2020.1832030.
Moulin-Stożek, D. and Metcalfe, J. (2020) 'Mapping the moral assumptions of multi-faith religious education', *British Journal of religious education* 42(3): 253–262. Doi.org/10.1080/01416200.2018.1556605.
Ofsted (2021) *Research Review: Religious education*. Available online: https://www.gov.uk/government/publications/research-review-series-religious-education (accessed 18 December 2021)
Pearce, R. T. (1979) 'Religious education and emotion', *British Journal of Religious Education* 1(4): 136–139. Doi.org/10.1080/0141620790010404.
Plato (2014) *Theaetetus*. Oxford: Oxford University Press.
Rudge, L. (1998) '"I am nothing" – does it matter? A critique of current religious education policy and practice in England on behalf of the silent majority', *British Journal of Religious Education* 20(3): 155–165. Doi.org/10.1080/0141620980200304.
Sikes, P. and Everington, J. (2004) '"RE teachers do get drunk you know": Becoming a religious education teacher in the twenty-first century', *Teachers and Teaching* 10(1): 21–33. Doi.org/10.1080/13540600320000170909.
Smart, N. (1968) *Secular Education and the Logic of Religion*. London: Faber.
Smart, N. (1989) *The World's Religions*. Cambridge: Cambridge University Press.
Smart, N. (2000) *World Philosophies*. London: Routledge.
Tolstoy, L. (1934 [1887]) *On Life and Essays on Religion*. Trans. A. Maude. Oxford: Oxford University Press.
White, J. (2004) 'Should religious education be a compulsory school subject?' *British Journal of Religious Education* 26(2): 151–164. Doi.org/10.1080/01416200420042000181929.
Wright, A. (1993) *Religious Education in the Secondary School: Prospects for religious literacy*. Fulton.
Wright, A. (2001) 'Dancing in the fire: A deconstruction of Clive Erricker's postmodern spiritual pedagogy', *Religious Education* 96(1): 120–135. Doi.org/10.1080/00344080121331.
Wright, A. (2015) *Religious Education and Critical Realism: Knowledge, reality and religious literacy*. London: Routledge.

8
WORLDVIEWS – A THREAT TO RELIGIOUS EDUCATION BUT IGNORED IN SCIENCE EDUCATION?

Michael J. Reiss

The possibility of religious education changing its character so that it explicitly includes non-religious worldviews, to the extent that the subject itself changes its name, is deeply contentious. It has unsurprisingly been welcomed by humanists (secularists) who have long been frustrated at their inability to colonise religious education, and has been seen by some within the RE community as a way of rescuing the subject from its perceived decline. Others, though, see the inclusion of non-religious worldviews as incoherent or 'selling out' and have raised a number of objections to the proposal, as discussed extensively in the other chapters of this book.

In this chapter I begin by providing an overview of the arguments concerning the place of worldviews in religious education and then examine the argument that school science should take account of worldviews. I go on to discuss recent calls for a different change to school science and religious education, namely that their curricula should focus on Big Ideas. I will argue that the reasons why Big Ideas have been advocated in school science and in religious education are similar and the suggestion has been similarly received in the two subjects, whereas the suggestion that worldviews be incorporated within them has been received very differently by the two subjects. I end by suggesting why this might be the case and discuss the implications that this may have for each subject.

Worldviews within religious education

All school subjects are debated with respect to their characteristics, their relationship with their 'parent' subject (religious education with religion, school science with science, etc), their aims, their content, and how they might be taught and assessed. In religious education, these debates have been long-lasting and have included such foci as the subject's importance (Watson 2012), its context-specific history (Barnes et al. 2012), the particular issues that attend faith schooling (Parker-Jenkins et al. 2005, 2014; Halstead 2009; Chapman et al. 2014; Pring 2018), its reception by students (Conroy et al. 2013) and its contribution to multicultural education (Smyth et al. 2013). More recently, other foci have been added, including the subject's role in tackling extremism (Miller 2013; Wilkinson 2018) and the argument as to how religious education should deal with what are sometimes referred to as 'non-religious worldviews'. For a recent, official review of the state of religious education in England, see Ofsted (2021).

The current debate around worldviews in religious education has been given particular impetus in England by the final report, after its two years of evidence gathering, of the Commission on Religious Education (2018). The Commission (CoRE) concluded that 'RE needs rejuvenating if it is to continue to make its important contribution; indeed if it is not to wither on the vine' (Foreword). The title of the final report was *Religion and Worldviews: The Way Forward – A National Plan for RE*, and it claimed:

> **We offer a new vision.** The subject should explore the important role that religious and non-religious worldviews play in all human life. This is an essential area of study if pupils are to be well prepared for life in a world where controversy over such matters is pervasive and where many people lack the knowledge to make their own informed decisions. It is a subject for all pupils, whatever their own family background and personal beliefs and practices. To reflect this new emphasis, we propose that the subject should be called *Religion and Worldviews*.
>
> *(Foreword)*

The Commission took a worldview to be 'a person's way of understanding, experiencing and responding to the world. It can be described as a philosophy of life or an approach to life' (CoRE 2018: 4). It saw one of the core tasks of education as enabling 'each pupil to understand, reflect on and develop their own personal worldview' (5) and argued that:

> Through understanding how worldviews are formed and expressed at both individual and communal levels, the ways in which they have changed over time, and their influence on the actions of individuals,

groups and institutions, young people come to a more refined understanding of their own worldview – whatever this happens to be – as well as those of others.

(CoRE 2018: 5)

The Commission noted that non-religious worldviews have become increasingly important in Western Europe and claimed 'the distinction between religious and non-religious worldviews is not as clear-cut as one might think' (6).

In response to the Commission's Report, the Religious Education Council for England and Wales (which established the Commission) itself commissioned an independent team of researchers to undertake a literature review on the concept of 'worldview' (Benoit et al. 2020). The resulting report chose to present its conclusions as a series of questions, including: whether worldview is inclusive of religion and non-religion or used as an alternative term to religion; whether worldview is a Western and Christian construct; and whether worldview refers to consciously thought out and articulated approaches to life or includes un-reflected elements.

Of course, the debate around the place of worldviews in religious education and education more generally was not initiated by the CoRE's report – Clive Erricker's 'Children and Worldviews Project' (Erricker et al. 1997) was influential, and see Hand (2012) and Aldridge (2015) for critical discussions of the range of ways in which 'worldview' is used that predate Benoit et al. (2020). Nevertheless, the Commission's report has given rise to a flurry of activity, of which this book is one instance. Somewhat unusually, autobiographic responses from members of the Commission or those who played a role in establishing the Commission have been provided by Cooling (2020) and Cooling et al. (2020).

Perhaps the most sustained critical examination of the CoRE's report to date has been provided by Barnes (2021). Barnes' article is wide-ranging; here, I concentrate on the parts of it to do with worldviews. Some of his criticisms of the Commission's arguments about worldviews are to do with terminology – notably their distinction between 'institutional worldviews' and 'personal worldviews' and their identification of humanism, secularism, agnosticism and atheism as worldviews, when it is clear that there is considerable overlap between them, while secularism:

> is typically characterised as the view that public and political institutions should be independent of religion. It does not constitute a worldview as such, only that there should be strict limits to the public

role of religions in society and that the state should be neutral between alternative religions and beliefs.

(Barnes 2021: 4)

Barnes also doubts that a study of agnosticism as a worldview will add much to a study of atheism, arguing that:

> A plausible case can be made for regarding atheism, agnosticism and Humanism, not as constituting independent and separate worldviews, but instances of the broader category of a naturalistic worldview – a relationship of tokens to type, in philosophical parlance. In the same way, Protestantism and Catholicism are examples of a Christian worldview. What is common to atheists, agnostics and Humanists is the conviction that all religions are without epistemic warrant.
>
> *(Barnes 2021: 5)*

For myself, this sounds convincing, though I would not be able to go as far as to agree with:

> The distinction often employed by philosophers (Rowe 2005) that atheism affirms the non-existence of God whereas agnosticism is the view that human reason is incapable of knowing whether God exists or not is for most people otiose; and certainly it is for most pupils in schools.
>
> *(Barnes 2021: 5)*

One of the things we try to do in science education – though I admit that we do not always succeed – is to get students to appreciate the extent to which scientific knowledge develops over time so that some scientific knowledge, at any one point in human history, is more robust than other scientific knowledge. Indeed, even the scientific theories considered most robust nowadays (e.g. Wegener's theory of continental drift) were often considered tentative when first proposed. The cognitive demands we thus make on students in school science do not seem greater than would be expected for them to distinguish atheism from agnosticism – something, indeed, that is already covered in many religious education courses.

A different point made by Barnes is his critique of the very notion of personal worldview, something that is core to the Commission's arguments:

> The issue is not whether everyone has beliefs, values, experiences and commitments, it is whether it is helpful to think of these collectively

as a *personal worldview*. People can hold a range of beliefs and values, not always consistent with each other or with some of their experiences or even with their professed self-identity: referring to a personal worldview may give the impression that what we believe and how we act possess a greater degree of coherence and unity than is the case for many. People are often not reflective or consistent in their beliefs. Whereas many will have an opinion about God and his existence and nature, few will have thought seriously or at length about this and about what constitutes human nature, the meaning of life and of human history, whether knowledge is available to us and how we distinguish what is morally right from what is morally wrong, and so on; and it is answers to these that philosophers tell us constitute a worldview. Many people and particularly the young and non-religious people do not espouse a worldview: they do not have a reflective philosophical view of the nature of reality, of the kind that is properly described as a worldview.

(Barnes 2021: 4)

A pragmatic (the term used by Cooling 2020) or educational (the term preferred by Barnes 2021) objection to the use of worldviews in religious education is that this increases the volume of material to be covered in religious education courses:

A careful reading of the CoRE Report suggests that by the end of Key Stage 4 a pupil could be obliged to study a minimum of ten or more different religions and worldviews – an onerous task, given that the law at present expects significant teaching about Christianity at each Key Stage (will the law have to be amended to accommodate this broader curriculum?). The requirement is also made that religious education takes account of 'the complex, diverse and plural nature of worldviews', i.e. 'the . . . diversity within worldviews' (2018: 5). How can teachers seriously do justice to so many traditions, while at the same time introducing pupils to their inner diversity? However charitably one interprets this broad-ranging and open-ended approach to content it ought to have been obvious to the authors of the Report that the religious education curriculum will inevitably become a summary review or a Cook's tour of religious and non-religious worldviews that will necessarily result in superficial teaching, simplistic learning and confused pupils.

(Barnes 2021: 7)

This is an important objection to the inclusion of worldviews – though it could be argued that the force of this objection is vitiated by the point that Barnes himself makes about the extent to which religious education courses already consider such issues, even if not necessarily under the heading of 'worldviews':

> One aspect of the critical element in religious education is that objections and philosophical criticisms of religions or aspects of religions are considered. Typically, attention is given by religious educators to the 'problem of suffering and evil', non-religious accounts of the origins of the universe, the relationship of science to religion, particularly that of the debate on human origins, that of evolution and its denial, that of creationism, and to non-religious perspectives on contemporary moral issues. It should not be thought that those who are opposed to systematic teaching about non-religious worldviews on the same basis as religions, such as Christianity or Islam, wish to remove or lessen this critical element from current practice: the essential content of secular worldviews is already integrated into religious education as criticism of religion.
>
> (Barnes 2021: 8)

Nevertheless, the point about courses being overladen is one that is common to religious education, science and many other school subjects. In my consideration below of 'Big Ideas' in both science and religious education, I indicate that one hope that educators who support the use of Big Ideas have is that this approach will slim down the curriculum, allowing the wood to be seen, as well as the most significant trees.

Worldviews within science education

The academic science education literature on why some students fail to understand certain aspects of science mainly concentrates on cognitive issues, including student misconceptions. A large part of school science education therefore consists of addressing these misconceptions – for example, the misconception that the natural state of affairs is for objects in motion to slow down (an Aristotelian notion, since, for Aristotle, the natural state of an object is to be at rest). This particular belief is in contradistinction to the way that science understands motion: since Newton it has been accepted that the natural state of affairs is for objects to continue to move with the same velocity (i.e., at the same speed and in the same direction) that they have unless acted on by a net force. To give one more example of a misconception that school science tries to correct, most people presume that a growing terrestrial plant gets most of its mass from the soil. The scientific understanding is that a growing plant gets most of its mass from the atmosphere via the process of photosynthesis, whereby carbon dioxide is captured, reacted with water (a very difficult chemical reaction, yet one that all plants manage) and used to synthesise sugars such as glucose and sucrose. Some of a growing plant's mass does come from the soil, including minerals that provide elements such as nitrogen, iron, phosphorus and sulphur that enable the plant to make proteins and other large molecules, but this contribution to a plant's mass is far less than that provided by the atmosphere.

For many years, science educators happily presumed that all that was needed for successful science education was to ensure that students understand science. In an oft-cited paper in the science education literature, Bill Cobern (1996) characterised the assumption that if students can see that scientifically orthodox conceptions are more intelligible, plausible and fruitful than other conceptions, they will come to accept these scientific conceptions. as a 'rationalistic view'. In recent decades, however, an additional perspective has come into view, particularly within biology. It has increasingly been acknowledged that students, even if they *understand* certain topics, may *reject* them because these topics may not mesh with their worldviews. The classic instance is evolutionary biology, which students from fundamentalist religious backgrounds not infrequently reject; other instances include anthropogenic climate change, vaccination advocacy and the use of animals for human ends.

The notion of worldviews is increasingly being employed in science education (Reiss 2018). For example, in the edited volume *Science, Worldviews and Education* (Matthews 2009), a number of philosophers, scientists and science educators use the thinking behind worldviews to explore a range of issues including whether science itself is a worldview and whether science can test supernatural worldviews. As other chapters in this volume discuss, the term 'worldview' is conceptualised in a number of ways. In *World Views: From Fragmentation to Integration*, Diederik Aerts et al. (1994: 17) state that 'A world view is a coherent collection of concepts and theorems that must allow us to construct a global image of the world, and in this way to understand as many elements of our experience as possible.' If one accepts such a definition, it makes sense to talk of a 'scientific worldview', though quite a number of scientists do not much like the phrase, because it suggests that a scientific perspective might not necessarily be superior to other perspectives. In science education, the notion of worldviews has increasingly been explored as a way of helping conceptualise why, despite the best efforts of many science teachers, so few students leave their schooling with the sort of scientific understanding and disposition that most science teachers wish they had. The principal conclusion is that school science fails to enable most students to see the world from a scientific perspective (Reiss 2011).

Nevertheless, for all that I (e.g. Reiss 2009) and a number of other science educators (e.g. Cobern 1996; Keane 2008; Taber 2013) are keen on the potential contribution of worldviews for science education, it cannot be said that most science educators, nor those responsible for science curricula, have been persuaded. This is not to say that the arguments for consideration of worldviews in science education have been furiously debated and rebutted; it's more that they are seen as less important than other considerations. Specifically, worldviews are likely to be alluded to only as explanations as to why students fail to understand what the designers of science courses want them to understand – whether we are talking about the theory of evolution, as discussed below, or such topics as climate change (where worldviews are used to explain climate change denial) or vaccine hesitancy (where, again, worldviews are used to explain why some people reject standard science). This is therefore in marked contrast to the reception accorded to the notion of worldviews in religious education.

Evolution

The concept of worldviews can be illustrated by examining the ways in which science and religion each attempt to explain how the Earth came to have the tremendous biodiversity that we see today.

The scientific understanding of this issue is far from complete but the narrative is a powerful one (Reiss 2009). Around 3.8 billion years ago, the earliest life evolved on Earth. Rather little is known with any great confidence about this early history, far less than is known, for example, about how stars form, grow and die. But scientists agree that by the time of the earliest fossils, life was unicellular and bacteria-like. Over the ages, natural processes, particularly natural selection (as discovered independently by Charles Darwin and Alfred Russel Wallace), eventually resulted in the 10 million or so species, including our own, that we find today.

The key point is that the scientific worldview that is associated with this standard scientific understanding is materialistic in the sense that it is neither idealistic nor admits of non-physical, and thus supernatural, explanations. There is much about the history of life on Earth that remains unknown. How precisely did the earliest self-replicating molecules arise? What caused the membranes that are essential for cellular life to exist?

How key were the earliest physical conditions – temperature, the occurrence of water and so forth? Where did life evolve – in a little warm pond (as Darwin speculated), on clays (Cairns-Smith's suggestion), in a hydrothermal vent, deep on the sea floor, or elsewhere? Despite this uncertainty, the scientific presumption is either that these questions will be answered by science or that they will remain unknown. Although scientists sometimes grudgingly admit that science cannot disprove supernatural explanations, scientists do not employ such explanations in their work, whatever their personal views; the few exceptions only attest to the strength of the general rule, though it needs to be admitted that a non-trivial number of scientists have adopted Intelligent Design theory, in which it is held that the complexity of life is such that it cannot have arisen by natural processes alone (Meyer 2009).

Religious understandings of the history of life and today's biodiversity are, of course, more diverse. Many religious believers, including many scientists (e.g. Ecklund 2012), are perfectly comfortable with the scientific account, either on its own or accompanied by a belief that evolution in some sense takes place within God's holding, whether or not God is presumed to have intervened or acted providentially at certain key points (e.g. the origin of life or the early evolution of humanity). But many other religious believers adopt a perspective that is not wholly concurrent with the scientific position. Creationism exists in a number of different versions but many people (about 40% of adults in the USA, fewer in other Western countries) believe that the Earth came into existence as described in the early parts of the Bible or the Qur'an and that the most that evolution has done is to change species into closely related species (Miller et al. 2006). For a creationist, it may be perfectly possible that the various species (about 350 extant) of parrots had a common ancestor (the scriptures are not concerned with contemporary definitions of biological species) but this would not be held to be the case for parrots, herons and falcons, still less for birds and reptiles, or monkeys and humans, or fish and flowering plants.

In this sense, creationism can be considered an alternative worldview to the scientific worldview when it comes to accounting for the diversity of life we see on the Earth today. One of the key points about worldviews is that it can be difficult for someone who has never inhabited a particular worldview to imagine what it is really like to do so – one reason, in my experience, why atheistic scientists are sometimes very patronising about creationists. In Christianity, of course, a creationist is also likely to think that the world will soon be coming to an end, very possibly in their lifetime, that there is a world to come and that the eternal fate of each and every one of us in that world depends on whether or not in this world we accept the teachings of scripture.

Big Ideas in science education and in religious education

It is widely agreed among science educators that school science too often consists of teaching isolated facts instead of attempting to develop an understanding of core ideas (Olson 2008). Osborne (2007) has argued that concentrating on isolated facts distracts students from seeing the beauty of science. In this sense, positive attitudes towards science could decrease because science is shown simply as atomistic events, so that students 'may miss the big picture' (Reiss 2014: 9).

In an attempt to address these problems, there has been a growing move among curriculum developers to argue that science education should consider 'Big Ideas' as ideas that are able to explain a wide range of scientific facts and phenomena (Metz 2012). These 'ideas enable learners to see connections between different scientific ideas' and when these are connected, it is easier to use them in new scenarios than other, unconnected ones (Harlen 2015a: 97).

The Big Ideas movement – for so it may validly be called – in science education had modest beginnings: a two-and-a-half-day residential seminar for 12 participants in a remote venue on the shore of Loch Lomond was paid for by Wynne Harlen using the money she was awarded for winning the 2009 Purkwa Prize. The resulting document *Principles and Big Ideas of Science Education* (Harlen 2010) was followed by a companion document *Working with Big Ideas of Science Education* (Harlen 2015b). Within a decade it had been incorporated into curricula in South Korea (Choi et al. 2011), Australia (Mitchell et al. 2016) and Chile (Bravo González and Reiss 2021) and influenced science curricula in a number of other countries.

The effects of the Big Ideas movement in science education have spread to other subjects, facilitated in England by advice given to the National Curriculum Review group by Tim Oates (2010) that students should study fewer things but in greater depth in order to secure deeper learning in subjects. In religious education, Barbara Wintersgill organised a three-day symposium at a remote farm on Dartmoor (there seems to be something about Big Ideas that means that they grow best in modestly funded writing workshops undertaken in remote locations), the fruits of which resulted in *Big Ideas for Religious Education* (Wintersgill 2017).

Big Ideas for Religious Education begins with a table that identifies 'Principles of Religious Education'. This is not unlike comparable lists in other religious education curricular documents, addressing the overall aim of religious education, its specific purposes and goals, as well as issues to do with progression, learning and assessment. The document then moves to identify four big questions that arise in religious education:

- If the content of the RE curriculum is to be reduced, on what principles or criteria should we decide what content is included?
- On what principles or criteria should we decide how the selected content should be sequenced for ages 5–18?
- How might the RE curriculum be presented in a more coherent way?
- How might we make RE more engaging for young people growing up in the 21st century?

(Wintersgill 2017: 6)

After extensive discussion as to what Big Ideas are (including the idea that they provide criteria for the selection and prioritising of subject knowledge in the curriculum, are transferable to events outside the classroom, are memorable, and capable of differentiation so that they may become the basis of progression) and are not (including that they do not provide a philosophy of education, do not presume any particular pedagogy, do not prescribe any specific content, are not themes or concepts found in individual subjects, are not intended to be a prescriptive programme, and do not assume which or how many religions and non-religious worldviews are being studied), six Big Ideas are identified:

Big Idea 1   Continuity, Change and Diversity
Big Idea 2   Words and Beyond
Big Idea 3   A Good Life
Big Idea 4   Making Sense of Life's Experiences
Big Idea 5   Influence, Community, Culture and Power
Big Idea 6   The Big Picture

(Wintersgill 2017: 15)

As the person who chaired the working party, I'll leave it up to readers to determine whether these meet the above-mentioned criterion of being memorable! To put some flesh on these bones, here are the suggestions for ages 5–7 and 14–16 for Big Idea 5 – Influence, Community, Culture and Power:

5–7

There are signs of religious and non-religious worldviews all around us and lots of evidence of their influence on our communities. Many local and national holidays are held at the time of religious or other festivals, and religious leaders are often important people locally. Several well-known traditional stories and songs reflect the ideas of religious traditions present in the community. Religions are not equally influential everywhere. Some places are more religious than others; some families are more religious than others. Most schools have children from different religions and non-religious worldviews and may have many who do not identify with any religion or worldview.

14–16

Religions and non-religious worldviews exist at several levels. Most people encounter religions at local level where they can make a difference to communities and individuals. At national level, everyone is affected when a religious or non-religious group influences the country's political and legal systems, its education system or the times of national holidays. Religious and non-religious groups also influence people's ideas about what is right and wrong and affect the way they respond to ethical issues. Some people see their role as one of offering a critique of prevailing social attitudes and practices. Religions and non-religious worldviews influence culture and community in places where they had power in the past and may still have it. Consequently, around the world countries and communities have very different relationships with religions and non-religious worldviews, from theocracies, where God is seen as the source of all authority, to secular states, which may claim to be neutral in matters of religion and belief. Many communities have become more diverse and have responded to this diversity in different ways. Changes in community are also reflected in the arts, which in most communities continue to remind people of their traditional religious identities while also being affected by contemporary religious and non-religious ideas. Most religions have a global presence and respond to the hardship that results from natural disasters, war, prejudice or disability. The relationship between religions, cultures and communities is both complex and controversial, since it can be peaceful and harmonious or can lead to conflict and disagreement. The appeal to ideas about a superior authority or vision represented by God, an authoritative text, a powerful leader or a compelling vision of the future may be used to justify social and political actions. This may lead to social and spiritual improvement, but it may lead to intolerance and violence.

Advocates of the approach of *Big Ideas for Religious Education* might argue that such an approach allows non-religious worldviews to be incorporated within religious education without leading to an impracticable expansion of content or to study of religions being diminished to 'make space' for study of Humanism, secularism, agnosticism and atheism.

Conclusions

As someone whose primary expertise is in science education, I find it fascinating that while both religious education and school science are currently exploring the possibility of Big Ideas playing a greater role in each subject (though see Freathy and John 2019), the reception that the two subjects have given to the suggestion that worldviews play a more central role has been very different. In science education, this suggestion has been enthusiastically adopted by a relatively small proportion of the community. Indeed, in my experience it is science educators who are particularly sensitive to issues to do with indigenous science and the rubbishing of religion by some scientists who are most likely to see the positive affordance of the notion of worldviews in science education. In religious education the situation seems rather different. Whilst there are a number of objections to the introduction of worldviews, here it seems that there is a widespread fear that to include worldviews, particularly non-religious worldviews, within the subject is to let the wolf into the sheepfold. In science, the idea of worldviews is often received with apathy; in religious education, often with fear and trembling.

Why this difference? It seems very possible that this is related to the general position of each subject in the school curriculum and in society more generally. For all that the classic work of Paul Hirst might envisage a place of near equality for science and religious education in the school curriculum (as for other forms of knowledge), one does not need to be a fully-fledged Bernsteinian (cf. vertical and horizontal discourses) to acknowledge that religious education is in a much weaker position in schools than is science. It is not surprising therefore that science typically reacts to suggestions that it should change with the indifference that the powerful can afford, whereas religious education reacts with angst, even defensively. The relative strengths of the two subjects in school, at least in England, are, of course, reflections of the relative strengths – and the on-going direction of change in these strengths – of the two disciplines in public discourse.

I therefore support the argument in both religious education and science education (Billingsley and Nassaji 2021; Pearce et al. 2021; Stones and Fraser-Pearce 2021) that there is value in students acquiring greater epistemic literacy during their school studies. However, while both subjects would do well to pay attention to worldviews and to introduce this concept to students, there seems no need for either subject to envisage changing its name.

References

Aerts, D., Apostel, L., De Moor, B., Hellemans, S., Maex, E., Van Belle, H. and Van der Veken, J. (1994) *World Views: From fragmentation to integration*. Brussels: VUB Press.

Aldridge, D. (2015) *A Hermeneutics of Religious Education*. London: Bloomsbury.

Barnes, L. P. (2021) 'The Commission on Religious Education, Worldviews and the Future of Religious Education', *British Journal of Educational Studies*. Doi: 10.1080/00071005.2021.1871590.

Barnes, L. P., Lundie, D., Armstrong, D., McKinnery, S. and Williams, K. (2012) 'Religious education in the United Kingdom and Ireland', in L. P. Barnes (ed.) *Debates in Religious Education* (22–51). London: Routledge.

Benoit, C., Hutchings, T. and Shillitoe, R. (2020) *Worldview: A multidisciplinary report*. Religious Education Council of England and Wales. Available online: religiouseducationcouncil.org.uk/wp-content/uploads/2020/10/20-19438-REC-Worldview-Report-A4-v2.pdf (accessed 20 December 2021).

Billingsley, B. and Nassaji, M. (2021) 'Secondary school students' reasoning about science and personhood', *Science & Education* 30: 967–991. Doi: 10.1007/s11191-021-00199-x.

Bravo González, P. and Reiss, M. J. (2021) 'Science teachers' views of creating and teaching big ideas of science education: Experiences from Chile', *Research in Science & Technological Education*. Doi.org/10.1080/02635143.2021.1919868.

Chapman, J. D., McNamara, S., Reiss, M. J. and Waghid, Y. (eds) (2014) *International Handbook of Learning, Teaching and Leading in Faith-Based Schools*. Dordrecht: Springer.

Choi, K., Lee, H., Shin, N., Kim, S-W. and Krajcik, J. (2011) 'Re-conceptualization of scientific literacy in South Korea for the 21st century', *Journal of Research in Science Teaching* 48(6): 670–697. Doi.org/10.1002/tea.20424.

Cobern, W. W. (1996) 'Worldview theory and conceptual change in science education', *Science Education* 80(5): 579–610. Doi: 10.1002/(SICI)1098-237X(199609)80:5<579::AID-SCE5>3.0.CO;2–8.

Commission on Religious Education (2018) *Final Report. Religions and worldviews: The way forward: a national plan for RE*. London: Religious Education Council of England & Wales. Available online: https://www.commissiononre.org.uk/wp-content/uploads/2018/09/Final-Report-of-the-Commission-on-RE.pdf (accessed 20 December 2021).

Conroy, J. C., Lundie, D., Davis, R. A., Baumfield, V., Barnes, L. P., Gallagher, T., Lowden, K., Bourque, N. and Wenell, K. (2013) *Does Religious Education Work? A multi-dimensional investigation*. London: Bloomsbury.

Cooling, T. (2020) 'Worldview in religious education: Autobiographical reflections on *The Commission on Religious Education in England: Final report*', *British Journal of Religious Education* 42(4): 403–414. Doi:10.1080/01416200.2020.1764497.

Cooling, T., with Bowie, B. and Panjwani, F. (2020) *Theos Report: Worldviews in religious education*. London: Theos. Available online: theosthinktank.co.uk/cms files/Worldview-in-Religious-Education-FINAL-PDF-merged.pdf (accessed 20 December 2021).

Ecklund, E. H. (2012) *Science vs. Religion: What scientists really think*. Oxford: Oxford University Press.

Erricker, C., Erricker, J., Sullivan, D., Ota, C. and Fletcher, M. (1997) *The Education of the Whole Child*. London: Continuum.

Freathy, R. and John, H. C. (2019) 'Religious education, big ideas and the study of religion(s) and worldview(s)', *British Journal of Religious Education* 41(1): 27–40. Doi: 10.1080/01416200.2018.1500351.

Halstead, J. M. (2009) 'In defence of faith schools', in Graham Haydon (ed.) *Faith in Education: A tribute to Terence McLaughlin* (46–67). London: Institute of Education, University of London.

Hand, M. (2012) 'What's in a worldview? On Trevor Cooling's *Doing God in Education*', *Oxford Review of Education* 38(5): 527–537. Doi: 10.1080/03054985.2012.722862.

Harlen, W. (2010) *Principles and Big Ideas of Science Education*. Available online: https://www.ase.org.uk/bigideas (accessed 20 December 2021).

Harlen, W. (2015a) 'Towards big ideas of science education', *School Science Review*, 97(359): 97–107.

Harlen, W. (2015b) *Working with Big Ideas of Science Education*. Trieste: InterAcademy Partnership. Available online: https://www.ase.org.uk/bigideas (accessed 20 December 2021).

Keane, M. (2008) 'Science education and worldview', *Cultural Studies of Science Education* 3: 587–621. Doi: 10.1007/s11422-007-9086-5 (accessed 20 December 2021).

Matthews, M. R. (2009) (ed.) *Science, Worldviews and Education*. New York: Springer.

Metz, S. (2012) 'Big Ideas', *The Science Teacher* 79(5): 6.

Meyer, S. C. (2009) *Signature in the Cell: DNA and the evidence for intelligent design*. New York: HarperCollins.

Miller, J. (2013) 'Religious extremism, religious education and the interpretive approach', in J. Miller, K. O'Grady and U. McKenna (eds) *Religion in Education: Innovation in international research* (121–133). New York: Routledge.

Miller, J. D., Scott, E. C. and Okamoto, S. (2006) 'Public acceptance of evolution', *Science*, 313: 765–766.

Mitchell, I., Keast, S., Panizzon, D. and Mitchell, J. (2016) 'Using "big ideas" to enhance teaching and student learning', *Teachers and Teaching* 23(5): 596–610. Doi: 10.1080/13540602.2016.1218328.

Oates, T. (2010) *Could Do Better: Using international comparisons to refine the National Curriculum in England*. Cambridge: University of Cambridge Local Examinations Syndicate. Available online: cambridgeassessment.org.uk/Images/112281-could-do-better-using-international-comparisons-to-refine-the-national-curriculum-in-england.pdf (accessed 20 December 2021).

Ofsted (2021) *Research Review Series: Religious education*. Available online: gov.uk/government/publications/research-review-series-religious-education/research-review-series-religious-education (accessed 20 December 2021).

Olson, J. K. (2008) 'Concept-focused teaching: Using big ideas to guide instruction in science.' *Science and Children* 46(4): 45–49.

Osborne, J. (2007) 'Science education for the twenty first century', *Eurasia Journal of Mathematics, Science & Technology Education* 3(3): 173–184.

Parker-Jenkins, M., Harta, D. and Irving, B. A. (2005) *In Good Faith: Schools, religion and public funding*. Aldershot: Ashgate.

Parker-Jenkins, M., Glenn, M. and Janmaat, J. G. (2014) *Reaching In, Reaching Out: Faith schools, community engagement, and 21st-century skills for intercultural understanding*. London: Institute of Education Press.

Pearce, J., Stones, A., Reiss, M. J. and Mujtaba, T. (2021) '"Science is purely about the truth so I don't think you could compare it to non-truth versus the truth": Students' perceptions of religion and science, and the relationship(s) between them: religious education and the need for epistemic literacy'. *British Journal of Religious Education* 43(2): 174–189. Doi: 10.1080/01416200.2019.1635434.

Pring, R. (2018) *The Future of Publicly Funded Faith Schools: A critical perspective*. London: Routledge.

Reiss, M. J. (2009) 'Imagining the world: The significance of religious worldviews for science education', *Science & Education* 18: 783–796. Doi: 10.1007/s11191-007-9091-9.

Reiss, M. J. (2011) 'How should creationism and intelligent design be dealt with in the classroom?' *Journal of Philosophy of Education* 45: 399–415.

Reiss, M. J. (2014) 'What place does science have in an aims-based curriculum?' *School Science Review* 95(352): 9–14.

Reiss, M. J. (2018) 'Worldviews in biology education', in K. Kampourakis and M. J. Reiss (eds) *Teaching Biology in Schools: Global research, issues, and trends* (263–274). New York: Routledge.

Rowe, W. L. (2005) 'Agnosticism', in E. Craig (ed.) *The Shorter Routledge Encyclopedia of Philosophy* (10). London: Routledge.

Smyth, E., Lyons, M. and Darmody, M. (2013) (eds) *Religious Education in a Multicultural Europe: Children, parents and schools*. Basingstoke: Palgrave Macmillan.

Stones, A. and Fraser-Pearce, J. (2021) 'Some pupils should know better (because there is better knowledge than opinion). Interim findings from an empirical study of pupils' and teachers' understandings of knowledge and big questions in religious education'. *Journal of Religious Education* 69: 353–366. Doi: 10.1007/s40839-021-00155-5.

Taber, K. S. (2013) 'Conceptual frameworks, metaphysical commitments and worldviews: The challenge of reflecting the relationships between science and religion in science education', in N. Mansour and R. Wegerif (eds) *Science Education for Diversity* (152–177). Dordrecht: Springer. Doi: 10.1007/978-94-007-4563-6_8.

Watson, B. (2012) 'Why religious education matters', in L. P. Barnes, *Debates in Religious Education* (13–21). London: Routledge.

Wilkinson, M. (2018) *The Genealogy of Terror: How to distinguish between Islam, Islamism and Islamist extremism*. London: Routledge.

Wintersgill, B. (ed.) (2017) *Big Ideas for Religious Education*. Exeter: University of Exeter. Available online: http://socialsciences.exeter.ac.uk/media/universityofexeter/collegeofsocialsciencesandinternationalstudies/education/research/groupsandnetworks/reandspiritualitynetwork/Big_Ideas_for_RE_E-Book.pdf (accessed 20 December 2021).

9
TURNING TO WORLDVIEWS EDUCATION INSTEAD OF RELIGION – HELPFUL SOLUTION OR EVEN MORE PROBLEMS?

A perspective from Germany

Friedrich Schweitzer

Introduction

On the occasion of the publication of the report 'Religion and Worldviews: The Way Forward: A national plan for RE' (Commission on Religious Education 2018) I was asked to contribute a brief response to this document (Schweitzer 2019).[1] In the meantime, a lively discussion about the CoRE Report has ensued, chiefly in the United Kingdom but also elsewhere. Independently of CoRE the topic of worldview education has been discussed in a number of countries and contexts in religious education (cf. Valk 2007; van der Kooij et al. 2016; Riegel and Delling 2019). In a few cases, authors from countries outside the UK have joined the discussion, for example, from Scandinavia (Bråten and Everington 2019). My own approach in this chapter should be viewed against the backdrop of its German authorship, not only in terms of my obvious lack of first-hand familiarity with the praxis of religious education in the United Kingdom but also in terms of the perspective used in this chapter. From a point of view outside the United Kingdom certain developments may be more salient than from within the country itself. To just mention one example: it seems that the issue of freedom of religion and correspondingly, of the relationship between state and religion implied by the construction of religion-related subjects at state-sponsored schools has not been receiving the attention it deserves in the United Kingdom discussion concerning CoRE. From the perspective of an outsider this is not only surprising but might indicate a serious lacuna in this debate. It should be clear from the beginning, however, that I have no intention of making German religious education the benchmark by which British religious education (or the new subject suggested by CoRE) could or should be measured. Such imperialist attempts have never proven to be helpful in the past and most likely, they will not be helpful in the future either.

In my earlier statement (Schweitzer 2019) I raised a number of questions which I want to repeat here as well because they may give readers a better understanding of my observations in what follows:

- What implications, for example, concerning the role of the state vis-à-vis religion and religious freedom does a centralised statutory curriculum, as suggested by CoRE, entail?
- Why does CoRE foresee a central role for school inspection (Ofsted) in improving religious education (or 'Religion and Worldviews') but not for educational research?
- Is there really a necessary relationship between the changes needed at system level concerning the curriculum and supervision of religious education on the one hand and changing from religious education to Religion and Worldviews on the other?
- Is it possible to improve (initial) teacher training which CoRE considers especially weak in its present shape, without clearly identifying an institutionally defined field of expertise and academic study to which the training should be related?

One may of course raise the question of whether a non-UK person should feel qualified to discuss critically a British report. It is certainly true that I am not familiar with the complex functioning of politics and school administration in the United Kingdom. Yet as indicated by the recent discussion on international knowledge transfer in religious education (see Manifesto 2019; Schweitzer and Schreiner 2021), more and more the future of this academic discipline should intentionally combine both attention and sensitivity to the regional and national contextuality of religious education as well as international research results from other countries and from international debates in the field of religious education. In other words, the future development of religious education has become an international issue, especially in Europe (quite independently of the European Union). The internationalisation of this discussion corresponds to the insight that decisions about religious education should be based on 'scientific' analysis and empirical research which can no longer be seen as limited to one's own country. Moreover, international-comparative aspects should also play a role, as a broader basis for considered judgments. From my perspective this holds true although, surprisingly, CoRE itself does not make reference to such considerations but presents itself as a document arising from a broad but only national context and drafted by a committee bringing together voices exclusively from the United Kingdom.

Facing the reality of religious education

It is probably fair to say that CoRE presents a picture of religious education in England which, in its critical clarity, surpasses all earlier readings I have encountered so far. While Gates and Jackson (2014: 83) report that the reality of religious education in England is commonly viewed as 'patchy', ranging from the excellent to the 'unsatisfactory' and Conroy et al. (2013) raise serious questions concerning its effectiveness, CoRE goes much further. Religious education is shown to be in poor condition, existing in ways which are lacking in dignity and which make it impossible to recognise or to develop the true potentials of the subject. For CoRE, the immediate consequence of such observations is that there is no more hope or use for improvements. Instead, the subject must change its very identity, from religious education to Religion and Worldviews.

The authors of the Report deserve praise for looking into the obviously serious problems religious education has to face in Britain today – being taught by teachers who have not been trained to do so, suffering from confusing aims or, even more, from being devalued altogether (for example, by being excluded from the EBacc subjects) and from coping with an increasing number of students who are disinterested in any kind of religious education. Since I consider children's right to religion and religious education a human right (cf. Schweitzer 2017), I can happily agree with CoRE's plea for acknowledging education in the area of religion and worldviews as a clear entitlement of all children. This positive impression concerning CoRE's willingness to face up to the dire reality of religious education in Britain is, however, counteracted by the use CoRE itself makes of this description. It does not serve as a starting point for careful analysis of the reasons behind the current unsatisfactory situation but immediately is made the stepping stone for recommending the transformation of the subject. This procedure fits best in a political arena where persuasion is key, not with empirical analysis where all hypotheses have to be tested and refined before they are allowed to be used as premises for further conclusions. Or, to put it differently, CoRE's way of arguing appears to be more rhetorical and psychological than logical. It is not possible, at least logically, to derive a particular new model from the shortcomings of the model it is supposed to replace. Many other options for a new model would be possible as well. For CoRE's model to be considered convincing must depend on the reasons offered for it.

From an international perspective one might also add to CoRE's evaluation of the deplorable situation of religious education that there have been very few empirical studies surveying the actual development and the quality of religious education in Britain. While empirical research has played a certain role in religious education in the United Kingdom (most of all through the well-known studies conducted by Leslie Francis and his teams), broader surveys and empirical investigations of its reality and effectiveness have remained rare (cf. as a recent exception Conroy et al. 2013; overview Schweitzer and Boschki 2018). The lack of such studies might well also be considered part of the problems which religious education is faced with today. In terms of the international discussion in general education as well as in religious education, it is now more and more taken for granted that the further development and improvement of schools and school subjects should be based on reliable empirical data. A true 'way forward' (as CoRE claims for itself) can hardly be identified as long as the map of the territory one wants to go through is at best a rough sketch. A first conclusion (which CoRE does not offer) could have been to identify the need for more representative research in order to get a better understanding of the current situation with its problems.

It is easy to see – and in spite of the questions raised so far – and also has to be admired that CoRE wants to take the shortcomings of religious education as it is presently taught not only seriously but also aims for identifying solutions which go beyond just patching up a situation that has become untenable. In other words, the attempt to change the whole system in order to guarantee thorough and long-lasting effects deserves praise and approval. The three main changes refer to a statutory curriculum, mandatory supervision by Ofsted, and a new wider scope for the subject in order to include religious as well as non-religious worldviews. In addition to this, the question of improving initial and advanced teacher education is addressed, though with less determination. While the basic intention makes much sense the concrete suggestions raise a number of further questions, beginning with the concept of worldview.

A compromised concept: The historical burden of 'worldview education'

The two most prominent examples of 'worldview education' (in German, *Weltanschauungsunterricht*) can be found with National Socialism and the

State Socialism of the GDR. The worldviews were different in both cases – National Socialist ideology or Marxism-Leninism – but the understanding of the educational task was quite similar. Pupils were to be 'educated' into the respective worldview, preferably such that they would become deeply convinced of its uncontestable truth. Later on, this kind of education – if it can be called education in any serious sense – was identified as indoctrination since it clearly bypassed any attempt of the pupils to critically assess what they were taught. In many ways, the two systems of worldview education can be viewed as the clearest examples of indoctrination through school and education in the western world, at least in the twentieth century but probably beyond as well.

In the German speaking countries the concept of 'worldview' has never recovered from this abuse, especially in education. In spite of its philosophical meaning and origins which cannot be reduced to its later ideological abuse, it would not occur to anyone who wishes to be taken seriously in the field of education, to suggest reintroducing 'worldview education'. Both historical types of worldview education functioned in parallel ways to making a totalitarian worldview the basis not only of all politics but, specifically, of education at school. This is why the German term *Weltanschauung* continues to be used in a descriptive manner but could hardly be found attractive as the designation of a (new) school subject in the twenty-first century. In other countries, for example in Norway, the concept of 'worldview' also carries with it a special history (cf. Bråten and Everington 2019). Even today, it remains tied to the Humanists as a group opposing the influence of the church and of Christianity. Parallels to this may also be found in other countries, among others again in Germany. The values pursued by these groups as stated in their mission statements typically remain vague, for example, by referring to 'science' and 'reason' as their basis.

Now, one could possibly argue that such historical legacies and burdens should not affect the discussion in the United Kingdom where neither National Socialism nor state socialism could take hold and where the Humanists are a small minority. It is certainly possible to take such a stance if one limits oneself to the United Kingdom. Yet in times of internationalisation and globalisation it has become harder to show no awareness of the international discussion. Moreover, the question may be raised if and what can possibly be learned from other countries. Why is 'worldview education' such a sensitive matter? Understood in today's sense, worldviews differ from other content, in that they offer a comprehensive interpretation of the world, its character and meaning. This interpretation includes the person who might take over the respective worldview, not only in terms of shaping that person's outlooks and understandings but – at least in many cases – also her or his lifestyle. In other words, the adoption of worldviews may have far-reaching consequences. At the same time, they may claim to be based on science (as in the case of socialist worldviews in the GDR or the Humanists today) but, upon closer scrutiny, it is unscientific beliefs they are based upon. It is easy to see that any combination of modern understandings of education and worldview education is intrinsically difficult and problematic. Most philosophers of education can probably only endorse the critical analysis or deconstruction of worldviews an adequate task for education – an assumption which does not seem to be shared by CoRE even where it refers to the 'critical' study of worldviews (2018: 35).

Worldview education and the issue of freedom of religion

Freedom of religion is one of the core human rights. The importance of religious freedom is no coincidence. It reflects the history of the relationship between religion and the state as well as the especially sensitive nature of this relationship. Religion is not an uncontroversial subject. It has never been uncontroversial throughout history, especially concerning the role of the state vis-à-vis religion. For a long time, it was considered legitimate for the state to regulate religious adherence, practices and even convictions of its citizens. The road to individual freedom of religion, now considered a core human right, has been long, and even today this right is not secured in many countries. Modern democracies are premised on freedom of religion which, in turn, excludes any attempt of the state to interfere with religious adherence, practices and convictions, unless it can be shown that they infringe upon the freedom of others.

The need for the democratic state to abstain from setting religious agendas also applies to state-sponsored education. In many ways, state-maintained schools can even be considered the true test case for religious freedom, in that pupils often have no choice but to attend such schools and because religious or irreligious influences in childhood and adolescence may well have lasting effects even in later life. This is the background against which the different models for guaranteeing religious freedom at school in different countries have to be understood, sometimes even implying that there should be no religious education in state-supported schools at all, as in France or in the United States of America. Other countries like Germany rely on a complex system of internal limitations for state influence on religious education, for example, by not allowing the state to determine the curriculum. In Britain, SACREs can be seen to fulfil a similar function by putting the syllabi in the hands of various non-state actors. Still other countries like, most of all, Sweden and, more recently the Canton of Zurich in Switzerland as well as Luxemburg, have opted for a type of teaching about religion based on complete neutrality of the subject concerning religion and worldviews.

It is this neutrality-based model which now seems to be preferred by CoRE as well. The suggestion is for a centralised small group of a 'maximum of nine professionals' to be in charge of the future of Religious Education (or Religion and Worldviews) (2018: 39). The SACREs are not to be abolished but to be transformed into a 'Local Advisory Network' (2018: 56). Yet questions of state influence which could be clearly strengthened at the expense of other stakeholders in the new model are not even considered by CoRE in this context. The only issue which is discussed concerning such implications is the right of withdrawal which the commission, rather 'reluctantly', wants to see upheld (2018: 67).

CoRE also does not consider the experiences which other countries have had with the neutral model of religious education. In Sweden, for example, this model was introduced about 50 years ago, yet it seems that the goal of neutrality has not really been achieved. One of the most recent investigations concerning Swedish religious education points towards serious breaches of neutrality because the allegedly 'neutral Religious Education' appears to teach Swedish pupils that being Swedish means being neutral and consequently, non-religious (cf. Kittelmann Flensner 2015). In other words, religious neutrality is equated with being non-religious and has turned religious education into a non-neutral subject – a tendency which, in Britain, was critically foreseen by Terence Copley (2005). In Luxemburg a new model with a focus on social cohesion was introduced as a replacement for traditional religious education. While neutrality is one of the aims the new subject is striving for, it seems that, in reality, it has led to an exclusion of religious topics altogether (cf. Ehret 2018). In a less spectacular sense the alternative subject of Ethics in Germany can also be quoted here. While Ethics is supposed to provide pupils with knowledge concerning religions by teaching about religions in a neutral manner, respective syllabi in fact indicate a receding attention to religion compared to philosophical topics and worldviews. So-called neutral models do not appear to be a good way to achieve quality religious education, at least judging from these experiences.

Moreover, what is the message of the neutrality-based model for minorities, for example, for Muslim children and their families? Is it due to their presence in Britain, they may wonder, that the system now has to switch to neutrality instead of allowing them a voice of their own, for example, by offering Islamic religious education as in a growing number of other European countries? From their point of view, the preference of neutral models may well appear as a tacit strategy to exclude them from equal rights.

To say it again, in all these respects my considerations should not be taken to mean that a certain model from another country should be adopted for Britain. Such transfers have never worked. Yet it would make sense to look at what experiences with similar models as the one suggested by CoRE are available and how they can be evaluated, among others in terms of how religion is treated in these models and of how effectively they support freedom of religion. That this question cannot be avoided becomes visible once one looks at what decisions about content imply, for religious education as well as for Religion and Worldviews.

The challenge of making decisions about content

The question of freedom of religion and state neutrality is not only a matter of *how* a subject is to be taught. Before that come decisions about *what* should be taught. What is important enough to be included in a syllabus and what not? And who should have the authority to make such decisions? As can be illustrated by another example from Germany, the introduction of a religiously neutral new subject in Brandenburg for teaching about 'Life Style-Ethics-Religious Studies' (LER, cf. Edelstein et al. 2001) in the 1990s, raises controversial questions. More concretely, the state of Brandenburg saw, in its initial syllabus, a need to teach pupils about which religions or worldviews are valuable for the future and which ones are not. Again, a clear breach of neutrality, in that the state claimed an authoritative role concerning different religions and worldviews. Moreover, how much space and time should be allotted to a particular religion or worldview? It is hardly possible to assume that the answer to this question can be given on neutral grounds. One may point to rules like the ones set by the British 1988 Education Act (the syllabus 'shall reflect the fact that the religious traditions in Great Britain are in the main Christian whilst taking account of the teaching and practices of the other principal religions represented in Great Britain'). Yet can British history, which has led to this kind of representation, really justify privileging certain religions over others? How can such privileging be reconciled with the claim to neutrality? In a similar way, the Norwegian state was taken to court because of privileging Christianity in the syllabus for a mandatory subject on Religion (a legal controversy addressed by CoRE, 2018: 65).

Such examples indicate that the principle of neutrality should neither be considered the solution to all problems nor should it be automatically considered the preferable principle for democracies. This consideration becomes more concrete once one turns to the question of which worldviews should be taught in school and whose worldviews these would be. As pointed out above, CoRE's reliance on the term worldview is surprising in that it shows no awareness of the historical contexts compromising this term, especially in connection with education. The Report points to the German *Weltanschauung* as the origin of the English neologism worldview (2018: 4) but neither National Socialism nor state socialism are even mentioned. This also explains why the content of respective worldviews promulgated by these regimes – racism, antisemitism, presumed superiority of the 'Aryans' in the case of National Socialism, materialism, superiority of the working class, the 'socialist personality' in the case of socialism – are not mentioned either. Had the Report done so it would also have been obliged to address the problematic nature of certain worldviews and consequently, the need for making critical judgments in this respect. Only by limiting itself to referring to worldview as a category in the abstract is it possible for CoRE to stay in line with its claim to neutrality. In other words, the correct observation of CoRE that today's situation can be characterised as diverse in respect to religions and worldviews, obviously is not enough. It should also be stated what limits are needed within this diversity concerning the hostility and bigotry of others. Antisemitism and hostility to Islam can also be called worldviews. Yet the Report remains silent about them (with the certain exception of 'extremism', but only in the context of what is criticised as 'a lack of understanding of worldviews' (2018: 28), which makes readers wonder if CoRE's understanding of worldview is limited to its benign varieties while problematic forms which often are more challenging in the context of education, are not taken account of.

In short, introducing a school subject called Religion and Worldviews automatically raises the question of which worldviews should be treated and who is responsible for their selection and presentation. Concerning the choice of worldviews to be addressed in school, the report tries to be as open as possible – excluding, however, one of the clearest examples of an explicit worldview, i.e. Communism, which, surprisingly, the report does not want to acknowledge as a worldview to be included in Religion and Worldviews (2018: 75) – possibly due to the respective discussions in the 1960s and 1970s when Marxism claimed a place in British schools next to Christianity and other religions. Yet on what grounds can

Marxism be excluded if it understands itself as a worldview? Who should have the authority for such exclusion? What are the criteria applied by the Report?

The obvious problem remains, of which worldviews deserve a place in the curriculum and what qualifies the encounter with them as educational. What should be the criteria for treating worldviews in school? And of no less importance, what does education mean in relationship to different worldviews? Again, the report remains rather vague in this respect, referring to 'refinement' as the aim of Religion and Worldviews (2018: 5): '... young people come to a more refined understanding of their own worldview'. What does this mean concerning, for example, fundamentalism and ethnocentrism, racism or, to mention some examples from different fields, neo-liberalism and evolutionism? How can they be 'refined'? Is 'refinement' an adequate aim in the case of 'prejudice and discrimination' (2018: 28)? It is obvious that CoRE does not have in mind that education should function according to such worldviews. Yet nevertheless, any decision concerning the content of teaching and the criteria applied in teaching is neither obvious nor innocent. All choices and selections of topics should be transparent, democratic and based on participatory procedures. Moreover, they should be informed by scientific analysis concerning both the respective worldviews themselves (including their implications for society) as well as education referring to worldviews.

Cooling (2020) argues that most objections against using the term worldview along with religion (as CoRE suggests) can also be raised against the concept of religion. Upon first glance, this seems to be indeed the case but in the context of education it is not convincing, for at least two reasons: From the perspective of sociological functionalism, worldviews and religions may appear the same. Yet as soon as one goes into more detail concerning the actual contents of both, which is inevitable for purposes of teaching, this functionalist interpretation turns out to be too undifferentiated. As has become clear above, not all religions and worldviews are the same!

Moreover, and more importantly, in the case of religion and religious education a number of checks and balances have been developed which are meant to prevent any infringement upon religious freedom. For this purpose, different countries have developed a whole variety of legal and systemic precautions which, in spite of the differences between them, follow the same logic of avoiding the privileging of a particular religious conviction by the state. Some of these regulations also include worldviews, but only in terms of legal protection for individuals and not on a systemic level. Such systemic regulations typically refer to the institutional level, concerning churches or other religious bodies. On the whole, in spite of the existence of institutional worldviews to which CoRE refers as one of the varieties under discussion, there are no equivalents for this in the field of worldviews, with the possible exception aspired to by Humanist associations.

Educational limits of neutrality in working with children and youth

In many countries, there is a tendency towards limiting religious education at school to neutrality and to 'teaching about religion'. This tendency also is reflective of the wish to make sure that the principle of freedom of religion is not infringed upon by state influence. Yet it is also evident that, in working with children and young people and in doing justice to their personal and existential questions and needs, teaching about religion is not enough. In England, Grimmitt's (1987) idea of introducing the additional dimension of 'learning from religion' has become a widely accepted basis for including more personal ways of dealing with religion or religions and worldviews. Similar tendencies can be found in many European countries (cf. the overview: Rothgangel, Jäggle and Schlag 2016 and the other volumes in this series). Moreover, it has been shown that teachers of religious education in various countries actually do not follow the schematic distinction between 'teaching about' and 'teaching from' or 'teaching religion' (cf. Ziebertz and Riegel 2009). The realities of the everyday classroom seem to require more openness and flexibility than the abstract ideas of neutral teaching allow for.

CoRE does not seem to take notice of such research results and developments, possibly because they come from other countries. Yet is it really still convincing in this day and age to only consider British experiences? Could it not be helpful, in the sense of the international knowledge transfer described above, to make use of international insights as well?

A school subject with no academic basis

In most cases in most countries and for most of history, the school curriculum has followed the idea that school subjects should be clearly related to a delineated field of study at university level, like English, Mathematics, Chemistry, History, etc. This does not only imply that teachers should have studied their fields of teaching at an academic level and should be certified in their expertise by respective degrees but that the content of the curriculum for a school subject should have a basis beyond school and beyond school administration or politics. This includes transparent criteria for what should be considered adequate for teaching and what not. This understanding does not exclude further developments, like combining different fields of study in order to create new school subjects. Yet it should always be clear what academic expertise is underlying a school subject.

Such an academic underpinning is a requirement of educational quality. This presupposition corresponds to another basic principle endorsed by modern philosophy of education – the requirement that the knowledge taught at school should be in line with the current state of scientific and educational research. While research as such is commonly not considered suitable for children and adolescents because it follows a logic different from that of teaching and learning at primary and secondary level, all knowledge taught at school should have been tested against the current state of research. Concerning the Bible, for example, it would not be legitimate according to this principle for pupils to still be taught that many parts of the Old Testament were written between 1000 and 500 B.C. Nor would it be acceptable if the understanding of evolution taught at school were still to follow the outdated assumption that certain traits or abilities acquired by parents which are of advantage for their survival will be passed on to future generations. On a more pragmatic level, the relationship between individual school subjects and academic disciplines opens up a field of public critical discussion which can be quite beneficial in that it prevents political committees from drawing up syllabi merely at will.

It is exactly this point which CoRE tries to circumvent by referring to quality training for teachers. But CoRE remains silent about which disciplinary expertise this would in fact require and how this expertise could in fact be obtained. There is agreement that there is no single academic discipline which is devoted to the study of worldviews. Consequently, worldview education is lacking an academic basis which would be comparable to other subjects. This lack is another reason why the subject would be vulnerable to political and ideological influences. One can of course point to the numerous disciplines in which the topic of worldviews has played a role – philosophy, anthropology, sociology, religious studies, Christian theology and Biblical studies as well as other disciplines (cf. Benoit et al. 2020) – yet it is hard to imagine that any one of these disciplines treats this topic as more than one of many topics. The lack of a clear relationship between worldview education and an academic discipline also entails consequences for teacher education which, because of their importance, deserve attention of their own.

How to train teachers for worldview education?

As already mentioned in the context of the foundations for instituting a school subject, in most countries it is assumed that teaching a certain subject should be based on respective expertise and that this expertise should or even must have been acquired in certified ways. The place for certified acquisition of such expertise is the field of higher education, i.e. universities or at least a teachers' college. How can such expertise be acquired concerning worldviews?

It makes sense that CoRE takes major offence at the current situation in Britain in which teachers of religious education often have no adequate training and have never acquired a degree in anything even close to religion. Yet if it is true that teachers lacking adequate expertise is one of the factors causing the problem, should the solution not also aim for clear provisions for the future in this respect? Where could and should a future teacher acquire expertise in Religion and Worldviews? As mentioned above, there are a whole number of different fields of study which have addressed topics related to this context – theology, philosophy, religious studies, sociology, psychology, cultural studies, ethnography, to mention just a few. CoRE remains vague in this respect, which is why it can be feared (or even argued) that the future of teacher education for the new suggested subject Religion and Worldviews does not look very bright. Instead, the confusion concerning the required expertise might just continue or could even increase, since the term worldview is even less defined than the term religion, especially concerning the academic expertise to be acquired for teaching it. Will it be enough for a teacher of Religion and Worldviews to have studied 'something' that touches upon worldviews? What expertise and which degrees in what fields will be considered acceptable? As long as such questions remain undiscussed, the possible shape of a new subject, Religion and Worldviews, remains vague, in general but also in terms of its possible realisation in schools.

How religious education could be improved without giving up the subject

CoRE seems to assume that religious education in its current form is beyond hope (for a new subject is being proposed in its place), therefore it is important to consider ways of improving religious education without losing it. Since religious education is not the only subject which has come to be viewed critically, for example, in the light of the results of international studies like PISA, it makes sense to consider the options which have been developed for improving their situation.

The most widespread possibility for improving the situation of a subject is based on the recommendation that teaching not only in general but in all subjects should have a stronger research base. In most cases, this implies empirical research, for example, examining different teaching strategies and their effectiveness concerning pupils' actual learning or competence development (for religion-related subjects cf. the contributions in Schweitzer and Boschki 2018). Moreover, the demand is that teachers should be familiar with research results and actually make use of them in designing their teaching. Surprisingly, CoRE does not show much interest in such expertise for teachers, not in the case of religious education nor concerning the academic qualification of teachers for the new subject recommended by CoRE. Indeed, there seems to be a certain scepticism towards research throughout the Report in general. The research on religious education itself is not quoted and no role for research is foreseen in the wished-for new subject.

CoRE claims to listen to a wide range of stakeholders. Yet it is easy to see that this is not identical with research-related insights upon which recommendations could be based. Internationally speaking, there is a clear tendency that evaluations of a subject as well as recommendations for its future development should not only be based, for example, on school inspection or even subjective evidence which often remains anecdotal, but should more and more rely on transparent and intersubjective investigations and scientific data. While CoRE claims to be based on research, this research is not really identified. As mentioned above, research on religious education allowing for generalisable results and robust insights has remained particularly rare in Britain. Might this be one of the reasons for the deplorable situation of religious education described and criticised by CoRE? If this holds true one may wonder why this should not also be changed in the future, quite independently of the designation and scope of the subject. Good teaching should be informed by research. Good school inspection needs to have a scientific basis it can rely upon.

May one then not also foresee a different future for religious education in Britain (and in other countries) as well? Should it not be possible to foresee a future existence for religious education, with a clear focus on religion(s) instead of a diffuse mixture of religions and undefined worldviews? This does not mean that worldviews – religious as well as non-religious worldviews – should not be addressed in religious education (see Barnes 2020: 108–110) or in other subjects, for example, in history or social studies (and its equivalents). Yet it must always be clear from what perspective they are being addressed and for what reasons particular worldviews are selected.

The challenges identified by CoRE concerning the status of religious education in schools are convincing. It does not make sense to continue with commitments and practices that ensure that it cannot flourish. There is a clear need for well-grounded curricular improvements and for better teacher education. Yet this could certainly be done without giving up the current balance between state and non-state influence on the subject and without taking up the rather ill-defined and compromised category of worldviews for renaming the subject.

In conclusion, I want to repeat my praise and agreement. Access to education concerning religion is a human right and indeed an entitlement of all children. This is what religious education should stand for, now as well as in the future.

Note

1 This chapter builds on my earlier article (Schweitzer 2019). It incorporates passages from this article but expands and elaborates the argument in the light of the later discussion about the Report and introduces additional material and research results.

References

Barnes, L. P. (2020) *Crisis, Controversy and the Future of Religious Education*. London: Routledge.

Benoit, C., Hutchings, T. and Shillitoe, R. (2020) *Worldview: A multidisciplinary report*. Religious Education Council of England and Wales.

Bråten, O. M. H. and Everington, J. (2019) 'Issues in the integration of religious education and worldviews education in an intercultural context', *Intercultural Education* 30(3): 289–305. Doi: 10.1080/14675986.2018.1539307.

Commission on Religious Education (CoRE) (2018) *Final Report: Religions and worldviews: the way forward*. Available online: commissiononre.org.uk/wp-content/uploads/2018/09/Final-Report-of-the-Commission-on-RE.pdf (accessed 6 December 2021).

Conroy, J. C., Lundie, D., Davis, R. A., Baumfield, V., Barnes, L. P., Gallagher, T., Lowden, K., Bourque, N. and Wenell, K. (2013) *Does Religious Education Work? A multi-dimensional investigation*. London: Bloomsbury.

Cooling, T. 2020. 'Worldview in religious education: Autobiographical reflections on the Commission on Religious Education in England final report'. *British Journal of Religious Education* 42(4): 403–414. Doi: 10.1080/01416200.2020.1764497.

Copley. T. (2005) *Indoctrination, Education and God: The struggle for the mind*. London: SPCK.

Edelstein, W., Grözinger, K. E., Gruehn, S., Hillerich, I., Kirsch, B., Leschinsky, A., Lott, J. and Oser. F. (2001). *Lebensgestaltung – Ethik – Religionskunde: Zur Grundlegung eines neuen Schulfachs; Analysen und Empfehlungen, vorgelegt vom Wissenschaftlichen Beirat LER*. Weinheim and Basel: Beltz.

Ehret, J. (2018) *Das Fach 'Leben und Gesellschaft' an den öffentlichen Schulen in Luxemburg. (K)eine Alternative zum Religionsunterricht?* Sankt Augustin & Berlin: Konrad-Adenauer-Stiftung.

Gates, B. and Jackson, J. (2014) 'Religion and education in England', in *Religious Education at Schools in Europe. Part 2: Western Europe*, edited by M. Rothgangel, R. Jackson and M. Jäggle (65–98). Göttingen: V&R Unipress.

Grimmitt, M. (1987) *Religious Education and Human Development. The relationship between studying religions and personal, social and moral education.* Great Wakering, Essex: McCrimmons.

Kittelmann Flensner, Karin (2015) *Religious Education in Contemporary Pluralistic Sweden.* Gothenburg: University of Gothenburg.

Manifesto (2019) 'International knowledge transfer in religious education: A manifesto for discussion', *Zeitschrift für Pädagogik und Theologie* 71(1): 90–95. Doi.org/10.1515/zpt-2019-0013.

Riegel, U. and Delling, S. (2019) 'Dealing with worldviews in religious education', *Journal of Beliefs & Values* 40(4): 403–415. Doi: 10.1080/13617672.2019.1618150.

Rothgangel, M., Jäggle, M. and Schlag, T. (eds) (2016) *Religious Education at Schools in Europe. Part 1: Central Europe.* Göttingen: V&R Academic.

Schweitzer, F. (2017) 'Children's right to religion in educational perspective', in *The Bloomsbury Reader in Religion and Childhood*, edited by A. Strhan, S. G. Parker and S. B. Ridgely (181–189). London and New York: Bloomsbury.

Schweitzer, F. (2019) 'Sacrificing Cinderella: Will giving up religious education help to establish a more promising successor?' *Journal of Beliefs & Values* 39(4): 516–522. Doi: 10.1080/13617672.2018.1542792.

Schweitzer, F. and Boschki, R. (eds) (2018) *Researching Religious Education: Classroom processes and outcomes.* Münster and New York: Waxmann.

Schweitzer, F. and Schreiner P. (eds) (2021) *International Knowledge Transfer in Religious Education.* Münster and New York: Waxmann.

Valk, J. (2007) 'Plural public schooling: Religion, worldviews and moral education', *British Journal of Religious Education* 29(3): 273–285. Doi.org/10.1080/01416200701479661.

Van der Kooij, Jacomijn C., de Ruyter, D. and Siebren Miedema, S. (2017) 'The merits of using "worldview" in religious education', *Religious Education* 112(2): 172–184. Doi: 10.1080/00344087.2016.1191410.

Ziebertz, H-G. and Riegel, U. (eds) (2009) *How Teachers in Europe Teach Religion: An international empirical study in 16 countries.* Berlin and Münster: LIT.

INDEX

Abrahamic traditions 106
academies 2, 6, 41, 47, 73, 101, 115n1
Aerts, Diederik 158
Agnew, Lord 6
agnosticism 83, 84, 102, 154, 155, 164
Agreed Syllabus, 1944 Education Act 45
Agreed Syllabus Conferences (ASCs) 7, 8, 26, 36, 41, 47–48, 59–60, 64, 66, 70, 71, 74
Agreed Syllabuses Committees 7
All Party Parliamentary Group on Religious Education 37n23
Alton, Lord 6
Anglican Church *see* Church of England
anomalies 80–81, 90, 95
Anselm, St. 52
antisemitism 177
Archimedes 51–52
ARE (Association of Religious Education) 68
Aristotle 157
ASCs (Agreed Syllabus Conferences) 7, 8, 26, 36, 41, 47–48, 59–60, 64, 66, 70, 71, 74
Association of Christian Teachers 62–63
Association of Religious Education (ARE) 68

ATCRE (Association of Teachers of Catholic R.E.) 34
atheism 83–84, 102, 120, 131, 134, 154, 155, 164
attentiveness 109–110, 111–112, 113, 115
Augustine, St. 52
Ayer, A. J. 120, 122

Baha'i faith 63, 83
Barnes, L. P. 102–103; critique of CoRE report 154–157
belief 47, 110
Benoit, C. 154
Big Ideas approach: RE (religious education) 22–23, 36, 152, 161–164; science education 152, 161, 164
Birmingham Agreed Syllabuses 8; 1975 48, 69; 1995 48; 2007 42, 48, 49, 74; 2020 74
bliks 121–122
Board of Deputies 6, 24
Board schools 72
Bourdieu, P. 57
Brine, A. 34
British values 72, 132–133, 134
Buddhism 63, 83, 88
Butler Act *see* Education Act 1944

calls for evidence, CoRE (Commission on Religious Education) 20
Carr, David 58

Catholic Church 35, 61
Catholic Education Service 6, 26, 37n3
Catholic schools 6, 25, 131
Central Schools Services Block (CSSB) 65
Chater, Mark 2, 13–14, 34
Chichester project 138
Children and Worldviews Project (Erriker) 141, 154
Chivers-Tharani, Amira 37n17
Christian Education Movement 93
Christianity 83, 85, 88, 93, 119, 126–127, 131, 133; and the 1944 Education Act 43, 45, 46; and the changing religious landscape 91, 92; Christian denominations and SACREs (Standing Advisory Councils on Religious Education) 65–66; Christian groups responding to CoRE 63; and creationism 160–161; decline of 136; as heritage 134; and indoctrination 134; persecution of Christians 6; Victorian period 139
Church of England 35, 68, 75; and the 1944 Education Act 45; Durham Commission 63; education office 20; *see also* National Society of the Church of England
Clarke, C. 31, 37n3, 40
classical models of RE (religious education) 136, 137–138, 139–149
climate change 158, 159
Cobern, Bill 158
coerced religion 134
'cognitive load' theory 24, 33
Cole, Owen 68
collective worship (CW) 41, 45–46, 67, 73
Commission on Religious Education *see* CoRE (Commission on Religious Education)
Communism 177
comparative religion 50
complacency, of critics of the 1944 Education Act 43, 47–49
complexity: and the name change 27–29; and the othering of faith 24–27; 'the complex turn' 21–24
concept-cracking model of RE 138
Confucianism 83, 145

Conroy, James 58, 94, 171
conscience clause 139
consensuality, of the 1944 Education Act 43, 47–49
consultation process of CoRE (Commission on Religious Education), Religious Education Council for England and Wales 19–20
Continuous Professional Development (CPD) 65–66, 91
Cooling, Trevor 9, 12, 14, 30–31, 33, 37n17, 77, 78–79, 82, 84, 85, 87, 89–90, 95, 100, 127–129, 131, 136, 154, 178
Copley, Terence 175
Copson, Andrew 37n21
CoRE (Commission on Religious Education) 18, 40, 99–103, 136–137, 169–170; Barnes' critique of 154–157; campaigns in support of 5, 8; and coherence 9–10; CoRE definition of worldviews 11, 29, 101, 137, 145, 153; DfE (Department for Education) response to 32; Initial Teacher Education and Continuous Professional Development 65, 66; insider perspective on 18–36; *Interim Report: Religious education for all.* (2017) 4–5, 20, 21; introduction and overview 4–8; methodology and consultation processes 19–21; neutrality-based model 175–176; religious groups responding to 62–63; similarity of proposals to those of the 1970s 69–70; and stakeholders 21, 29–30, 35–36, 182; syllabus content 9–10, 176–177; and teachers 5; *see also* LANs (Local Advisory Networks for Religion and Worldviews); 'Religion and Worldviews' proposed name change; worldviews approach, CoRE
'counter-culture' movement, 1960s 92
Cowper Temple clause 72
Cox, Edwin 69
CPD (Continuous Professional Development) 65–66, 91
creationism 160–161
'critical realism' 127

critical realist (religious literacy) model of RE 138
CSSB (Central Schools Services Block) 65
Culham St. Gabriel 28
Cupitt, Don 139
curriculum: curriculum making 114; decolonisation of 142, 143; *see also* LANs (Local Advisory Networks for Religion and Worldviews); SACREs (Standing Advisory Councils on Religious Education)
Cush, Denise 37n17, 99
CW (collective worship) 41, 45–46, 67, 73

Daoism 83
Darwin, Charles 146, 159, 160
Davidson, Donald 104
Dawkins, Richard 36, 122, 134
decolonisation of the curriculum 142, 143
deconstruction model of RE 138, 145–146
deconstruction of religions 84–86
DfE (Department for Education) 19, 20, 21, 22, 26; PoS (Programmes of Study) 64; response to the CoRE report 32
Dharmic traditions 106
difference 23, 44, 52, 141; Commission on Religious Education as a safe space fro discussion of 18, 26
Dinham, Adam 20
discernment 109–110, 112–113, 115
diversity 8, 9, 23, 35, 45, 46, 83–85, 129–132, 131–132, 156; as a Big Idea 162
Doctrines 35
'Does Religious Education Work?' project 94
Durham Commission 63
Durham Report 70–71

EBacc 41, 171
Education Act 1888 139, 176
Education Act 1944 14, 40–41, 42, 59–60, 115n1; analysis and criticisms of 43–53
Education Act 1996, Section 375 7

education, purposes and functions of 108–110
Education Reform Act 1988 42
educational research, lack of 170, 172
empiricism 122, 126
Enlightenment 139
epistemology 126
Equalities Act 2010 110
Erriker, Clive 89–90, 141, 143, 145, 154
Erriker, Jane 143, 145
essentialisation of religions 140, 142–143
ethics 35, 122
ethnocentrism 178
ethnographic (interpretive) model of RE 138, 141, 143–145, 144
European Convention on Human Rights 110, 119
European Court of Human Rights 133
evangelicals 28
Everington, Judith 63
evolution 158, 159–161, 178, 180
existentialism 83, 102, 145
Expert Invitees to Commission Gatherings, CoRE (Commission on Religious Education) 20
extremism 153, 177

faith, othering of 24–27, 34, 35
faith schools 2, 25, 30, 34, 41, 47, 153
Federation of RE Centres 63
Flew, Anthony 120–121
Folgero v. Norway 133
Forster Education Act, 1870 72
France: state relationship with religion 174
Francis, Leslie 172
Frazer, J. G. 50
Freathy, Rob 58–59, 60, 74
free schools 2, 25, 41, 47
freedom 109, 112
freedom of religion 169, 170, 174–176; checks and balances on 178–179; 'freedom of religion or belief' 119
fundamentalism 178
'Fuzzy Epistemology' 38n24

Gadamer, H.-G. 33, 129, 130
Gates, B. 171

GCSE examinations: GCSE Reform, 2016 21–22, 24; Religious Studies 73, 115n2
Genders, Nigel 20
Georgiou, Gillian 33
Germany: law governing RE 60; LER (Lifestyle-Ethics-Religious Studies) teaching 175, 176; National Socialism 172, 173, 177; professionalism 58; state relationship with religion 174
Goldsmiths (University of London) 20
Grimmitt, Michael 136, 137, 138, 141, 147, 148, 179

Hall, John 5, 32
Hall, Stuart 78
Hampshire County Council: *Living Difference III* (2016) and *Living Difference IV* (2021) 108, 110
Hare, R. M. 121–122
Harlen, Wynne 161
Heidegger, M. 86, 129
Heraclitus 132
hermeneutics 33, 35, 85–86, 106–107, 128–129, 131
Hick, John 121
Hinds, Damien 5, 6, 25
Hinduism 83, 88, 144; Hindu groups responding to CoRE 63; stereotypes of 143
Hirst, Paul 164
Hockerill Trust 28
Holloway, Derek 20, 37n21
Holm, Jean 68
Holy Qur'an 146
'horizon' theory 33, 129
Horn, Klaus-Peter 58, 63
Hull, John 68
human development model of RE 138, 141
Humanism 11, 28, 31, 35, 83–84, 91, 102, 144, 154, 155, 164, 173, 174, 179
Hume, David 121, 130
Husserl, E. 129

ICE (Institute of Christian Education) 59

illiberal nature of critics of 1944 Education Act 43, 45–47
incommensurability 129
independent schools 45, 47
indigenous science 164
indigenous values, beliefs and practices 144
individual worldviews *see* personal worldviews
individualism: RE Council Review 4
indoctrination 134, 173
Initial Teacher Education 65, 66, 170, 172
Institute of Christian Education (ICE) 59
institutional worldviews 11, 82–83, 84–85, 102, 103, 154, 179; *see also* worldviews approach, CoRE
intellectual engagement/humility 111, 112, 113, 115
Intelligent Design theory 160
interpretation 126–129
interpretive (ethnographic) model of RE 138, 141, 143–145, 144
interpretive religious education 87–89
Islam 83, 88, 146; and the changing religious landscape 91, 92; Muslim groups responding to CoRE 63; and the neutrality-based model 175–176; stereotypes of 143

Jackson, J. 171
Jackson, Robert 87–88, 89, 90, 141, 143
Jainism 63, 83
Jehovah's Witnesses 83
Judaism 83; and the 1944 Education Act 45; Jewish groups responding to CoRE 63; professional advisors 61
judgement 51

KS1 30
KS2 30
KS3 30, 72–73
KS4 22, 36, 72–73, 156; GCSE Reform, 2016 21–22, 24
KS5: GCSE Reform, 2016 21–22, 24
Kueh, Richard 33
Kuhn, Thomas 78–81, 123–125, 127, 129

Lakatos, Imre 125–126
Lane, Frances 20
LANs (Local Advisory Networks for Religion and Worldviews) 7, 26, 65–66, 67, 175
Latter Day Saints (Mormons) 83
legislation, and RE 5–6
LER (Lifestyle-Ethics-Religious Studies) teaching in Germany 175, 176
'life-stance' 89
Liverpool 73
Local Advisory Networks for Religion and Worldviews (LANs) 7, 26, 65–66, 67, 175
local authorities: and the 1944 Education Act 45; and proposals to reform RE 46; and SACREs (Standing Advisory Councils on Religious Education) 66; see also ASCs (Agreed Syllabus Conferences)
Lockyer, Rudi 32–33, 37n17
logical positivism 119–120, 122, 126
Loosemore, Alan 68
Luxemburg: state relationship with religion 175

MacPherson, Duncan 37n8
Marxism 177–178
materialism 120, 177
MATs ('Multi Academy Trusts') 115n1
Matthews, M. R. 158
Meyer, Karlo 86
Mitchell, Basil 70
morality, theory of 122, 132–133
Mormons (Latter Day Saints) 83
Muijs, Daniel 37n6
'Multi Academy Trusts' (MATs) 115n1
mutability 23

NAHT: submission of evidence to CoRE 63
'narrative pedagogy' 89
narrowness, of critics of the 1944 Education Act 43, 45–47
NASACRE (National Association of SACREs) 2, 37n3, 54n8, 63, 68, 74
National Association of Teachers of R.E. (NATRE) see NATRE (National Association of Teachers of R.E.)

National Body of Religious Education Experts 26
National Curriculum 41; PoS (Programmes of Study) 64–65
National Entitlement 7, 9, 10, 21, 23–24, 26, 30, 35, 65, 66, 67, 101; DfE response to 32; implementation of 33
National Socialism, Germany 172, 173, 177
National Society of the Church of England: Durham Report 70–71; professional advisors 61; and SACREs (Standing Advisory Councils on Religious Education) 66; 'Understanding Christianity' programme 25–26; see also Church of England
National Survey, CoRE (Commission on Religious Education) 20
NATRE (National Association of Teachers of R.E.) 34, 62–63; School Workforce Data survey 72–73; submission of evidence to CoRE 63
natural selection 159
'naturalism' 120
neo-liberalism 178
neutral rationality 126
neutrality 175–176, 176–177; educational limits of 179
'new legal settlement' for RE 40–43
Newman, J. H. 36
Newton, I. 157
Nietzsche, F. 127
nihilism 131
non-religious worldviews 10, 44, 47, 49–53, 77, 82, 83, 91, 102, 136, 138, 144–145, 152, 153–154
Non-Statutory National Framework 2004 9, 48–49
Norway 173, 176

Oates, Tim 161
Ofsted 26, 27, 37n3, 73, 93, 170; *Ofsted Research Review Series: Religious Education* (2021) 148, 153
ontology 126
Orchard, Stephen 93
Osborne, J. 161

'other religions' 47, 87–88, 144
othering, of faith 24–27, 34, 35
Owen, Peter Lefroy 68

paganism 83
Panikkar, Ramon 105–106, 115
paradigms/paradigm shifts 78–81, 90–91, 123–126, 127, 148; worldviews approach as a new paradigm for RE 77–79, 87–90, 91–95
Parker, Stephen 58–60, 74
paternalism, of critics of the 1944 Education Act 43, 47–49
perception, philosophy of 104
permissiveness, of the 1944 Education Act 43, 45–47
personal worldviews 22, 85–86, 89, 91–92, 100, 102, 103, 107, 110, 113, 114, 123, 153–154, 155–156; *see also* worldviews approach, CoRE
Peterson, M. 11
Pett, Stephen 33
phenomenological (world religions) model of RE 137–138, 140–141, 142, 144
'Philosophy, Religion and Ethics' proposed name change 28
physicalism 120
PISA international comparative study 181
Plato 132, 133
pluralism, of the 1944 Education Act 43, 45–47, 53
plurality 109, 110, 112, 131–132; and classic pedagogies 145
Plymouth Teacher Network 37n3
PoS (Programmes of Study) 64–65
post-colonial scholarship 143, 144
post-confessional RE (religious education) 87, 92–94
post-modernist philosophy 128, 130
Powerful Knowledge theories 21
Practices 35
primary education 30, 73; Religion and Worldviews education 66; teacher training for RE 101
professionals 74–75; and the CoRE review 56, 61–62; CW (collective worship) 67; Initial Teacher Education and Continuous Professional Development 65, 66; LANs (Local Advisory Networks for Religion and Worldviews) 65–66; meaning of 'professional 56–57; model for study of professionalisation 58–61; PoS (Programmes of Study) 64–65; professionalisation of RE in the 1970s 68–74; promotion of particular view by 67–68; in religious education literature 57–58; religious groups 62–64
Programmes of Study (PoS) 64–65
progress, in science 123
proselytism 72
Protagoras 132
Public Evidence Sessions, CoRE (Commission on Religious Education) 19–20

qualification 109

racism 177, 178
Rastafarians 83
RE Council *see* CoRE (Commission on Religious Education); Religious Education Council of England and Wales
RE (religious education) 101; alternative proposal for 108–115; Big Ideas approach 22–23, 36, 152, 161–164; as a 'Cinderella subject' 138; classical models of 136, 137–138, 139–149; and conflicting truth claims 145–146, 147; content decisions 176–177; 'crisis' in 91; enlarging the scope of 50; as a human right 171; improvements to without giving up the subject 181–183; international perspectives on 170–171, 172, 173–174; and interpretation 126–129; and judgement 51; learning of young people who have no religious belief 138–142, 146; legal requirement for 41; neutrality-based model 175–176; parents' 'right' to withdraw child from 1, 45–46, 175; as part of education in the public sphere

108–110; post-confessional 87, 92–94; professionals and professionalisation 46, 57–58, 68–71, 74; proposed name change to 'Religion and Worldviews' 21, 27–29, 32, 34, 35, 36, 42–43, 47, 69, 99–100, 101, 153, 170, 171; purpose of 3; reality of current situation 171–172; reification of religious traditions 142–145, 146–147; 'religious education community' 5, 8, 19, 20, 33, 48, 49, 99; religious education literature 57–58; 'Religious Education' proposed name retention 28, 36; and self-knowledge 51–53; teaching of 111–113; weaknesses in 72–74, 171–172

reactionary nature of critics of the 1944 Education Act 43–45

reason, theory of 122

Regelski, T. 56, 57, 61, 63

reification of religious traditions 140, 142–145, 146–147

relativism 70, 81, 124–125, 126, 145–146

relevance 26–27

religion: changing religious landscape 91–92; deconstruction of 84–86; philosophy of 120–121; relationship with the state 169, 170, 174–176; Smart's six/seven-fold dimensional account of 12–13, 82; *see also* RE (religious education)

'Religion and Belief' proposed name change 28, 29

'Religion and Ethics' proposed name change 27–28

'Religion and Worldviews' approach *see* worldviews approach, CoRE

'Religion and Worldviews Education' (RWE) *see* worldviews approach, CoRE

'Religion and Worldviews' proposed name change 21, 27–29, 30–31, 32, 34, 35, 36, 42–43, 47, 69, 99–100, 101, 153, 170, 171

Religion and Worldviews: The way forward (CoRE, 2018) *see* CoRE (Commission on Religious Education), Religious Education Council for England and Wales

'Religion, Beliefs and Values' proposed name change 31

'religion or belief' 119

'Religion, Philosophy and Ethics' proposed name change 28

'Religion Values and Ethics,' Welsh Government 34

'religious education community' 5, 8, 19, 20, 33, 48, 49, 99

Religious Education Council of England and Wales (RE Council) 37n3, 67, 68; 'A review of religious education in England' (2013) 1–4, 5, 7, 9, 40, 48, 71–72; PoS (Programmes of Study) 64; RE teacher recruitment and training 69; *Religious Education for All* 4–5; 'What future for the Agreed Syllabus?' 68–69; *Worldview: A Multidisciplinary Report* (2020) 154; *see also* CoRE (Commission on Religious Education)

'Religious Education' proposed name retention 28

religious illiteracy 134

'Religious Instruction' 119

'Religious Knowledge' 119

religious life, living of 110–111

religious literacy 26; religious literacy (critical realist) model of RE 138

religious sensitivity, of the 1944 Education Act 43–45

'Religious Studies' 119

research, as a basis for subject teaching 182

responsiveness, of the 1944 Education Act 43–45

Robinson, C. 99

Robinson, Philip 37n21

Russell, Bertrand 123

RWE ('Religion and Worldviews Education') *see* worldviews approach, CoRE

SACREs (Standing Advisory Councils on Religious Education) 2, 5, 7, 20, 24, 26, 30, 36, 41, 59–60, 61–62, 68, 71, 73, 74, 75, 91, 174–175; committee structure 65–66; and CW (collective worship) 67;

replacement of by LANs (Local Advisory Networks for Religion and Worldviews) 65; submission of evidence to CoRE 63
Sahajpal, Sushma 36
Salter, Emma 10
Samples, K.R. 11
Schools Council Working Paper, 1971 19
Schweitzer, Friedrich 10
science: challenge of 118–121; nature of 125; *see also* paradigms/paradigm shifts
science education 155; Big Ideas approach 152, 161, 164; misconceptions in 157–158; worldviews in 152, 157–161, 164–165
scope, of RE 50
secondary education 86; Religion and Worldviews education 66
secularisation 42, 49, 53; and the religious landscape 91–92
secularism 83–84, 102, 154–155, 164; secular nature of critics of the 1944 Education Act 43–45
self-knowledge 51–53
Sex Education, parents' 'right' to withdraw child from 15n1
Shaw, Martha 20
Shinto 83
Sikhism 83, 143
Smalley, Paul 68
Smart, Ninian 12–13, 22, 82, 87, 89, 137, 140, 144
social anthropology 126, 130
social media 130
social mobility 21
social sciences 126
socialisation 109
'sociology of knowledge' 126
solipsism 123
Sophists 132
stakeholders 21, 29–30, 35–36, 182
Standing Advisory Councils on Religious Education (SACREs) *see* SACREs (Standing Advisory Councils on Religious Education)
state, relationship with religion 169, 170, 174–176

State Socialism, GDR 173, 174, 177
Stopes-Roe, H. 89
studio schools 41
subjectification 109
subjectivism 124
Sullivan, John 37n8
superiority 177
Swanwick conference, 1934 59
Sweden 175
Switzerland 175
syllabuses: content decisions 176–177; local production of 7–8; *see also* LANs (Local Advisory Networks for Religion and Worldviews); SACREs (Standing Advisory Councils on Religious Education)

teacher education and training 65, 66, 180–181; CPD (Continuous Professional Development) 65–66, 91; Initial Teacher Education 65, 66, 170, 172
teachers: and the 1944 Education Act 45, 49; associations of 34; and conflicting truth claims 145–146, 147; professional advisors 61; and professionalism 58; RE Council and RE teacher recruitment and training 69; right of excusing from RE and collective worship 45–46; and SACREs (Standing Advisory Councils on Religious Education) 66; subject expertise of 24; and syllabus development 62; teaching of RE 111–113; *see also* teacher education and training
Tharani, Amira 9, 36n1
theology 27, 36
toleration 132–134
Tolstoy, Leo 52, 139, 142
transcendence 105
TRS-UK 8
truth 132–134

uniqueness 112
United States of America: state relationship with religion 174; U.S. Constitution, First Amendment 119
University of Exeter 22

vaccine hesitancy 158, 159
verification theory 120–121, 122, 124
Vienna Circle 119–120, 121
voluntary aided schools 6, 45, 67
voluntary controlled schools 45

Wainwright, Allan 68
Wallace, Alfred Russel 159
Warwick Religions and Education Research Unit 143
Weber, Max 57
Weil, S. 111, 112, 113, 114
Welsh Government: 'Religion Values and Ethics' 34
Weltanschauung ('worldview') 22, 54n9, 118, 173, 177
West Riding syllabus, 1922 60
'Westminster Faith Debates' 40
White, J. 138
Williams, Shirley 69
Wintersgill, Barbara 22–23, 37n3, 161–162
Wittgenstein, Ludwig 43, 129–130
Woodhead, L. 31, 37n3, 40
world religions 87–88, 119; world religions (phenomenological) model of RE 137–138, 140–141, 142, 144
'worldview education,' as a compromised concept 172–174
worldviews approach, CoRE 52–53, 69, 81–84, 99–103, 152–154; alternative proposal for 108–115; Barnes' critique of 154–157; content decisions 176–179; definition of 11, 29, 101, 137, 145, 153; educational issues with 103, 106–108, 113; and freedom of religion 169, 170, 174–176; institutional worldviews 11, 82–83, 84–85, 102, 103, 154, 179; lack of academic basis for 179–180; as a new paradigm for RE 77–79, 87–90, 91–95; non-religious worldviews 10, 44, 47, 49–53, 77, 82, 83, 91, 102, 136, 138, 144–145, 152, 153–154; outline and overview 8–14; personal worldviews 22, 85–86, 89, 91–92, 100, 102, 103, 107, 110, 113, 114, 123, 153–154, 155–156; philosophical issues with 103–104, 113; philosophy of 118–134; PoS (Programmes of Study) 64–65; purpose of 133; and reification 143–145; 'Religion and Worldviews' proposed name change 21, 27–29, 30–31, 32, 34, 35, 36, 42–43, 47, 69, 99–100, 101, 153, 170, 171; retreat to 121–123; support materials for syllabus writing 9, 13; theological issues with 103, 104–105, 113
worldviews, in science education 157–161, 164–165
Wright, A. 141, 143
Wright, Kathryn 33

Yeaxlee, Basil 59
Young, Michael 21

Zoroastrianism 83

For Product Safety Concerns and Information please contact our EU
representative GPSR@taylorandfrancis.com
Taylor & Francis Verlag GmbH, Kaufingerstraße 24, 80331 München, Germany

www.ingramcontent.com/pod-product-compliance
Lightning Source LLC
Chambersburg PA
CBHW051613230426
43668CB00013B/2088